pine for me

haircuts and heartthrobs
book three

Swati M.H.

Kismet Publishing

Copyright © 2025 by Swati M.H.

All rights reserved.

No part of this book may be reproduced in any form or by any electronic or mechanical means, including information storage and retrieval systems, without written permission from the author, except for the use of brief quotations in a book review.

This is a work of fiction. Names, characters, businesses, places, incidents, and events are either a product of the author's imagination or used fictitiously.

Cover: Cover Me Darling

Editing: Silvia's Reading Corner

also by swati m.h.

Haircuts and Heartthrobs Series:

Pretend For Me

Pitch For Me

Elements of Rapture Series

Adrift

(Forbidden, single dad/nanny, grumpy/sunshine, age gap)

Ascend

(Marriage of Convenience, single-mom, friends to lovers romance)

Ablaze

(Brother's best friend, friends-to-lovers, one bed, firefighter romance)

Abyss

(Enemies to lovers, dad's best friend, workplace romance)

MomComs Series

Mother Pucker

(Hockey star, single mom, reverse age-gap, doctor/patient romcom)

Feel the Beat Series

My Perfect Remix

(Single-dad, friends-to lovers romance)

My Beautiful Chaos

(Fake-relationship, second chance romance)

My Darling Neighbor

(Enemies to lovers, surprise pregnancy romance)

Fated Love Series

Kismet in the Sky

(Slightly forbidden, second chance, workplace romance)

Surrender to the Stars

(Enemies to lovers, hospital romance)

content warning

Content warning: This book is intended for mature audiences. It includes sensitive themes like fertility struggles, miscarriage, and divorce which may be triggering for some readers. Please read with your mental health in mind.

To all the hairless pussies, the actual main characters in this series—stay bald, bold, and beautiful.

nisha's crying in my car playlist

"Hello" by Adele
"All Too Well" by Taylor Swift
"Un-break My Heart" Toni Braxton
"Say Something" by A Great Big World, Christina Aguilera
"Without You" by Mariah Carey
"All I Ask" by Adele
"Kill Bill" by SZA
"The Scientist" by Coldplay
"Just Give Me A Reason" by P!nk, Nate Ruess
"It's So Hard to Say Goodbye to Yesterday" by Boyz II Men

prologue

Nisha - Sixteen Years Ago

Our breaths ghost over our faces, transparent against the sparkling sky. Our chests rise and fall dramatically with each long, quiet pull of air after having climbed what felt like an unending hill.

The cold ground, sparsely dusted with mossy green grass, provides little in the way of comfort. But it's not the comfort of the earth I seek, anyway. Not when *my* earth is lying right next to me—shoulders touching, fingers entangled, hearts embracing.

Silence stretches out above us, as expansive as the dark sky. But in contrast to its vastness, the silence is familiar, intimate and calming. It's as if we're the only two people looking up into this very patch of the universe. Like it belongs to us.

"It looks unreal, somehow," I breathe, eyes skimming over the ethereal green waves dancing in the midnight sky. "Man-made instead of something created by nature."

It was the first time in my sixteen years that the Aurora Borealis could be seen in Boston. And though we had school tomorrow, Dad granted me my wish to see it, miles from home and the city. As long as I was with *him* . . .

The boy my heart had claimed.

The one it beat for, out of rhythm and achingly loud, whenever he looked at me like he was doing now. Like I was the wonder and not the magical sky.

"Beautiful," he whispers, and I stop myself from turning to him, from meeting his eyes or his lips.

Because what if in that first kiss, we stilled the magic?

What if my heart went back to beating like normal?

But deep down, I knew that wouldn't be the case. It would never be the case. Because he shone brighter than every twinkle on the clearest night. Because his magic was inconceivable, yet lying right beside me.

"Didn't you say your name meant 'night' in Sanskrit?" I hear the grin in his voice.

He feels my silent nod.

"I guess your parents knew what they were doing when they named you. Nisha Arora, Northern Lights of the night sky." His voice takes on a husky edge, and I wonder if he can hear the butterflies taking flight inside my chest. "It's like they knew you'd be the most beautiful thing to see, even in complete darkness."

This time I do turn to face him, bringing our lips millimeters apart. "That has to be the cheesiest thing anyone has ever said to me."

His grin—God, *that* grin—coupled with the ever-present mischief in his chocolate browns, makes me feel like I'm floating.

"I always aim high," he says.

Above us, the aurora dances the way my soul does in his nearness. As if it knows it's found its other half.

"*Little Borealis,*" he murmurs, testing out the nickname he'll call me for years to come. "My personal northern lights."

And then he's kissing me, beneath an impossible sky and countless possibilities. Anchoring me to him when all I know how to do is float.

The magic doesn't still.

It magnifies. Defies. Solidifies.

Like it's been waiting for this exact moment, under this exact sky, to settle into something that feels . . . like home. Like forever.

He may say I'm his light in the dark, but he's the sun—the one who lights up galaxies and tethers planets.

I'm just lucky to be caught in his orbit.

I don't know it yet, but that nickname will follow me. Through the brightest days and the darkest nights. Through near and far, laughter and tears. Through vows made . . .

And promises broken.

It's a name that spans a love so eternal and soul-deep, it'll save us . . .

Before it destroys us.

one
nisha

The Clam Jam

PIPER MENON

We're on month one of Patton Pierce's San Francisco invasion, and I have heard nary a peep from our friend, Nisha Arora. Either she's secretly gargling his balls or she's still denying he didn't just move into town to win her back.

SARINA ARORA

Technically, he's been in and out of town for the past few months, but he just met with Troy last week.

Anyway, we both know my sister is the master of denial and secrecy. I still remember when my parents found her vibrator in high school, and she told them she thought it was a back massager.

NISHA ARORA

Or MAYBE—and this is a radical thought—he's just here to work with Troy like he said and there is no subterfuge happening.

PIPER MENON

See how she's trying to gaslight us while using big words? She's a master, I tell you!

NISHA ARORA

[GIF of Judge Judy massaging her temples]

KAVI CASE

Wait, are you guys saying she's secretly seeing her ex-husband? SPILL THE TEA, Nisha! What sort of back-alley dicking is happening under our noses!?

PIPER MENON

The nefarious, hedonistic sort, consisting of midnight trysts and whispered, "Fuck me harder, Hollywood," while we're all sound asleep like baby chihuahuas under our mother's teats.

BELLA MEYER

You never cease to amaze me with how much strange imagery you can put into one sentence.

RANI MEYER

@Nisha Arora, are you seriously getting railed by your ex behind our backs? How dare you go against the sacred values of this girl tribe and withhold filthy details of each toe-curling orgasm!

MALA MEYER

The nerve!

Pine For Me

NISHA ARORA
What in the actual fuck are you guys going on about? I haven't seen Patton since Troy's retirement party six months ago. You were all there, and we didn't say a word to each other.

KAVI CASE
Yeah, but the tension was so hot and thick between you two, I thought the room would go up in flames.

NISHA ARORA
The only thing thick in that room was everyone's imagination. In any case, I certainly HAVEN'T been gargling any of his body parts, Piper!

PIPER MENON
But you want to. Don't even try to lie. Your stalking history of his IMDB page will testify against you.

NISHA ARORA
I DO NOT stalk him! I looked him up ONE TIME, and that was only because he was co-starring with Henry Cavill, and I felt sorry for Henry in that scenario.

SARINA ARORA
Bitch, please. You look him up so much, our browser at the salon autocompletes "Patton Pierce shirtless" anytime someone punches in "P".

```
[Nisha Arora has left the chat]
[Piper Menon has added Nisha Arora to the chat]
```

Swati M.H.

PIPER MENON

> Okay fine, Neesh. We all know you don't use the salon computer to look him up. You're too prim and proper to diddle your fiddle at your place of work.

NISHA ARORA

> Jesus. It's too early in the day to have a migraine. You guys need psychiatric help. And another hobby besides my vagina.

PIPER MENON

> Your vagina is this group's collective hobby. And given that it's the only one in this group to have grown back its hymen, we feel compelled to force it out of retirement.

NISHA ARORA

> My vagina is not in retirement! It's just . . . on a break.

KAVI CASE

> Hasn't it been seven years?

PIPER MENON

> Girl, that's not a break; that's a coma. At this point, it's been dormant for so long, I bet we could carbon date it.

RANI MEYER

> LOL! I literally choked on my coffee. <crying-laughing emoji>

NISHA ARORA

> I truly hate every single one of you. And also, need I remind you of Micah? Things may not have worked out with him, but we did, you know, try.

Pine For Me

SARINA ARORA

That was so two years ago, and if by "try," you mean you laid there thinking about the sweater you were going to knit for Rome while he jack hammered you like he was trying to dig his way to China, then sure, you get an A for effort, sis.

NISHA ARORA

It wasn't Micah's fault. I'm just . . . hard to please.

PIPER MENON

As I recall, Patton never had a problem pleasing you.

NISHA ARORA

Yeah, well, he also never had a problem being MIA when I needed him most.

BELLA MEYER

Has he tried to get in touch with you yet?

NISHA ARORA

He texted me a couple of days ago with a "Hey".

SARINA ARORA

And you're JUST telling us?! Especially me! Does sharing a womb, where you took up most of the goddamn room by the way, mean nothing to you anymore??

NISHA ARORA

Calm your tits. I didn't think it was a big deal.

Swati M.H.

PIPER MENON

Wasn't a big deal?? "Hey" is literally code for "I'd like to fuck you over the nearest flat surface." When Dev messages me with a "Hey," I know I'm about to be face down, ass up on the kitchen counter within the next hour.

BELLA MEYER

TMI, but also, did you respond to Patton, Nisha?

NISHA ARORA

No. Also, who gave him my new number?

SARINA ARORA

Not me. You might betray me—keeping secrets and shit—but I would never!

NISHA ARORA

<eye-roll emoji> Your flair for the dramatics today is second only to your seventh-grade stage performance where you pretended to faint and elbowed Sammy DeWalt in the eye. Kid walked around with a black eye all week.

SARINA ARORA

It's not my fault he forgot where he was supposed to be and ended up behind me during the most important performance of my life!

PIPER MENON

I didn't give him your number, either. I haven't spoken to your ex since you guys separated.

Pine For Me

KAVI CASE

[Gif of Eddie Murphy overreacting to juicy gossip]

MALA MEYER

Damn, @Nisha Arora. So you left him on Read? I can't decide if that's ice cold or hot as fuck. Serious boss move.

NISHA ARORA

Look. Yes, he's in town shooting for his next big blockbuster, and of course I'm happy that he's living his dream. But the way I see it, we moved on from each other seven years ago, so I no longer owe him an immediate response to his messages.

RANI MEYER

Okay, but, real talk. When was the last time you both had an actual conversation?

NISHA ARORA

A little more than a year ago when I went to L.A. for the taekwondo tournament. He was in the audience, and we chit-chatted after my students competed.

SARINA ARORA

WHAT? That's it. I'm revoking your sister card.

PIPER MENON

You "chit-chatted" with your ex-husband, whom you haven't spoken to in years, a year ago, and we're JUST finding out??

NISHA ARORA

Again, it wasn't that big of a deal. Just a casual conversation.

KAVI CASE

But if it was such a "casual conversation," why not mention it earlier?

PIPER MENON

Yeah, like during the dozen girls' nights we've had since?

SARINA ARORA

Because my sister is a lying liar who lies! What else happened, Nisha? And don't you dare say "nothing," or I will literally bring a bouquet of helium-filled balloons to your house right this second!

BELLA MEYER

Hehe, I always forget about her balloon phobia. It's even more hilarious because Nisha's a total badass in every sense of the word.

SARINA ARORA

Nisha? Details. NOW!

NISHA ARORA

Ugh! Okay, so we had dinner, too.

PIPER MENON

WHAT!?

MALA MEYER

[GIF of woman slapping her hand over her mouth in shock]

RANI MEYER

This just keeps unraveling. Next she's going to tell us there was naked time after said dinner.

Pine For Me

KAVI CASE

OMG! Was there naked time after dinner?

NISHA ARORA

No! Of course not! We just . . . caught up. WITH clothes firmly in place! Geez!

SARINA ARORA

I can't believe you've been sitting on this for almost a year. What the hell, Neesh!

PIPER MENON

You know what? I don't know about the rest of you ladies, but I'm certainly not satisfied with the paltry details of this so called "chit-chat" with her hot-as-fuck ex-husband. I feel like our tight-lipped bestie isn't giving us the entire story.

Perhaps we need some "truth serum" in the form of her favorite margarita to get her talking. I propose an impromptu ladies' night at my place Saturday.

KAVI CASE

Saturday works for me. What about you guys?

BELLA MEYER

Works for me.

MALA MEYER

I wouldn't miss it!

RANI MEYER

Same. I'll be there.

NISHA ARORA

I won't. But you guys carry on.

SARINA ARORA

> Literally purchasing balloons as we speak. Oh, and telling Dad you're keeping secrets. Bet he'll have something to say about that . . .

NISHA ARORA

> You're the actual devil, you know that? FINE! I'll be there!

PIPER MENON

> Perfect! Saturday it is. Oh, and Nisha, hope you're ready because I'm going to have an entire interrogation list prepared. By the end of the night, we're going to know everything from what you ordered for dessert to how many times you thought about climbing him like a horny koala in heat.

NISHA ARORA

> Ugh. See you Saturday, you absolute monsters.

two
nisha

Living in that Third Act

I fight the smile threatening to break through as I read this morning's messages from my best friends again. They are relentless when it comes to what they've all decided is their life's mission: my love life.

Too bad they're bound to be disappointed.

It's not that I've sworn off men or anything dramatic like that; I've just sworn off fairy tales.

Phone rolling against my palm, I lean back against the driver's seat, letting the soft tunes from my "Crying in My Car" playlist fill the silence both in my car and inside my bones. It's a mix I created, equal parts heartbreak ballads and moody songs that give my bruised heart validation, that I listen to religiously every morning on my way to work.

I'm a hairstylist for a luxury men's salon I own with my sister Sarina, and my best friend, Piper. We opened *Haircuts and Heartthrobs* a few years ago when we all found ourselves in the same city after having endured our own forms of trauma and drama. But on the side, I also teach taekwondo at a *dojang* owned by my friend, Micah. Actually, I'm not sure if we're *friends*, but more on that later.

Even from a young age, I thrived on discipline and

routine. So, after watching a taekwondo match on TV as a teen, I asked my parents to sign me up for classes. And now it's become a part of my life, grounding me, especially when my life feels out of control.

I stare at the house across from mine. Yeah, I'm one of those people who likes to back into a parking spot so I can pretend I have my life together. It's probably the same reason my bedsheets have hospital corners and my books are arranged by color.

There isn't a stack of magazines at my salon that doesn't get tidied up first thing in the morning or a throw-pillow that isn't fluffed twice—just in case.

After all, isn't it true that if you fake something long enough, it'll eventually start to feel real?

Except, I've been waiting for that reality to kick in for almost seven years.

As if my eyes and brain finally connect, I realize there's something different about the house today—it's no longer on the market. The hideous yellow and purple realtor sign that offended my retinas for the past three months is finally gone, replaced by a simple red "sold" sign.

Thank the Lord. Hopefully now I'll get some decent neighbors, instead of the circus show that lived there before. The Cockburns—yes, that was their actual last name, and no, I will never not snort-laugh like a juvenile when I'm reminded of it—had turned living in peaceful suburbia into a free WWE viewing. Between the couple's nightly driveway spats and their adult son revving up his motorcycle like he was trying to launch himself to Mars, our entire block lived in a state of audio trauma.

And ever since my sister Sarina and her eight-year-old son Rome moved out of the house next door, and into a much grander one with her now-fiancé, former star pitcher for the Bay Area Blazers, Troy Winters, I felt like I had no one to meet at the fence and whisper, "Jesus Christ. Not again," when the Cockburns would hit their nightly sound pollution quota.

It's been strangely quiet around here, not because I miss the chaos but because I miss Sarina and Rome.

Thankfully, I was able to buy the property from my sister and get a renter in it—a middle-aged traveling nurse named Nancy—but I'd be lying if I didn't say I miss being able to pop over in my pajamas and collapse on her couch to say absolutely nothing or steal my nephew to watch Star Wars reruns at my place.

In any case, whoever is moving into the house across the street has to be an improvement over who was there before.

I glance down at the phone on my lap, still displaying the messages that took me down this internal spiral. The thing my friends don't understand—the thing I'm not able to voice to them without seeming broken or bitter—is that I already had my shot at a happily-ever-after.

With my best friend no less.

And it left me faithless and hollow.

Patton and I dove headfirst into love at the age of sixteen and thought we would conquer the world together when we got married at twenty-one. Except, it all turned upside down. We didn't conquer the world as much as it conquered us. That same love that made us unstoppable started to tear us apart.

It wasn't for a lack of love—God knows we always had plenty of that—it was everything else. The distance that grew between us when life got hard. The dreams that pulled him so hard, I was often left standing alone, wondering if I'd ever be enough to make him stay.

In the end, the love that bound us together was the very thing that pulled us apart. In the end, that love wasn't enough to bridge the gap between who we were and who we wanted to be.

So, at thirty-two, it's not that I'm afraid of love; in fact, I relish watching it bloom all around me. All my best friends are in fulfilling, soul-stirring relationships. My father met the man of his dreams not too long ago and is once again happy after having lost my mom to an aneurysm years ago. Even my cynical twin, who used to run from athletes, found her forever match in Troy, a former baseball pitcher.

No, I'm not afraid of love.

I'm afraid of being an afterthought to someone who consumes all my thoughts.

I'm afraid of making space in my hopes and dreams, only to realize I never had a place in theirs.

Seven years ago, I walked away from my life in L.A. with Patton, leaving behind our shared home and a *Dear John* letter pinned to the fridge. Since then, I've been slowly rebuilding a life I can call my own, from my array of potted plants to the home gym I assembled, piece by piece.

Seven years of coming to terms with the fact that it took two to create what we had, and two to allow it to break.

But coming to terms with the past is a far cry from wanting to relive it. Or revive it, no matter how much my well-intentioned friends insist I should.

They have it in their heads that getting back with Patton would be some huge romantic story, like we're two characters from a chick flick he's starred in. But real life isn't a screenplay where love conquers all and the third act is saved by some poignant grand gesture.

Sometimes love just isn't enough.

Sometimes you end up living in that third act, content with an ever-after, even if it doesn't come attached with the "happily" you always pictured.

I click over to Patton's text, the three-letter message my friends believe is some grand romantic opening for a second chance. But what they see—what they *hope*—as another opportunity for love, I see as a temptation to walk a path I had already left behind.

It's just as clear to me now as it was that evening in L.A. after the taekwondo championship. The night of almosts and maybes. The night of what-ifs and perhaps . . .

The night I remembered that some doors needed to stay closed, no matter how your heart begs for you to walk through them again.

But even now as I look down at my screen, some small traitorous part of me still flutters at the sight of his name. It's a part that never quite accepted our ending—*the dissolution of us*—that's always belonged to him. And though it took seven years to convince the rest of me that I made the right decision that night, I won't deny there are days I still have to say those reasons out loud.

My dad and my girlfriends think I haven't moved on, but they're clearly not seeing all the ways I have. I've built a great life here, running a thriving salon, teaching kids an art I'm proud to pass on, and training my body until it's practically a weapon. Not to mention that I regularly volunteer at the local homeless shelter, cutting hair for free.

I have friends who love me, a family who supports me, and a house where I might live alone, but at least I'm not living each day waiting . . .

For him to come home.

No, some paths are meant to be traveled once and then left behind.

My gaze flicks to the time on my phone before I place it into its designated sleeve inside my purse. Time to head to the *dojang* for tonight's charity spar.

I shift into drive, eyes on the road, and shove all thoughts of Patton's three-letter lure from my mind.

three
nisha

In Life, In Love, And On
The Mat

My feet find the familiar feel of the rubber mats, and my lungs fill with the scents of sweat, old sparring gear, and disinfectant. The scent composition might make someone else's nose wrinkle, but it instantly puts me at ease.

Tonight's charity spar has drawn quite the crowd with approximately twenty volunteers in comfortable clothes, chest guards, and headgear who look like extras on a low-budget remake of *Gladiator*.

They mill around with palpable nervous excitement, likely wondering if they'll walk out of here on one or two legs. I suppose even knowing you're in good hands, sparring against fifth and sixth *dan* black belts, the idea of getting your ass handed to you in front of an entire audience doesn't reduce the flow of adrenaline . . . or visible armpit stains.

Twice a year, my *dojang* hosts this charity spar, encouraging experienced martial artists from the community to spar its four instructors, including me, for a few controlled rounds. It's our way of giving back to youth programs and spreading the word about our center, while offering people a chance to go toe-to-toe with a black belt in a safe environment. In the past seven years I've been a part of this *dojang*, it's become one of our most anticipated events.

"Good evening, everyone! I'm Nisha Arora, but here you can refer to me as *Sabumnim* Arora, which is the Korean title for instructor," I call out, sweeping my gaze around the room to the various new faces. "Remember, sparring is about form, technique, and control, not ego. We're here to raise money for foster families around the Bay Area, not to end up in the emergency room."

A few chuckles ripple across the crowd, and a soft laugh escapes Micah's lips to my left. I don't have to look at him to know his eyes are pinned on me.

"As a reminder," he says, stepping forward and addressing the crowd with an easy confidence. His English accent has some of the ladies in the room raising an interested brow. "We'll be breaking out into rotations where you'll get two-minute rounds with each instructor, or *sabum*. We'll be using the World Taekwondo rules and scoring system. Remember, you only score with legal techniques, so keep your head-butts and elbow strikes for your next Black Friday shopping spree."

His comment earns him more confident chuckles, and his eyes light up when he catches the smile I've turned his way. But my smile falters when I see the spark of hope once again reflecting inside his irises.

Micah's not a bad guy—a little socially oblivious and gossipy, but he's also funny and confident. Perhaps a little overconfident.

We dated for a few months a couple of years ago. Let me rephrase: we fell into a pattern of going out to dinner after class, then falling into bed. Soon enough, however, I realized that was all it was, a sort of Netflix and chill without the Netflix.

Which would have been fine if his bedroom game was as impressive as his roundhouse kick.

Don't get me wrong, Micah was plenty enthusiastic, pummeling me like he was trying to exorcise a demon and rolling his hips like Shakira's backup dancer. But, unfortunately for me—and him—he was like an English Springer Spaniel. Tail wagging, he'd eagerly bound off to fetch a stick but would, disappointingly, always come back with a dried leaf.

I suppose that's not completely on him, either, considering no one's bedroom game has been up to par since . . . well, since *him*. The man who no longer has space in my mind and the only man for whom I didn't have to put on a Broadway-worthy performance just to convince him—and myself—that "yes, that's the spot" when it absolutely wasn't.

I thought Micah and I were on the same page when I put the brakes on the "chill" part of our arrangement, but judging by the way he's looking at me, it seems I misunderstood.

Clearing his throat, Micah addresses the crowd once more. "If you happen to deliver a legal knockout technique that hinders your opponent from continuing, you'll automatically win by knockout. Any questions?"

My gaze sweeps the room again, taking account of the shaking heads, the determined set of shoulders, and the shuffling feet. And then—

A prickle, like the touch of electricity on wet skin.

A tug, like the whisper of emotional déjà vu that heightens my awareness and awakens my intuition.

Something shifts the air around me, along with my heartbeats, and my eyes dart to find the cause. It's as if my body already knows what I'll find before my mind has caught up.

It's the same way my eyes involuntarily found him last year at the taekwondo championship, dressed inconspicuously and obscured by the crowd, yet impossible to miss.

And the way I felt his presence in the room six months

ago, before my eyes had even confirmed it, when he came to ask Troy for his help on a new role. A role, coincidentally, playing an injured baseball star, living in the Bay Area.

Or the way my soul connected with his across a similarly crowded *dojang* all those years ago, when we were just teens. Connected and sealed.

Because the man has the magnetic pull of the Earth, always has.

I inhale sharply when my eyes land on him.

Taller than the rest, with shoulders set so confidently, they make his chest look like an immovable wall. He's utterly unfazed by the nervous energy in the room.

His stance is casual, deceptively easy. His hands are clasped loosely in front of his waist, serving to draw the eye to the stretch of his biceps straining against the sleeves of his fitted long-sleeve black shirt.

His eyes, the molten chocolate I've drowned in again and again, are lined with lashes as dense and dark as the hair underneath his headgear. They're fixed on a spot straight ahead, as if purposely avoiding my inquisitive stare. The rest of his face is covered beneath a black balaclava tucked under his headgear, presumably so no one recognizes him as the world-famous celebrity he is.

But I don't need to see it to *know* it's him.

A jaw dusted with the kind of insufferable stubble that makes my thighs clench on reflex. A mouth and lips so sinfully kissable and annoyingly smug, even a simple smirk has the power to undo seven years of my hard-won resistance. And the faintest sprinkle of freckles—*God, those freckles!*—over his nose and cheeks, a testament to the time he spends in the sun, and a constellation I could trace even with my eyes closed.

I lift my fingers to my neck, feeling my pulse hammering beneath my skin.

He's here.

I know it's him as surely as I know my reflection in the mirror. But just as that conclusion locks into place, his covered face turns. His dark eyes lock with mine, unblinking and . . . certain.

I stand motionless, breathless—perhaps even pantiless—as I suppress the urge to disconnect our standoff and run for the nearest exit.

"Nisha?" Micah's voice jolts me out of my mind trap, and I straighten my posture. "How about you start with this set of five here?" He waves his hand toward five volunteers who look to be of different skill levels. "From each set, each *sabum* will choose an overall winner. And that winner will then choose a final instructor to spar with for a chance to win the grand prize. We'll address ties if they occur."

Letting out a relieved breath, I nod, motioning for my group to follow me to the far side of the mat while forcing myself not to look at the masked man again—the one I'm ninety-nine percent sure is my ex-husband. Though, shamelessly, my ears stay acutely trained on his whereabouts like horny bats.

"*Sabumnim* Choi will take this group," Micah announces, and with a quick glance in their direction, I notice Patton follow four other volunteers behind Instructor Choi toward the opposite side.

Good. The farther away from me, the better.

For my sanity.

And my increasingly traitorous underwear.

Perhaps I can get through this evening without having to confront him and whatever his reason is for being here.

Because one thing is clear: his walking in here was not by mistake, nor was it a sudden philanthropic itch. Although, to be fair, he has donated almost half of his earnings to charitable causes over the years, like an incredibly hot, ridiculously ripped, and recently bathed Keanu Reeves.

Because Patton is all lean and lethal muscle with a soft heart, smelling like expensive body wash and the promise of orgasms.

No, he didn't walk in here on this particular Friday night to risk getting recognized by every person with a smartphone because he wanted to raise money for foster families. He walked in here for something else.

Me.

I suppose I shouldn't be surprised, though I was hoping Troy could have kept his mouth shut a little longer, given we're practically family at this point, and family is supposed to look after one another, but I also know my ex-husband.

Once he's determined to do something, be it obtaining a black belt with two broken toes, securing a lead role in the next Scorsese film, or irritating the shit out of his ex-wife by spontaneously showing up to her events, he'll let nothing stop him. It's the same reason he does his own stunt work, like flying off a bridge on a motorcycle, having had zero experience with motorcycles.

The kicker of it all? The bastard usually comes out unscathed!

Well, not today.

Fifteen minutes later, having done some simple combinations with my group, I've just finished winning the spar with one of the men—a middle-aged fourth *dan*—when impressed murmurs from the crowd have us all turning toward the noise.

I suppress my groan.

Of course, it has to be him—Patton fucking Pierce—having executed what seems to have been a flawless tornado roundhouse, followed by a spinning hook kick that stops millimeters from *Sabumnim* Choi's chest guard. He finishes the combo with a textbook back kick that, if he'd intended it to, would have sent his opponent flying backward.

A sense of nostalgia washes over me, mixing with that familiar pang that rises anytime I'm in the vicinity of my ex-husband.

The way his agile body does his bidding. The way each muscle flexes and yields as if well-versed in the choreographed movements. It's both utterly beautiful and extremely irritating to watch.

"Flawless technique!" *Sabumnim* Choi commends, awe and reverence lacing each syllable. "Where do you train?"

Patton straightens, his chest barely moving, despite having seemingly defied physics just seconds ago.

"Here and there." His eyes flick to me, and his gaze sends goosebumps over my arms. "But I learned with some of the best."

Pretending not to have heard, I swivel my gaze back to my group, murmuring something about getting back to it. I pretend his natural athleticism and ability to command a room doesn't evoke the very thing I've worked years to bury—that attraction that's always at the surface.

Once each group has completed their rotations, each instructor picks their winner. It's no surprise when *Sabumnim* Choi picks the masked man some in the room have nicknamed "The Ninja," though I've had to stop my eyes from rolling each time I've heard it.

Micah claps to get everyone's attention before glancing at Patton. "That was quite the training and skill you showed today, Master Luca—"

One of the ladies from my group searches my face, and I realize I've gasped audibly when Patton's middle name confirms his identity.

"We'll start with you. Who would you like to spar against next?" Micah asks, giving Patton a curious smile.

My heart somersaults inside my chest preemptively, my instincts knowing exactly who the bastard is going to choose, exactly who he came here for.

Patton turns, his eyes dragging up my legs and torso in a slow perusal before coming to rest on my face. Even under his headgear, his brow hitches, and though I can't see it, I know the asshole is giving me one of his smug smirks, too.

His chin lifts. "*Sabumnim* Arora."

With my eyes still pinned to Patton's, I don't have to look at Micah's expression to know he can feel the tension between us.

"Very well," Micah says as the crowd shifts to give me and Patton the center of the mat. "*Sabumnim* Arora, if you accept, please proceed."

I nod, stepping forward before rolling my shoulders while Patton moves to his spot facing me. His deep brown eyes are deceptively calm, like the earth before a catastrophic quake.

And we're just two fault lines about to collide once again.

We bow, formally. We've danced this dance before. The muscle memory is the same, whether on a mat or a mattress.

I get into my fighting stance, forcing my inner calm to come forth, and Patton mirrors my movement, winking at me like the sly bastard he is. He's always known how to get under my skin.

The command to begin barely rolls off Micah's tongue before Patton comes at me. Because of course he does. It's always been in his nature to make the first move.

In life, in love, and on the mat.

His front kick is aimed at my head, controlled and powerful, snapping like a thunderclap before a downpour, but I sidestep it easily. Too easily.

The asshole is holding back.

"Really?" I taunt, circling him. "Is that the best you've got, or are you just out of practice?"

His eyes crinkle at the corners, giving away the tilt of his lips I can't see. "Just warming up, Little Borealis."

The endearment throws me off momentarily, causing that same familiar but unexpected pang to rip through me. As if he's struck me without having done so.

I channel the irritation and hurt into a lightning-fast roundhouse, aiming at his ribs. He blocks it, but he knows he's struck a nerve. Too bad for him, struck nerves don't count for actual points.

"Don't call me that," I snap as we circle each other again.

That ever-present grin is back in his voice. "What should I call you then? Mrs. Pierce?"

My anger flares, and I strike him using an illusion step he doesn't see coming.

"Point!" Micah calls.

"You lost Mrs. Pierce seven years ago," I grit, blinking back the sting in my stupid eyes.

He takes advantage, trying a kick combination that scores him a light touch to my chest guard. The lightest controlled touch as compared to the uncontrolled thwack mine had made.

"Point!" Micah calls out again.

"No, Little Borealis, that's where you're wrong," he says, not even a little out of breath. "You see, I never lost you . . ."—he watches me reset my stance, coming closer and dropping his voice—"you ran."

I lunge, launching at him with a spinning hook kick to his head that he only barely avoids.

"I see you've missed me," he teases.

"Keep talking, and I'll aim where it really hurts."

He laughs, the deep throaty timbre of his chuckle threatening to send familiar shockwaves through me. But I shirk them off, hyper-focused on my task.

Shifting into a back stance, I fire off a double roundhouse

—one that he blocks and another he barely evades by millimeters. But I hear the hard exhale of his breath, knowing he's getting worked up.

Good.

He tries to sweep my leg, but I jump over it and land with my elbow to his chest guard, making him stumble.

"Point! Thirty seconds left on the clock!" Micah warns.

We reset to center, and this time, my ex-husband comes at me with a tornado kick and a combination that would have impressed me a long time ago when we used to train together in a *dojang* similar to this one. But I'm not a teen anymore.

And I'm certainly not the twenty-something woman who waited around while he chased his dreams.

I slip under him. Using his momentum against him, I sweep his leg just as he lands. He goes down hard, rolling just in time to avoid my follow-up kick and making the crowd gasp.

I shake my head. "Give up, Hollywood."

He springs back up, eyes determined. "With you? Never."

This time I come in hot with a triple kick combo—low, high, and spinning axe kick—and the bastard manages to block all three. Clearly, he's kept up with his training.

But when he charges at me, I meet him halfway, catching him off guard when I feign left, then come around with a spinning back kick that lands precisely at the center of his back.

He hits the mat with a satisfying grunt.

"Final point for *Sabumnim* Arora!" Micah calls.

The crowd takes a relieved inhale before erupting into applause.

Patton blinks at me from the mat, and I can see the curve of his maddening smile stretched beneath his balaclava. Asshole *wanted* this outcome, not even giving me the satisfaction of a fair win.

I extend my hand down, though all I really want is to punch him in his stupid, smug face.

"Want to tell me why you're here?" I ask in a hushed voice veiled under the crowd's murmur.

His hand envelops mine, and for a beat, no one else exists. Just us.

"This *dojang* or this city?" he asks softly, pulling me closer so I'm hovering over him. "Either way, it's to chase you."

four
patton

Treat-me-so-good,
Gooseberry

I groan, stuffing my pillow under my chest and turning to relieve the pressure off my back. There isn't a visible bruise there, but damn, she got me good.

The thought makes me smile.

She makes me smile.

She kicked my ass last night but I suppose that's nothing new. Between the two of us, she was always better—at landing a kick, a punchline, or an exit.

And damn if she isn't still the most magnificent thing to step on a mat, all lethal grace and controlled power. Just the way she was when we were teens, taking after-school taekwondo classes at the same *dojang*. I loved those hours on the mat, especially because they meant I could spend more time with the girl from school who was slowly becoming more than my best friend, but theater was always my true calling.

From as far back as I can remember, I always wanted to be an actor. And while the path was often unclear and rocky, I had one constant—a girl who always believed in me, even when I didn't believe in myself. Whether it was our school's small stage or theaters all across the world, she was my biggest fan.

Until I lost her somewhere along the way.

The memory of last night seeps back in—her sharp kick, the rage burning in her eyes, and the way she shivered when I told her I was here for her—and I can't help the grin that spreads across my face.

I tested that tightly-held control of hers, and I have neither a regret nor an apology to offer for it. Not for last night, at least.

Because my regrets and apologies span years.

Just as the scent of fresh paint, new sheets, and cardboard register in my senses, reminding me I spent the night in my new house, a wet, slobbery tongue drags across the bottom of my foot.

Perfect.

Usually I have the wherewithal, even in my sleep, to keep my feet under the blankets for this very reason, but clearly, that final kick last night knocked that out-of-whack, too, besides just my back.

"Morning, buddy," I mumble, hearing his nails tap across the hardwood as he lumbers around my bed to give me one of his signature disappointed and judgmental stares. "Give me five more minutes okay?"

Bob, all one-hundred and twenty healthy pounds of him, is somehow the oldest-looking two-year-old bloodhound in existence.

With the droopy jowls of a grumpy old man nodding off on his porch rocker, eye bags that could double as suitcases, and enough sagging skin to suggest he's seen some shit in his day, Bob looks like he's one dog treat away from retirement.

But as tired and despondent as his eyes might look, they're just a front. Because under that droopy facade is the soul of a Tasmanian Devil with a penchant for theatrics.

For example, he just collapsed on the floor, as if he's been shot, with the most outrageous sigh ever heard. As if my asking for *five extra minutes* was akin to telling him he'll be going hungry for a week, or *God forbid*, that he'll never have another Starbucks pup-cup.

The flowery bra he stole out of a box in my closet—one of the only things my ex-wife accidentally left behind—lies on the floor next to him like a trophy from a scandalous night. I swear, he walks around with it clasped in his mouth all day, like he's waiting to clasp it on in case he's asked to walk a *Victoria's Secret* runway. And no matter how many times I've tried to sneak it away from him, he's found it, giving me an "*I'm on to you*" stare, reminiscent of Robert De Niro from *Meet The Parents*, and taken it back.

He stares back at me when I open one eye to look at him. *Dammit*! I should have pretended to have gone back to sleep!

He sighs again, a flutter catching his jowls.

Jesus. This dog.

"Fine," I groan, flinging my blanket off and wincing when my back protests.

I slowly haul myself out of bed, running a hand through my hair before dragging it over my face. I check the time on my phone—seven twenty-three. So much for sleeping in.

But I suppose I need to get moving, anyway. I'm meeting Troy and his friends for brunch this morning.

I've already met with Troy twice this past week—once to get to know him, and once to talk more about the elbow injury that took him out of the MLB for a year. It's the same injury that he came back from to win the last World Series and quickly became the inspiration for my next movie.

I might have had *other* reasons for insisting on making this film—personal, unfinished business—but artistic integrity and a heroic story were an easier sell to my agent.

So when Troy suggested brunch with his friends, knowing I'll be in town, shooting for the next few months, I didn't hesitate. Besides, my ex-sister-in-law's new fiancé strikes me as a solid dude overall, so hanging out with him is far from a hardship.

Theatrics forgotten, Bob jumps to his paws behind me, trusty bra in his mouth as I make my way to the bathroom to brush my teeth, then to the kitchen. I try not to stub my toe on one of the few boxes I told the decorator not to open as I make my way there.

How she and her team managed to furnish this home—curtains, paintings, and all the shit that makes a house feel lived-in—only hours after I purchased it, is beyond me. But I guess that's what I pay them for.

And speaking of purchasing this home, if I hear what a "professionally irresponsible" decision it was from my team once more, I'm going to start handing out pink-slips.

Yeah, I get it; it's not the sort of home a Hollywood A-lister might settle down in. Sure, there are security guards posted at the gated entrance to this upscale private neighborhood, but the homes themselves aren't walled off, or hidden behind iron gates or towering hedges. Just tree-lined streets, kids riding their bikes, and front porches decorated with potted plants and swings.

It's the kind of normalcy my heart has been searching for since . . . *her*. Since that one fucking fateful night seven years ago, when I came back to an empty house and a goodbye letter I still carry around with me.

This was the kind of life I'd promised her we'd have, but never delivered.

Yet another regret to add to my long and weighty list.

So when Troy casually mentioned that the house across from my ex-wife's was on the market, I considered it fate.

Some might call it stalking, but eh, tomato, tomahto.

Of course, since I purchased the place, my team went into panic mode, installing cameras, arranging security detail around the neighborhood, and monitoring everything as if I'd just been elected president. And though they're pissed at me for not letting them ask the neighborhood to sign NDAs, I told them to relax. I didn't move here to sit inside a bunker; I moved here to breathe . . .

And execute my plan.

If that means I'll be photographed here and there, well, la-dee-fuckin'-da. There are enough pictures of me on the internet to satisfy even the craziest fans, so what if there's one more?

That doesn't mean I'll be stupid and purposefully get recognized or photographed. Hence, the reason I wore the balaclava and gave my middle name at the *dojang* last night.

Plus, there's also Nisha's privacy to think about. She never cared much about getting photographed when we were married, as long as the paparazzi kept a respectful distance, but I wouldn't want to put her in the limelight again without her consent. It's why I'm going to make a concerted effort to be low-key and fly as much under the radar as I can.

With Bob waiting patiently—okay, more like he's watching my every move like a hired P.I.—I take a cup out of the cupboard and place it under the kind of coffee machine that looks like it requires an advanced degree to operate.

I've just pressed what I think is the *"Make My Coffee and Don't Explode"* button when my doorbell rings.

Bob's reaction is completely over-the-top, as is everything my dog does.

First, he lets out a low gruff, drops the bra from his mouth, then charges the door with a bark loud enough to wake the neighborhood. Then, squaring his shoulders, he plants himself in front of the door, staring at the doorknob as if daring it to turn. He gives two more barks for good measure.

When I don't rush behind him with equal fervor or concern, he drags his droopy, judgmental gaze to me. I can practically hear him say, *"What the fuck, man? Am I the only one who gives a crap about becoming the next headline on a true crime show? I'm too pretty for this shit."*

"Christ, Bob. It's probably just Alex," I mutter, referring to my publicist as I walk toward him. "You know the asshole doesn't believe in weekends or boundaries . . . or normal working hours."

But when I open the door, it's not Alex on the other side. It's an Amazon box.

Bob approaches it like he's a Homeland Security agent, sniffing it for explosives, drugs or, God forbid, butterflies.

Yeah, my ginormous dog is terrified of butterflies or moths or basically any other harmless winged insect. A couple of weeks ago, a small blue butterfly landed on his nose when he wasn't suspecting it, and he practically fainted. Seriously, his tail was tucked so tight against his belly, he looked like a corgi.

Don't ask me why he is the way he is. At this point, I've just accepted it.

The thought makes me smile because it reminds me of someone else I know. Tough as nails on the outside, with that sleeve of tattoos I've traced with my fingertips, coal-dark eyes that miss nothing, and that beautifully stubborn jaw I've felt against my lips. She's also the same woman who's deathly scared of balloons.

I learned that the hard way when I showed up to our high school with a huge bouquet of helium balloons for her seventeenth birthday. Until then, I'd never heard my tenacious, nearly unflappable best-friend-turned-girlfriend scream. She'd run like it were a rabid bear. The funny thing is, I'd bet every dollar in my account that she *could* take on a rabid bear . . . and win.

I pick up the box, bringing it inside with a curious Bob following me, and pull my phone out of my pajama pocket to check my messages. Perhaps my assistant or my decorator ordered something and sent me a message about it. It wouldn't be the first time.

When Bob lets out a dramatic whine—either because he thinks I'm not working fast enough or he's worried for my safety—I set the box down on the kitchen counter and grab a knife.

The tape gives way and the flaps open easily to reveal . . .
Uh, what the hell?

I lift a package containing edible underwear in "Peachy Cream".

Brows furrowing, I set it aside, only to lift out a dildo. There are six more below it in varying colors, sizes, and electrical modes. One even looks like Darth Vader.

"What the hell is this?" I mumble, confused.

At this point, I should put the items back since *clearly*, they're not for me. But my curiosity gets the better of me, and I forage through the packing material to find edible lubricants, with names like "Swirl-me-more, Melon" and "Treat-me-so-good, Gooseberry". There are also silk handcuffs in varying colors. And, Jesus Christ, don't even get me started on the number of condom boxes. Like a fucking lifetime supply!

Feeling guilty for having intruded on someone's private life, I quickly toss the items back into the box, closing the flaps.

That's when I see it.

My ex-wife's name and address.

This time, it's me who stares at it like it's a ticking bomb.

And that's when it hits me—a prickle of something I haven't felt in a long time. Something I've only felt with, and for, one girl in my entire life.

Jealousy. Dark, raw, and completely irrational.

Or maybe it *is* rational?

Who the fuck knows.

Who did she order these for? The question burns my chest like it's been doused with acid.

Who is she planning to wear edible underwear for? Who gets to watch as she uses those... those dildos? Does she allow him to use them on her? Does she let him watch as she gasps? As she screams his name?

It's that fucking instructor, Michael or Micah or whatever the hell his name was, isn't it? I'd taken one look at him last night and seen his thoughts written all over his smug face. He'd seen her, touched her the way only I had before.

Heat works up my neck, my hands rounding into fists. My thoughts turn murderous as I continue to glare at the box. I have half a mind to drive over to his *dojang* and put my fist through his pretty-boy face.

Instead, I take a long breath, reminding myself that I'm a grown man, so I can't act like a petulant teenager, even if it's exactly how I feel. And that Nisha has the right to date whomever she wants.

And I have a right to want to rearrange his face however I want.

Bob, with his emotional support bra hanging from his mouth again, taps his nails on the hardwood. It's his way of asking me why the fuck I'm losing my shit.

"Well, because this shit..." I wave to the box. "You don't buy this kinda shit for just anyone, Bob. Edible underwear and lube? Seven different kinds of vibrators?!" My jaw hardens as I speak to him. "This is for someone you're planning to spend a lot of naked time with. You wouldn't understand because you're always naked. And you literally have no balls."

Bob's tail droops, his eyes finding a spot near my feet.

I bend to scratch behind his ear. "Sorry, buddy. That was a low blow. See how this box is already coming between us? It's making me feel... unhinged."

I run a hand through my hair.

"Should I just head across the street and tell her it was a delivery mix-up? I suppose it's as good a time as any to let her know I'm her new neighbor. She's not going to be thrilled either way."

I pace around my large island and listen to Bob sigh dramatically, like he's an exasperated housewife from a nineties sitcom.

"A part of me wants to demand answers, you know? I get it; we're no longer together. But what about what happened last year? I thought it meant something. It meant something to me, at least."

I point a weighty finger at him. "You know I haven't been with a single woman in years. And all I've done since last year is work on this plan." I pull at the ends of my hair with a fist. "This fucking plan that may be fucked because she's fucking someone else!"

Bob can't appreciate the many different ways I've used the same word in one sentence. Instead, he flops on the ground again, dragging his treasured bra—a constant reminder of my ex-wife—over his ear with a paw, looking like he needs a smoke.

"Fuck it," I declare, clipping on Bob's leash and grabbing a ball cap to place over my head. "We're going over there."

Tongue hanging out, Bob jumps to all fours, finally giving me a look of respect.

With the box in one hand and my dog's leash in the other —him leading, of course—the walk across the street feels like the longest one of my life.

I don't pause to admire her warm-toned stucco home with its broad driveway, oversized windows, and patio that looks like something out of a home and garden magazine, with ivy-wrapped stone columns, hanging lanterns, and enough potted plants to be considered a rainforest.

Instead, I march forward with my heart hammering inside

my chest. My heart didn't even beat this hard when I jumped out of a plane for my last film.

Bob, meanwhile, is as calm as a cucumber—bra in mouth, nose to the ground in full-on inspection mode, and tail wagging. When we reach Nisha's front patio, he immediately does a forensic exam of the potted plants and anything else within sniffing distance.

With one hand gripping his leash, I ring her doorbell just as Bob starts circling one of her potted plants that looks like a rare and expensive tropical monstrosity.

My stomach drops, and I immediately tug on his leash, bracing for impending calamity.

"Bob, no!"

But I'm too late.

Because right as Nisha's door swings open, my beast of a dog lifts his leg and starts to take the longest piss of his life.

five
nisha

I Love a Good Peach

Grabbing the three beanies I knitted this week from the drawer in my closet, I place them into the large tote I'm carrying. I also pack my knitting needles and the work-in-progress sweater for Hector, just in case I get a chance to work on it between clients. It'll be light blue with a dark gray neck and hem that will make his piercing blue eyes pop.

Going over to the drawer next to the one with my knitting supplies, I throw in a few travel-sized deodorants and bottles of SPF. I remember someone—was it Janice or Becker?—said they had run out.

My eyes land on the time displayed on my phone. It's still early, but sometimes the traffic to the shelter can be unpredictable on the weekends. And if there's one thing I can't stand, it's being late to anything.

Okay, it's one of *many* things I can't stand.

Like people who speak too loud, too close—or, hell—just too much. And if any of that talking is done while they're eating, say, a banana, making that smacking-slurping sound like they're trying to give oral to the fruit, I will self-detonate.

A shudder goes down my arms as I shake off a violent case of the heebie-jeebies at the mere thought.

I'm just walking down the hallway toward my living room when the doorbell rings.

I frown, checking my watch again before adjusting the strap of my tote bag over my shoulder. Who could it be at this time of the morning?

The sound of a man's deep and admonishing voice fills my ears as I turn the lock and swing open my door, coming face-to-face with . . .

Wait.

Why am I coming face-to-face with my ex-husband?

Again.

My eyes take in the scene before me. Patton, with eyes as big as saucers under a Bay Area Blazer's cap, is holding a cardboard box in one hand and a leash that leads to what can only be classified as a large bear in the other. Said bear has one hind leg up, slightly shaking in mid-air, and is now peeing directly into my Thai Constellation Monstera—the same plant I've nurtured for the past four years with as much care as one would give a newborn.

"What—"

My shocked voice is abruptly cut off by Patton's. "Nisha, hey! Shit."

He flicks an embarrassed and desperate glare at his dog before tugging on his leash, but I'm still processing what the hell is actually happening on my patio.

My mouth opens and closes like a fish out of water as I watch droplets of urine trickle down the pristine white pot.

Four years.

Four years of devoting myself to its beautiful foliage.

Four years of following a regimented watering schedule, gently pruning and cleaning its beautiful green and white leaves like I was detailing a Rolls Royce, and this overgrown mutt has turned my prized plant into his very own toilet.

"Patton Luca Pierce, why is your dog peeing on my

Monstera?" My voice is deadly calm as I bring my gaze back to my ex, making him flinch.

He knows this voice better than almost anyone. It's the same one I'd use when he told me he'd once again miss Christmas or another anniversary because he was going to have to stay back for reshoots in Germany or Prague or Timbuktu.

Patton winces but quickly masks his face with a thoughtful expression. "Did you know that the Monstera is known to attract growth and positive energy in Feng Shui? Bob's naturally drawn to positivity, you see. He saw it and decided to contribute to the vibe."

"By *peeing* on it?"

"He's a generous boy. A thoughtful boy." Patton shifts on his feet, visibly sweating under my glare. "So, fun fact—the Thai Constellation actually became a status plant in the 1970s—"

"Are you seriously trying to distract me from the fact that your dog is *still* peeing on my plant with historical trivia?"

It's widely known that there are very few Hollywood celebrities with as much historical knowledge as my ex. It's both an extreme turn-on and a severe irritation.

"Fuck, I'm so sorry," Patton says hastily, shifting the box in his hand awkwardly while yanking on his dog's leash once more with the other. "This got delivered to my house, so I came to drop it off. I probably should have let Bob do his business first."

"You think?"

A flush settles on the tops of his cheeks, his dark scruff making it more obvious, and I force my eyes not to soften.

I know the man all too well: give him an inch and he'll take a mile. And right now, with him wearing those black, low-slung pajama pants that hug his trim waist and a white undershirt stretching around his chest and arms—doing little to hide the packs of abs I know are underneath—my eyes *really* want to soften.

But I won't let them. I'll keep them hard as steel. As cold as the Alaskan winter. As unmoved as a wall of concrete.

Still, how does the man manage to look more attractive every year?

Dragging my gaze from him, I look at the box in his hand. And that's when his words finally register. *His house...?*

"What do you mean, this box got delivered to *your* house? My stuff hasn't been delivered to your house in ages..."

Having finally finished his plant-watering, Patton's dog, *Bob*, sniffs a trail across my patio, coming to a stop at my feet, where he drops...

Wait...

I recognize that bra.

I've been looking for that bra!

But what if it's someone else's? Maybe it just *looks* like the one I used to have. What if it's actually a trophy from the last leggy model I saw draped over my ex-husband's arm in a tabloid photo?

"Is that my bra?"

Patton rubs the back of his neck sheepishly. "He's, uh... attached to it."

My brows furrow. "Why do you still have it?"

But before Patton can answer, Bob's nose wiggles, taking quick inhales of my black combat boots. He trails up my bare legs to the crotch of my ripped denim shorts before taking a long, shameless inhale.

"Wow. Oh, please," I drawl. "Go right ahead. Make yourself at home."

Patton's lips pull into that infuriating grin that's unlike anyone else's, the one that's haunted me since I was sixteen. "What can I say? Bob's always had discerning taste, just like his dad. Plus, remember that bit I said about him being drawn to positivity?"

I wrap my arms around my chest, drawing Patton's eyes to my breasts, before raising a brow. "He's also clearly a pervert, *just like his dad.*"

Patton shrugs, unfazed. "Can't blame the guy for going after what he wants." As if appreciating the encouragement, the droopy-eyed behemoth wags his tail, sniffing more fervently to find any spot on the bottom half of my body he can reach. "Besides, you can't open the door wearing those shorts, showing off that midriff, and expect a man, or his dog, not to notice."

Patton's gaze follows a trail up my torso, taking in my cropped white tank top with the kind of appreciation that should annoy me. But my brain isn't cooperating at the moment, acting no different than this dog at my crotch, desperate for every morsel of attention it can get.

And my body? It's all too eager, swaying toward him like it's being pulled by a magnet. When his eyes linger on my lips with an intensity that literally has me perspiring—and not because of the July heat—I stutter in a breath.

Get it the fuck together, Nisha. Remember why you left him? No? Well, let me remind you: Patton Pierce puts nothing before his aspirations, and that includes his wife.

And that's when my brain reboots and I repeat my question, snatching the box from his hand with more force than necessary.

"Why would you get a box delivered for me at your house?" I inspect the name on the shipping label, confirming it's mine, before realizing the seal has already been slit. "And if you knew it was mine, then why did you open it?"

I'm just prying open the flaps with one hand when Patton throws a thumb over his shoulder. "Oh, the delivery person must have just gotten the house number wrong. You know, since I live right across the street from you now."

My hand freezes mid-rummaging, and my eyes snap to meet my husband's—uh, ex-husband's—earthy brown ones. "Wh–what do you mean you live across the street from me?"

Having gotten enough from my crotch and clearly not giving a shit about my body going into fight-or-flight mode, Bob makes his way over to smell the other plants on my patio.

God, please don't let him *vibe* with their positivity, too.

Patton tries to mask his smirk, turning to look over his shoulder at the beautiful mid-century modern we both damn well know he's talking about. "I mean, I moved into the house across from you yester—"

"No." My heart rattles inside my ribs like a caged bird, and I shake my head, cutting him off. "No, that can't be true. I didn't even see a moving truck or . . . or movers. How could you have . . .?" My voice shakes, getting higher with each word. "And why? Why would you move there when there are literally a million other homes in the city? Mansions, penthouses . . . castles with moats!"

You know, all the things he was working those long hours for. All the things he always wanted. More than he wanted anything or anyone else.

I look to the left and right, examining the quiet tree-lined street. "And do you know how absolutely insane it is for you to live here? You won't have the kind of privacy and security you need. You'll have paparazzi swarming—"

Patton leans in, bringing with him the scent of bergamot, fresh mint, and something familiar, something uniquely and devastatingly him, and the rest of my words die on my lips.

"Breathe, Little Borealis." His eyes peer into mine before dropping back to my lips. "I get what this looks like—"

"What it *looks* like is that my ex-husband, who is possibly the biggest star on the planet, is hell-bent on ruining my sanity by showing up, not just to my *dojang* last night, but moving into the house in front of mine."

I don't mention the fact that I haven't stopped thinking about his parting words—*"Either way, it's to chase you."* They were a nod to the question I asked him that evening a year ago —why didn't he chase me if he missed me so much?

Patton pulls his cap off his head, sliding long fingers through his disheveled dark hair before placing it back on again. I know him well enough to know he's using the time to think about his response.

"Look, you know I'm going to be working with Troy at that old baseball field nearby. A lot of the shooting for the movie will likely be there as well, so I'll be in town longer than I expected—"

"How much longer?"

He shrugs again, but there's something in his eyes. Something less nonchalant than the casual gesture he's trying to mask it with. "Months. A year, possibly."

"A year?!" The panic surging inside me can't be stopped from rising to the surface. "Patton—"

"As I was saying . . ." He tilts his head, but I don't miss the flicker of hurt that passes over his features in response to my outburst. "I'll be working nearby—on set most days—so I figured I'd find a place around here instead of living out of hotel rooms and trailers the entire time. When Troy told me the house across from yours was on the market—"

"Troy told you about the house?" My mouth hangs open.

Why would Troy do that? My soon-to-be brother-in-law might be crazy about my sister, but he's not crazy enough to meddle in anyone else's life. Sure, I haven't given him the details about my and Patton's separation, but he knows enough. I'm sure my sister has filled him in, too, given she practically lived through the ordeal with me.

My sister . . .

My thoughts whirl as dots connect inside my head. Troy *wouldn't* have told Patton about the house, unless . . .

That little traitor! She always had a soft spot for my ex-husband. As did my dad. As did Piper. And most of the female—and some of the male—population in the world.

Honestly, if my mother were alive, I bet she'd bake cookies and take them over to his house to welcome him to the neighborhood.

Basically, everyone I love is a backstabbing Brutus and will be hearing from my lawyer. Or at the very least, they'll be getting an earful from me later.

"Yeah." Patton clears his throat. "Actually, I need to head back to get ready. I'm meeting him and some of his friends for brunch."

Oh, dear God. This just keeps getting worse.

"You're meeting the Six Schlongs for brunch?"

"Pardon?"

I shut my eyes and take a calming breath.

He's meeting the Schlongs. At this point, he might as well become a part of *The Real Housewives of Beverly Hills*. Those guys, namely Dean Meyer, are worse than a pack of gossip-hungry hyenas.

"Right." I force my voice to sound normal, given everything I've had to process in the past ten minutes. Speaking of which . . . *Dammit*, I'm going to be late! "Well, don't let me keep you. I need to get going, too."

Patton's gaze shifts to the bag at my side, but if he's wondering where I'm headed, he doesn't ask. Instead, he nods toward the box, that mischievous smirk barely in his control.

"I have to ask . . . seven vibrators, Neesh? Is it like one for each day of the week, or does *Michael* need mechanical assistance?"

"Michael? What are you—" I start, my head snapping back and my brows furrowing in confusion.

But then, like a movie where the dubbing is off, my brain catches up with what he's just said and the blood drains from my face.

Seven vibrators.

Oh, no.

Oh, no, no, no, no.

My eyes dart to the box in my hand and then to the smile on his smug face, and I realize that the asshole isn't just making an assumption; he's seen the contents of the box.

"It's one thing to accidentally open someone's mail," I grind out, mortification staining my cheeks. "It's another to *inspect* it."

Patton's smirk widens. "What can I say? After I saw the 'Peachy Cream' edible underwear, my curiosity got the best of me." He winks. "You know how much I love a good peach."

My face flames so hot I'm shocked my hair doesn't catch fire.

"You're disgusting. And those aren't—it's not what it—" I take in a fortifying breath, dropping the box on my entryway chair. "Those aren't for me. Well, they're not *all* for me. They're for Sarina's bachelorette party."

Patton's brow quirks. "So, which ones *are* for you? Let me know if you need help giving them a go."

I roll my eyes, pretending his words don't affect me, pretending I don't remember what it was like to say yes to him. "I don't. But thank you for the generous offer."

"Why? Because of Michael?"

My eyes narrow slightly, picking up the tick in his jaw and the way his fist balls at his side. But I don't dignify his question with a response. Because if he wants to think there's something going on with me and Micah, then let him.

"Thank you for dropping by, Patton. It's been a real *treat*. But if there's no other surprise you need to drop on me"—I look pointedly at the dog, now snoring with his tongue sticking out on my patio floor like a hungover frat boy—"or if your dog is—"

"Bob," Patton cuts in, mock-offended. "His name is Bob. Not 'Bob' like your seven battery-operated-boyfriends, but Bob, like the World War II hero who received the Dicken Medal for his bravery."

I blink at him, and then at said dog, with his leg twitching in deep slumber. The only medal he looks like he's earned is "Outstanding Achievement in Couch Potatoing".

"Right. Well, unless *Bob* needs to relieve himself on more of my plants, I have somewhere I need to be."

"Those are all the neighborly surprises Bob and I had planned for you today." Patton pulls on the bill of his cap. "You're welcome, by the way."

As if knowing we're at the end of our conversation, Bob bolts upright with energy I didn't know he had. Capturing my bra in his mouth, he gives me a droll look before trotting off the patio.

Patton trails after him, but just before he steps off the last stair, he looks over his shoulder at me, the previous humor in his tone completely gone. "Oh, and Nisha?"

"Yes?"

"Get rid of Michael."

I suppress the need to throw something at him. "Excuse me?"

"You heard me."

The fucking nerve of this guy. If he thinks he can just show up here and demand I "get rid" of someone seven years after our divorce, he must be certifiable.

"No, I clearly didn't. I don't know a Michael. I know a *Micah*."

"Sounds like a guy who drinks oat milk and uses rosemary as deodorant. Like I said, get rid of him."

My mouth drops open.

Before I can even formulate a response, Patton continues down the path, putting distance between us. But then, halfway to the sidewalk, he glances back at me once more.

This time, that hard edge in his jaw softens, and that same smile—the one that has me thinking about kisses under a warm sun and whispers in bed—graces his face.

With a lazy salute, he winks. "See you around, Little Borealis."

I don't answer. Instead, I close the door slowly, like if I shut him out, this will all have been something I'd just imagined.

But I know it's not.

Because he's here. Living across the street. For possibly a year.

A year of watching him come and go every day. A year of him parading women. Because if the tabloids are to be believed, the man has dated everyone except Siri.

A year where I slowly lose my peace, my sanity, and possibly everything I've worked to regain.

And this time, I won't get to leave first.

six
patton

Being Assholes is Part of Our Charm

"Holy shit, we're having brunch with Patton Pierce," blurts a man with shoulder-length dirty blond hair, pulled into a half bun.

He looks a lot like the guy to his left, who has shorter hair but the exact same piercing blue eyes, making me wonder if they're brothers.

I can't help but grin at his enthusiasm as we settle into our seats in a private dining room of an upscale restaurant in the Financial District.

Troy goes around the table doing introductions, starting with the guy with the man-bun. "Patton, this is Dean. Dean, try not to spring a boner in the first five minutes."

"Hey!" Dean raises his hands, eyes wide and offended. "My boners are reserved just for you, Troy. No need to get jealous, my friend."

"Pretty sure Mala—you know, that gorgeous wife of yours and my sister-in-law?—might have something to say about that," says the similar-looking man next to him, confirming that indeed, they are brothers.

Pointing to the other brother, Troy continues, "And this is

Garrett. He and Dean are twins, but Garrett is the one with the brain-to-mouth filter."

Dean shrugs. "That may be, but I'm the better-looking one. And for the record, Mala gets all my *actual* boners. She knows my worship of Troy is purely based on his athletic prowess."

Garrett reaches out a hand for me to shake. "Nice to meet you, man. Watched a few of your movies, and both my wife and I are big fans."

"Thanks," I respond with a genuine smile.

Troy continues with the introductions, pointing to each of the three other guys. "Hudson, Darian, and Dev. Hudson owns one of the largest excavation companies serving the West Coast, Darian is Dean and Garrett's younger brother, and one of the most level-headed men I know. Too bad he got stuck with Beavis and Butt-Head as brothers—"

"Hey!" Dean and Garrett say together, but it doesn't stop Troy.

"And on the other side of Garrett is the one and only Dev Menon. I doubt he needs much of an introduction."

I reach out to shake each of their hands. "No, he doesn't. Pretty sure Dev Menon is more famous than God himself."

And that's not an exaggeration by any means, given the dude is one of the richest and most powerful men on earth.

Dev waves a dismissive hand. "Pretty sure the guy with the Oscar at this table deserves that credit. I just happened to get lucky in tech; you're the one with the actual talent, Patton." He smiles at me. "My wife, Piper, tells me she knew you were going to be on the big screen even back in high school."

"She was the most intuitive of our group," I say, forcing a smile as memories flit through my brain.

"Was she also the most unhinged of the group?" Dean asks, making everyone at the table chuckle. "Because she definitely has that title in this group."

"Says the man who's still thinking about getting Troy's face tattooed on his ass cheek," Darian says dryly. With dark hair and eyes, he looks nothing like his brothers, but based on the fact that they're sitting next to each other and have been teasing each other nonstop, I get the feeling they're close.

"Art is self-expression, baby bro," Dean retorts, reaching to ruffle Darian's hair, but giving Dean a murderous glare, Darian flicks his hand away. "You wouldn't understand, since your favorite way of expressing yourself is wearing a color besides gray once a year."

Darian flips Dean off before taking a drink of his water, making everyone chuckle.

"Actually, Piper had us all figured out before we did ourselves," I answer, turning to Dev again. "How is she, by the way?"

"She's great!" Dev's eyes brighten, and the adoration in them at the thought of his wife is clear. "We have a little girl named Ariana who's almost one."

I congratulate him, recalling the quick message I sent to Piper on Instagram after she posted a picture of her baby. She'd only responded with a "Thanks!" but I still remember how that one word had strummed the hollowness that had been growing ever since Nisha left.

I take a sip of my water, keeping my face neutral.

It was never a secret that Sarina and Piper were closest to Nisha, given one is her fraternal twin, the other her best friend. But the four of us got close in high school. In fact, we remained that way for years after. But when Nisha left, I wasn't just cut off from my wife—my best friend and the love of my life—but some of my closest friends, as well.

Friends I considered family.

The only real family I'd ever had.

I know the blame for the loss of my marriage lies largely

with me. I own that. But seven years of silence from the others?

Seven years of missed birthdays, holidays, and celebrations? Seven years of stalking their lives through their social media posts, and nothing more? Seven years where none of them—except for my ex-father-in-law—ever checked on me?

None of that was easy to swallow.

And since my ex-wife has her socials locked down like a fortress—much like her feelings about me—the only way I could see how she was faring was through stalking Sarina and Piper's posts, looking for a rare glimpse of her.

I'm forced from my thoughts when the waitstaff enters the room with large trays of food, apparently from a prefixed menu. The only thing we're asked to order are our drinks.

When they've left, and we've all taken helpings of truffle scrambled eggs, pancakes with elderflower syrup, and some sort of fancy tomato tart, I turn to the quietest man in the group, the one sitting to my right. He's been acutely focused on his plate, like he's hoping to disappear inside it.

"So, Hudson, you own an excavation empire? Not sure I know anything about that sort of business. What does that entail?"

Hudson puts his fork down, an obvious hitch in his voice that gets everyone's attention. "We, uh . . ." He clears his throat and tries again. "We . . . we . . ."

"Dude," Garrett asks slowly, squinting at him. "Are you having a stroke?"

The other guys around the table seem just as bewildered, and I gather this isn't something they've ever witnessed with their friend.

Hudson throws an irritated glance at Garrett before tossing a similar glare around the table, nostrils flaring as he takes in a breath like he's trying to compose himself.

I place a hand on his shoulder. "You good, man?"

"Yeah. Yes." Hudson responds before taking a sip of water. "I'm fine. Just . . . a huge fan, actually. I don't watch much TV, but my wife and I never miss your movies. *Fatal Facets, Pilots of the Pacific, Credit Card Millionaire, Truly Yours Again* . . ."

A pin-drop silence falls over the table, and I swear no one moves.

I keep my gaze pinned on my plate, because if I look up and catch anyone else's, I will absolutely lose it.

It isn't unusual for people to get a little flustered when they first meet me, but watching Hudson, a man who likely has thirty pounds and two inches over my six–foot–one height, get tongue-tied? It's pretty fucking funny.

I get the sense that not much rattles him, that he's likely the most calculating and stoic of the group. So watching him stammer even has his friends in shock.

"Holy shit," Troy whispers, clearly covering his smile behind a napkin.

"Jesus," Dean follows, both disgusted and stunned. "Hud, is that a tear at the corner of your eye, or do they just water more since you're so ancient?"

Hudson gives Dean a scathing look. "Shut the fuck up, asshole. Firstly, I'm only a couple of years older than you. And secondly, I'm a hundred times more composed than you were the first time you met Troy."

"We can all vouch for that," Dev agrees and turns to me. "Dean has an altar dedicated to Troy in his bedroom."

My brows rise, and I look over at Dean to see if he'll argue, but he just smiles proudly.

"Let's not forget the pajama bottoms he wears each night with Troy's face on them," Garrett adds, taking a bite of his tart.

Darian nods. "He didn't wash his hand for days after shaking Troy's for the first time."

"True story." Dean nods. "But it was more like weeks."

"Fucking nasty, bro," Garrett condemns. "The sad thing is, I don't know if you're kidding."

"I'm not."

I can't help but laugh, my previous melancholy over having lost touch with my childhood friends lifting off my shoulders.

Troy mentioned these guys multiple times this week, telling me how they'd become his closest friends, and I can see why. Twenty minutes in their presence, and I already feel like I've known them for twenty years.

"It's fine," I say, looking at Hudson, who is once again staring at his plate. "I'm flattered, actually. Honestly, you guys all seem more interesting than me, but can we all forget that I actually starred in *Credit Card Millionaire*?"

Dean nods somberly. "Not gonna lie, man, that one was pretty terrible."

I laugh, though that familiar anguish threatens to pull me under. Not only was it a terrible fucking movie, but it was the last straw that broke my marriage. "You have no idea how many times I've wished I could go back in time and make a different choice."

It's then that the waitstaff comes in, and I'm spared from the way Dean's eyes narrow on me. I get the feeling that under the class-clown act lurks a man who misses nothing.

"What were you going to say about your company, Hudson?" I ask, taking a sip from my latte.

Hudson finally seems to have settled his nerves, some of what I think is his usual sternness coming back in his demeanor. "We displace earth for large construction sites like buildings, malls, and so on and so forth."

"He's being modest," Troy adds. "His company excavated the Blazers' baseball field."

"Wow," I say, impressed.

"Speaking of which," Dean chimes in. "How long are you planning on being in San Francisco, Patton? How's it going hanging out and learning to pitch from the legend of all legends himself?"

I take another sip of my coffee, buying myself a moment to think. "Probably a few months, maybe a year. And as for working with Troy? It's been amazing. In just two meetings, I feel like I've learned intricacies of pitching that I never knew. It'll definitely take a while and a few more lessons from Troy before I actually *look* professional on-screen . . . as professional as an actor can look, that is."

"Several months or a year?" Dev chimes in, and dammit, I'm not quick enough to stop him from asking the rest. I might not know the guy well, but his smirk says he gives zero shits about putting me on the spot. "But didn't you just buy a house here? Specifically, across the street from Nisha?"

The entire table goes quiet once again, except for the sounds of forks clattering against plates.

"Well, isn't that one hell of a coincidence," Dean says with a shit-eating grin. "And Dev, are we talking about *Nisha Arora*? The ex-wife of our Hollywood guest of honor today?"

I pinch the bridge of my nose. The asshole knows damn well which Nisha he means.

"Why yes, yes I am, Dean," Dev responds, playing along.

"So let me get all this straight because"—Garrett whistles before he grins—"it's a doozy. A Hollywood A-list celebrity decides to film a baseball movie in San Francisco, based on his ex-sister-in-law's new fiancé's career. He then buys a house in a 'regular' neighborhood, instead of staying in a highly secure condo, and it just *happens* to be across from his ex-wife?" He looks around the room exaggeratedly, getting their nods. "Did I get all that right?"

I should have asked more questions or maybe politely declined when Troy asked if I wanted to meet his friends.

"The neighborhood is secure enough," I hedge. "My team even added more security around it."

"I don't know about you guys," Hudson says, trying to suppress a smile, "but this sounds more like a strategic plan than a coincidence."

Clearly, he's recovered from his bout of speechlessness, though a part of me wishes he'd go back to sputtering again.

"Some may even call this 'strategic plan' a stalking operation," Darian muses with an amused expression.

"Hey now, guys," Dean says, turning up his hands in mock defense. "Perhaps Patton just couldn't find a condo of his liking in one of the largest cities in the U.S."

"It's likely the same reason he didn't like any other screenplay besides the baseball one," Troy adds sarcastically, inciting the same shit-eating grins on every face around the table. "Not that I'm complaining!"

Wow.

Et tu, Troy?

I run a hand through my hair, squeezing the back of my neck, realizing that I've walked right into a trap set by these guys.

"Look," I say, not able to hold back my smile, but refusing to give into them cornering me. "It's not like I'm hiding out in her basement or anything. I told Troy I was looking to buy property, and when he mentioned the house across from her was on the market, I decided to act on it."

"Sure, sure," Dev says, grinning. "This all makes sense. You absolutely *didn't* move here under the guise of filming a baseball movie to win back your ex-wife."

I give him an "are-you-serious?" face. "I *am* filming a baseball movie!"

"Sure, sure."

"It's actually romantic," Hudson says into his mimosa. "In

a 'not advisable and will probably end badly' sort of way, but romantic, nonetheless."

I take a breath, hating how hard I'm having to work to suppress my damn smile. "I might have just met you all a half-hour ago, but I already think you're assholes."

Dean raises his glass. "That's the spirit! Welcome to the club, man. Being assholes is part of our charm!"

Darian side-eyes Dean. "Some of us are bigger assholes than others."

Without missing a beat, Dean pulls him into a headlock and kisses the top of his head. Darian shoves him off, both of them laughing like they're twelve and not grown adults.

"But seriously," Dev says, bringing everyone's attention back to me. "Are you trying to get her back? You're part of the Schlongs now, so anything you say will stay in the circle of trust."

"The *Schlongs*?" Why do I feel like I've heard the name before?

Troy nods, pulling out his phone and typing something while he speaks. "It's our group chat—the Six Schlongs Hen Party. It'll be Seven Schlongs now since I'm adding you to it."

I swear, I only understood fifty percent of that, but when my phone buzzes in my pocket, I see I've been added to a new group chat.

"Well?" Hudson asks, pushing his empty plate away and leaning back in his chair to look at me. "Are you trying to get her back?"

Over the past almost-decade since I've been in the spotlight, I've had to be careful with who I trust. And I've learned the hard way that when you have money and fame, most people aren't after the real you.

But something about this group is different. Perhaps it's the way they couldn't give two shits about my celebrity status or the fact that they've welcomed me into their group so easily

—already giving me shit like we've known each other for ages. Whatever the case, I find myself wanting to trust them.

Hell, maybe I've been craving friendship just like this. It sounds sappy as shit even in my own head, but it's the truth.

I run a hand down my face. "You know what? Yes. I moved here hoping to win her back. After Troy was injured and then had that incredible comeback, I proposed the idea for this movie to the right people in the industry. When it seemed like they were interested, my only condition was that it be filmed here."

Troy raises his brows, and I can't tell if it's in offense or in admiration. "So you used me to get closer to my sister-in-law? Do I have that right?"

"Yes."

"Damn." He pauses before nodding. "Well, I respect that."

"What happened between you two, anyway?" Hudson asks. "I mean, is it truly 'irreconcilable' like the tabloids stated?"

"Clearly, Hudson hasn't been stalking you online or anything," Garrett says dryly, to which Hudson just flips him off.

I take a long breath. "That's a story for another night. But no, it wasn't irreconcilable in the unforgivable sense. Nisha and I never stopped loving each other. We just . . ." I drag my teeth across my bottom lip as memories, both good and painful, dance across my vision. "I didn't prioritize what mattered, and I've been paying for it ever since."

The guys go quiet. A couple of them nod, whether in understanding or support, I can't be sure.

"But what's your actual plan?" Dean asks. "Knock on her door and ask her to chat every day?"

I smile, recalling doing exactly that this morning when I went over to deliver her package. God, she looked fucking beautiful—my Little Borealis—dressed in those shorts and that tank top, showing off her sleeve of tattoos. Her dark, glossy hair skimmed her toned shoulders, and she smelled like pomegranates.

Always like pomegranates.

And when her shocked eyes found mine and those delectable lips of hers turned downward, I swear, I wanted to fist my hand in her hair and drag her mouth to mine, if only to cover that scowl. If only to hear her gasp before I tasted her pomegranate-flavored lip gloss again.

Years later, and my ex-wife is still the most beautiful woman I've ever seen, even pissed.

I'm just about to answer Dean, just about to tell him that I don't really have much more of a plan than that, when Troy cuts in, "What are you doing next weekend?"

My brows furrow. "Not sure yet. Why? What's happening next weekend?"

Troy smiles, raising his brows at the rest of the guys in some sort of silent exchange. They all nod before Troy answers, "The Schlongs and Clams bachelor and bachelorette party."

I still don't understand most of that sentence, but I have a feeling my plan to get my ex-wife back just got hijacked by six guys I barely know.

seven
nisha

Calm Down, Hannibal Lecter

With my mouth pursed to one side, I stretch the partially knitted sweater over Hector's broad back, gauging it for size. It needs to be larger to fit him.

"You're knitting that for me?" Hector asks, his blue eyes connecting with mine through the mirror. "That's very kind of you, Ms. Arora."

I frown. "Hector, how many times have I asked you to just call me Nisha? Anyway, I was hoping to have it done before your interview at the warehouse, but it might be another week before I can finish it."

He smiles, the lines around his mouth deepening. "That should be plenty of time. The interview isn't for ten days." He pauses, examining the gray and blue colors of the sweater. "I can't remember having something so nice before."

I place the sweater back in my bag, mentally calculating how many more rows I'll need before reaching for my clipping shears.

I picked up knitting over seven years ago. And while the reason I started carries the weight of a loss—multiple losses, in fact—I still can't completely shake, my hands continue to reach for the yarn. Maybe it's my way of calming my racing mind; maybe it's the only connection I have to the version of me from that time.

A version that used to be full of promise and hope.

A version of me who used to dream.

Squeezing his shoulder, I give him a tender smile. "You deserve all the nice things, Hector. Including a fresh cut that'll show off those beautiful eyes of yours."

His weathered freckled cheeks tint pink. "It'll help me look more put-together, that's for sure. And if I get the job, who knows? I might be able to take Abby on a date. Though, it's like pulling teeth to get her to even look at me."

My eyes soften. "She's a tough nut to crack. I get the feeling she's a little . . . standoffish."

"That she is. But I think I'm wearing her down. She even whispered a hello to me in the lunch line today."

I run my fingers through his towel-dried salt and pepper hair, thinking about the frail woman who I've seen around here recently.

She's likely no more than fifty, but her pale green eyes, almost translucent skin, and thinning dark hair makes her look much older. And it's clear that with her hollowed cheeks and several missing teeth, life hasn't been kind to her.

I started volunteering at this homeless shelter nearly five years ago, giving out haircuts to all who needed it. About a year in, they converted one of the storage closets into a makeshift salon for me. While the shelter installed a shampoo sink, I donated a salon chair, mirror, and continue to keep it stocked with products. The space is shoebox-sized and bare-boned, a far cry from the opulent luxury salon I co-own, but it has everything I need to get the job done.

I start on Hector's sides, snipping away what seems like two months of growth. He's in his sixties and has been one of the regulars here for the past two years. Like many others, sometimes he stays at the shelter, sometimes he doesn't.

He doesn't volunteer his reasons as to what brings him in from time to time, and I'm not one to push for answers. Everyone deserves to tell their story on their own time, and if they don't, well that's a fair choice, too.

God knows, there aren't many who know my entire story.

The thought makes me smile because, even as it occurs, I realize staying tight-lipped about anything has become increasingly difficult considering my group of girlfriends.

They're like nosey FBI agents with carte blanche access to every interrogation tactic known to man like wine, memes, and emotional manipulation.

I'm already regretting letting it slip that I had dinner with Patton last year. Ever since then, our group chat has lit up. Apparently, we're all meeting tonight for the sole purpose of making me "spill the tea".

They all already know the reasons I left him seven years ago.

Sarina, Piper, and my dad held me through the loss and heartbreak. Even now, I just need to think about that very last night—with my back against the bathroom door, trying to gulp in air as tears streamed down my face—for the grief to come bubbling to the surface.

It was the type of heartache I wouldn't wish on my worst enemy.

And I dealt with it on my own.

And while I only met the rest—Rani, Bella, Mala, and Kavi—at Piper's wedding a couple of years ago, we formed a bond not unlike mine with my sister and best friend. So, during a girls' night out last year, over a few tubs of ice cream and boxes of tissues, I told them everything.

And in those tears we shed together, I realized that my circle had expanded, and so had my heart. Because I can confidently say that while these women might not have known me through every chapter, they love me as if they have.

But none of them, not even Sarina or Piper, know what happened last year. That I barely managed not to slip under the same tide again—a tide I'd almost drowned in the last time.

Fifteen minutes later, I unclasp the cape around Hector's neck and brush the loose hair from behind his ears. Hector's blue eyes shine a little brighter, and his jaw seems more defined than when he sat down. It's a small change, but the joy that comes from helping someone feel a little more like themselves again hits me every time.

"You know," I say, smoothing some gel into a few strands of his hair. "I think this warehouse job is going to be great for you. It'll be steady hours and pay. I have a good feeling about it."

Hector rises from the chair, checking himself out in the mirror with a satisfied grin. "I hope so. It'll be—" His words are cut off when both our eyes land on the woman standing at the entrance. "Oh, hey, Abby! I was just talking about you with Ms. Arora, here."

"Nisha," I remind him.

"Oh?" Abby asks hesitantly, her voice raspy like that of a long-time smoker. She pulls her sleeves almost to the middle of her palms, shifting from one foot to another. "Okay . . ." She looks down past Hector, as if resigned to whatever he may have said about her, convinced it was bad.

Hector takes a step toward her, but falters when she stiffens, though his smile holds. "I was just telling her that maybe my new haircut will help me land a job so I can finally ask you out on a date."

Abby's eyes give nothing away, almost as if Hector hasn't spoken. Instead, they slide down, focusing on her fidgeting hands. My chest tightens at the way Hector's shoulders deflate, but he turns to me with a polite smile and a murmured thanks before sliding past Abby, telling her that he'll see her later.

I offer her a smile. "Are you here for a haircut, Abby?"

Her tired eyes find mine. "If . . . if it's not too much to ask."

I run a sanitizing wipe over my chair, waving her toward it before reaching for a broom. "Not at all. Come sit down. I'm Nisha, by the way."

Abby settles in the chair as I sweep the loose hair into a bin. When I come to stand behind her, she fingers the ends of her hair at her shoulder. "I have quite a few split ends . . ."

I run my fingers through her hair, studying it. It's definitely damaged, likely from being in the sun, poor nutrition, or stress. It's probably from all those things. But while it's wispy, it's still soft. "You do, but there's nothing a little trim and shaping can't fix. How about you come over to the shampoo bowl with me?"

Abby does as I ask, lowering her head into the sink.

A minute later, I'm lathering her hair with shampoo, watching as her shoulders finally relax and some of the wariness in her eyes subsides.

"Are you from around here, Abby?"

I regret my question instantly when I watch that flicker of peace she'd just obtained crash and disappear.

She moves her head from side to side. "No. From the East Coast."

"Me, too," I say, hoping to ease whatever tension I'd just stirred. "I grew up in Boston, but life sort of brought me to California."

Abby's eyes flick to mine for a moment, but she stays quiet, tugging on the ends of her sleeves.

Seriously, leave the woman be, Nisha. It's clear she doesn't want to talk to you. You don't even like to talk!

Resolute, I rinse her hair, careful not to let the water spill into her ears.

But then, as if my brain no longer controls my mouth, I hear myself ask, "What brought you to San Jose?"

Jesus. Shut up! Why do you care what brought her here?

Her throat bobs, and I'm positive she won't respond. But then she surprises me. "Just something I'm searching for."

And this time, I leave it at that.

~

"Wait. He said *what*?" The beer bottle in Kavi's hand freezes on its way to her mouth.

I roll my eyes before massaging a temple with two fingers. "His exact words were 'Get rid of him'."

Mala bursts out laughing, leaning back on the massive sectional sofa she's sharing with Sarina, Bella, and Rani. "Oh, this is gold! And you didn't correct him to let him know that you're not even dating Micah?"

Shrugging, I take another sip of my pineapple margarita. "Why should I? Plus, maybe if he thinks I'm dating someone, he'll stay away."

Rani snorts. "I get the feeling that Patton staying away isn't in the cards for you."

"Man's got it bad, sis," Sarina adds, folding her legs under her before pulling a throw blanket up to her waist.

"Yeah, well, he's a few years too late to have anything bad. And I'm not getting rid of anyone, especially because he said so. Seriously, the fucking nerve."

"What did I tell you girls about having to attend two weddings this year?" Sitting on an oversized cozy chair next to me in her living room, Piper lifts her index finger off the cocktail glass she's holding to wave it over everyone but me.

The room looks like a Pinterest board fell in love with a

billionaire, adding flair and chaos to his meticulous life. Which is exactly what Piper did when she married Dev.

It's all hand-scraped wood floors, plush carpets, buttery leather sofas, and throw blankets in every color that cost more than my mortgage. Have I had to suppress my mild urge to straighten and fluff some of her throw pillows? Yes. But I've controlled it on account of not appearing insane.

There's a professionally created cheeseboard on the enormous stone table in the center of the room, with all sorts of artisanal cheeses, dried fruits, and cured meats. But there's also a massive glass bowl full of Hot Cheetos. Because, as per Piper, it's "balance".

"The man is in town to win his ex-wife back," she continues. "And he isn't going to stop with just moving into her neighborhood . . . He wants to move back into her panties."

I glare at my best friend before turning it to my sister.

We aren't identical—her long, tight curls to my straight, shoulder-length hair, her golden tanned skin to my deeper undertones, her coffee-brown eyes to my onyx—but there's no mistaking we're sisters.

And where she's soft curves in that femme fatale kind of way, I'm lean and edgy in a switchblade kind of way.

I'd sent her a text after this morning's impromptu visit from my ex-husband.

ME

> Did Patton move into the house in front of mine because of you? I swear to God, Sarina, I will go back in time and eat you in the womb so that Mom never had twins.

Her response made me want to strangle her even more.

SARINA ARORA

> OMG, calm down, Hannibal Lecter. I just innocently told Troy to let Patton know that the house was for sale, and that you could often be seen watering your precious plants wearing your tiny shorts from its front windows. How were Troy and I supposed to know Patton would actually buy the damn house?

"Don't even think I've forgotten that this is all your fault," I say to my sister, who pretends to hide behind her wineglass. "You're the reason I'm going to be wary every time I open my front door."

Sarina's shoulders shake as she tries to conceal her laughter. "But what if it's his dog peeing on one of your marigolds or something?"

Oh, this little shit is asking for it today.

It's no surprise my friends and sister had a field day, bowling over with laughter, when I told them about the lovely greeting from Patton's dog this morning. How he'd urinated on my plant, then proceeded to sniff me like I was hiding narcotics inside my vagina.

I also told them about how Patton had shown up to the *dojang* the night before.

And because none of them are questioning my accusation of my sister, I have a strong suspicion they all knew she'd crafted this plan.

"Firstly," I mock seethe, "if you think I'd waste my soil on budget seasonals like marigolds, then you don't know me at all. Secondly, I hope that dog and his owner like surprise showers, because I'm going to be installing a motion-triggered sprinkler system around my plants."

"But doesn't that mean anyone on your porch would get wet?" Bella asks, clearly over-analyzing my half-baked plan.

"Like, a legitimate delivery guy or an unsuspecting Bible thumper?"

I take another sip of my favorite cocktail, relishing its sweetness. "It's like that old saying: one dog's overactive bladder ruins it for the entire neighborhood."

"I don't think I've ever heard that say—"

"Now you have," I state. "It was a proverb born from pain around 500 B.C. when a floriculturist in Mesopotamia lost his prized mulberry tree to an obnoxious donkey named Walter. He cried for a few days, then he invented the fence."

"You just made that shit up, didn't you?" Bella blinks. "You're both brilliant and weird."

"I made it relevant, Bells. History was written by the emotionally damaged and fiercely vengeful."

Piper cackles, walking to the large bar area behind the sectional. "I think I'm going to need that embroidered on a sweatshirt."

Sarina smirks. "Have I mentioned my sister has a curated playlist called 'Crying in My Car'?"

Kavi nearly spits out her beer. "No! It's *actually* called 'Crying in My Car'?"

I shoot my sister another one of my famous death glares. "Don't you dare..."

"Yes," Sarina answers delightfully. "It's all sad-girl anthems and breakup ballads. The first time I heard it, I thought someone had died."

"Shut up. It's a good playlist."

"Babe, it's almost entirely made up of Adele's rage songs."

I shrug. "She gets me *and* my rage."

"Okay, but going back to what Piper said. I think she's right." Kavi places her empty beer bottle on a side table. "I think Patton is trying to get you back. Especially after what he said about Micah."

I stay quiet, hoping my mixed emotions aren't written all

over my face. Because it's exactly how I feel: jumbled up and turned around.

A part of me—the part that's been detached and dormant for so long—is stirring awake, wondering if it really is as simple as they're making it. That perhaps my ex-husband moving into town is some type of Nicholas Sparks-level love declaration.

But the other part—the part that still nurses old wounds from time to time—is suiting up with additional armor. Because she's the one who remembers those nights alone. She's the one who recalls wondering where she sat on his priority list. And she's not ready to just hand over those keys because her ex-husband has decided, *seven years later*, that he misses her.

"But why now?" Rani asks, gathering her hair into a topknot. "Why after all these years?"

"I have a feeling it has something to do with what happened last year," Sarina answers. There's a gleam in her eyes that I don't like one bit. Like she already knows that whatever happened will only help fortify her plan to play Cupid.

"Which brings us to why we're here," Piper says, bringing a tray of—*oh, God*—shot glasses brimming with green liquid. "To get the tea! To commemorate this occasion, I appropriately made green tea shots for us!"

A few of us groan, but we all reach out to grab a shot glass. There's no point in arguing with her. Unless you're pregnant, a recovering addict, or it's against your religion, the woman is going to pour the shot down your throat anyway.

"Salud, bitches!" Piper chimes as we clink glasses and throw back the shots. She puts her empty one back on the tray before looking at me. "Now. Don't you dare skip a single detail."

eight
nisha

Not Asking For Forever

One Year Ago

I tune out the roar from the bleachers—the various national flags, the distant yells from proud parents and family, the scattered applause.

My focus is locked on my student, Sydney, as she blocks a chop kick from her opponent and pivots to land a clean kick to her side.

"Good," I whisper to myself, though my hands ball at my sides. In my right hand, I'm gripping my protest card so tight, it's threatening to slice through skin.

I'm waiting—*fucking daring*—Sydney's opponent to try something sketchy again. She's a German girl who's built like a tank and probably eats toddlers for breakfast. How the hell did she even get into the featherweight class? There's literally nothing feather-like about her.

Sydney, on the other hand, is all long legs and refined kicks. The kind that makes her look like she's meant for ballet until they're trying to crack your spine. But right now, she's off balance coming off a clinch, the mat squeaking under her feet as she tries to stay upright but can't.

It's as if I've willed the scenario into existence when her opponent delivers a sharp kick a second after Sydney hits the floor. Not only was that kick unnecessary, it was completely illegal.

Or it *should* have been.

I wait for the referee to call it. He doesn't.

What the hell?

I shoot to my feet and hold the protest card up like I'm trying to stab someone with it. "Coach challenge! That should have been a *gam-jeom*."

The ref calls for a pause, separating the two fighters. And while Sydney is back on her feet, her eyes flick to mine, wondering the same thing—*why isn't the ref calling textbook bullshit?* A grounded opponent taking a kick? That should have been an automatic deduction. And it's not like I'm the only one who saw it.

I give Sydney a short nod, letting her know I've got her, but inside, I'm fuming. My eyes are locked on where the judges are reviewing the footage on their monitors while my fists park themselves on my hips.

And that's when I feel it—that strange pull that starts inside my chest, like a string tugging me upright. It stiffens my spine, making me turn to find the cause.

I scan the bleachers, already searching before my brain can even register it. It's then that they land on the tall figure partially hidden behind two massive men, who are likely part of his protection team.

He's wearing an oversized hoodie with a cap and sunglasses, but I'd know that set of shoulders, those unfairly plush lips, and that stubbled cut of his jaw anywhere. Not because any of those features belong to a man who's been gracing *People's Sexiest Men* list for the past five years, but because he's starred in every single one of my damn dreams since the moment I left him.

Hell, the man could have worn a paper bag over his head, and I'd probably still recognize him.

But why is he here?

Why now?

And while I know he loves taekwondo as much as I do, I've never seen him at one of these competitions before.

Is he here for me?

My eyes flick back to the judges before the ref announces the deduction of a point from Sydney's opponent and the girls go back to finish the round. But my mind is still stuck on the man in the bleachers, begging my eyes not to betray its command.

My attention stays on Sydney, and I watch the way her posture changes. There's a fire in her eyes, a determination in her stance—the *I was just warming up, but I'm about to own you kind*—as she lands three solid kicks in succession. She delivers them like claps of lightning, the last one landing just as the buzzer sounds.

And just like that, the match is over with Sydney winning by two points and advancing to the semifinals. While she doesn't win the next one, she earns herself—and our *dojang*—a bronze medal, which is a huge feat on its own.

After a long embrace, where I tell her how proud I am of her, Sydney pulls back, eyes shining and breaths still heavy from the exertion. Her parents have joined us near the exit.

"I can't believe I did it," Sydney says, clutching her medal over her chest. "I can't believe I got this far."

"I can," I respond easily, because it's true. "You're one of the hardest working athletes I know. It's not a surprise to me at all."

"Thank you for always believing in me, *Sabumnim* Arora." Sydney beams, looking from her parents to me. "Would you like to come to dinner with me and my family?"

My gaze flicks to the man standing near a pillar behind

her, his two bodyguards hovering close, blending in about as well as Madonna in Amish country.

I give Sydney's shoulder a final squeeze before nodding my thanks to her parents. "You guys go on and celebrate. I have something I need to catch up on."

With that, I make my way over to the man watching me approach as if mesmerized. His glasses are gone, but his hood is still up, as if that will stop anyone from recognizing one of the most recognizable faces in the world. But I guess he doesn't care much about that if he's risking being here.

His eyes grow darker, richer, with each step I take, and his lips tilt upward. His bodyguards assess me warily, likely wondering if I'm a threat, given I'm charging at their ward like I'm either going to kiss him or kill him.

Honestly, it could go either way.

Coming to a stop in front of him, I try to get straight to the point. Annoyingly, his familiar bergamot and mint scent permeates my thoughts, diminishing some of my tartness.

"What are you doing here?"

We're hidden enough by the pillar and his security detail that Patton brushes back the hood over his head, his jawline looking anything but casual.

He lifts one shoulder. "I wanted to see you."

"You wanted to see me," I repeat. "*Why?*"

I refuse to acknowledge the way my heart gallops in his presence. In fact, I've never had a regular heartbeat around this man. Not when we were dating, not when we were married, and certainly not now. I'm not sure if he made the damn organ stronger or weaker.

"Can I not want to see my best friend?"

I huff out an incredulous laugh. "Yeah, well, we're not best friends anymore, are we, Patton? In fact, I'd hedge to say we're pretty far from that after six years of radio silence."

His gaze drops to my wrist, a smug smile threatening to emerge on his face. "And yet you're still wearing our bracelet."

I stand up taller, nostrils flaring.

I knew I should have gotten rid of the damn thing after all these years. And while I took off my wedding ring a year after the divorce was finalized, for whatever reason, I didn't have it in me to cut the permanent bracelet we'd gotten as teens, his silver to my gold.

"I didn't want a perfectly good piece of metal to go to waste."

His smile says he knows I'm lying to both of us. Dropping his eyes to his own wrist, he says, "Yeah, me, too."

I nod, readying myself to turn around and leave. "Well, this has been swell—"

"And as for the years of silence, who wanted that, Nisha? Who asked for that?"

Yeah, me. I asked for that. Because I needed that.
But fuck him for following through.

I suck in a slow, calming breath. "I'm not going to do this with you here, Patton—"

"Then don't." He steps toward me, swallowing hard. "Not here, not anywhere. Have dinner with me."

"Why?" The bitterness leaks out before I can contain it. "So we can rehash what happened and come to the same conclusion—that you chose your career over me and I chose to be okay with it? Until I wasn't. Until I had to live the most excruciating night of my life alone because you weren't there?"

Though he doesn't flinch, his eyes close for a moment too long, confirmation that I've hit my mark.

My throat feels dry. It's not like I want to hurt him. I know what happened between us wasn't all on him. But it's as if just his presence alone has the power to bring everything bubbling to the surface, making it all seep out through angry, bitter words.

But the truth is . . . I miss him.

I miss the boy I fell in love with and the man I watched him become.

I miss my best friend. My husband. The only person who could make me laugh until I cried, and the only person to have turned real tears into laughter.

I miss him, dammit. With every hollow breath, with a longing set inside my bones. I don't know when I'll get over him.

Patton takes my hand, and though the current that zips through me should have me pulling back from his touch, I let him.

Maybe because I'm tired of pretending to be strong, unfeeling, and okay. Maybe because I've spent the last six years building walls that he's managed to crumble in a mere six minutes. Or maybe because his hand feels warm and familiar against my cold one.

"No," he says softly, shaking his head. "I'm not here to rehash or defend my mistakes, Little Borealis. I've been living the consequences of my decisions, day in and day out. I'm asking you to put it all aside for just a night. A few hours. Hell, I'll even take one hour if that's all you'll give me."

"But why?"

His rich brown eyes hold my charcoal ones, and in them I see a reflection of my own longing. "Because I miss you, plain and simple."

The corners of my eyes prick, betraying tears threatening to spill as I recall the messages he sent me the first year after we separated. Messages saying he missed me and wanted me back. Messages I left unanswered. Like clockwork, he sent them daily. Until I asked him not to and changed my number.

Because I couldn't survive them.

Hell, I barely survived without them.

But I had to do what was right for me at the time.

But now? With him saying those words aloud and my hand still inside his . . . do I have any fight left?

"I don't know, Patton," I say finally, but we both know I'm not saying no.

"I'm not asking for forever, Little Borealis. Just dinner."

That shouldn't have sent a stabbing pain through my ribs, but I barely stop myself from rubbing my chest.

I pull my hand out of his grasp. Not because I want to, but because I need to. Because, with just one touch, he has me breaking all rules and resolve. If I don't reset and give myself a little distance to think, he'll have the power to break a lot more. To take a lot more.

I glance away, thinking of another way to stall. "I'm leaving L.A. tomorrow morning."

"Then I guess we need to make tonight worth it."

A beat passes between us, with his victory shining through his smug smile before I've even provided an answer.

I sigh, shaking my head and knowing I'm being reckless.

But it has been so long since I have.

"Send me the address. I'll meet you there in an hour."

nine
nisha

Let Me Feed And Water You

One Year Ago

I squint as the road curves upward into the hills, turning into a stretch of dark asphalt with nothing but scant shrubs flanking both sides and the lights of L.A. glittering somewhere in the distance.

He'd sent me the address, along with a message saying, `The road will be a little windy, but don't fret.`

Don't fret?

Don't. Fret.

My maps app practically had a panic attack getting here, and he says, "*Don't fret*"?

I spot the small turnout ahead and slow down. The tires of my SUV crunch gravel as I pull up next to a sleek black Escalade I assume is his car, given the two familiar faces of the men from his security team loitering around it like they're coming off the set of *Men in Black*.

Both give me nods as I climb out of my car, wordlessly directing me toward a short wooden bridge that looks like it was built approximately five-point-two million years ago. The "guardrails" on this thing are frayed ropes that look like they'll give out if a bird perches on them.

I lean forward, peering across the bridge for a sign of Patton before taking a tentative step. And if I die, I hope whoever recovers my body at least comments on my winged eyeliner technique, curved and pointed like a dagger.

Footsteps rustle on the other side, and a moment later, Patton emerges, smile stretched and those earthy eyes twinkling against the setting sun.

His gaze travels over the ribbed black tee that shows off my sleeve of tattoos, distressed black jeans tucked inside black combat boots, and my shoulder-length, stick-straight black hair waving in the breeze.

Patton drags his tongue over his bottom lip, slow and deliberate, and I don't have to worry about whether I'm still his type. The desire in his expression says he's still imagining me beneath him.

Moaning his name. Clawing at the sheets. Meeting him, thrust for thrust.

He's the only one who's ever made my body rev. The only one who's ever held the keys.

I clear my throat, forcing away the memory. "Let me guess . . . you've been planning my murder for six years, and today's my lucky day."

He laughs, his voice low and rough, hitting me square in the chest. I'll admit, it's a sound I've been dying to hear. Not through his movies or his interviews. Not through the million videos I have of us on my phone from all those years ago. But in real life.

"Relax," he says, striding across the suicide bridge like it's the damn red carpet. He reaches for my hand, pulling me behind him like we haven't just reunited after six years. Like I'm still his and this is all just normal. Like we didn't just spend years missing our friendship or love.

I know I did.

A part of me, hardened by time and pride, wants to pull back and tell him that we don't do this anymore. But the other part—the traitorous, hopeful, and a little slutty one—has always given in when it comes to him.

"I brought tacos," he says while my eyes stay glued on our locked hands.

I take careful steps behind him, not daring to look down at the rocky creek a hundred feet below. I'm not scared of much, but there's brave and there's stupid. And right now, my one partially working brain cell is waving a red flag.

Patton turns to look over his shoulder at me. "Plus, if I wanted to kill you, this would be too cliché. I mean, give me more credit than that. I'd be way more creative."

"Well, that's refreshing to know."

"I'd probably come over to your house and fuck up your color-coded closet, stab your seasonal throw pillows, and rip pages out of your neatly stacked magazines."

I gasp. "So you'd kill me by giving me a heart attack. You're a monster, Pierce."

He chuckles again, and I remember how easily we used to make each other laugh.

"You won't think I'm too big a monster when you see the margaritas I also brought."

"Pineapple flavored?" I ask as we make it to the other side of the bridge.

"Uh, yeah. Do you take me for an amateur? It's still your favorite, isn't it?"

I give him a simple nod, but a bit of the ice I'd formed over the years loosens in my chest. The fact that he remembered something as simple as my favorite drink after all this time . . . It shouldn't feel like a big deal, but it does.

I look up as I trail behind him, and that's when I see the flannel blanket at the end of the cliff, secured by a couple of large rocks. In the middle of the blanket sits two bags of tacos I recognize from a food truck we used to frequent and a large cooler.

"Can't believe *Cheeky Mike* still has his food truck," I say, feeling breathless for reasons I don't want to admit.

"He's grown the business, actually. He has six or seven trucks all around town now."

"His tacos were always my favorite."

"I know," he says, stopping at the edge of the blanket to share a meaningful look with me.

But that look is cut short at the sound of my stomach rumbling, making us both chuckle.

Patton waves at the blanket. "Come. Let me feed and water you."

I laugh, recalling how he always said that to me when I was PMSing, hangry, or just stressed. It was so silly and stupid, but it was . . . us.

Taking my boots off, I reluctantly climb on, something inside my head telling me this—whatever this is—could be dangerous.

I haven't seen or talked to the man since our divorce was settled, and now, just like that, he's back in my life out of nowhere?

It's just for a few hours, Nisha, says the slutty, sex-starved girl inside my head. She's the reason dreams of other hot Hollywood men turn into dreams about my ex-husband. *Just live a little, bitch. Like he said, he's not asking for forever. Not again. You can leave at any time, as long as you don't die falling to that creek going back.*

As Patton pours me a glass of margarita, I watch the tiny city lights dance like gems in the distance below us. The wind rustles through the short brush and trees, lifting my hair, and for a moment, everything feels . . . exactly how it should.

Patton plants himself beside me, handing me a taco and

drink. Our thighs brush, and so do our forearms, as we eat and drink, sending little goosebumps racing across my skin that have nothing to do with the breeze.

"Did you know there's no concrete origin story for the margarita?" Patton asks, taking a sip from his glass. "There are several theories; some say it was created during the American prohibition, and some say it was created by a bartender for a showgirl who was allergic to everything but tequila."

I smile, studying the glass in my hand.

I'm not big on drinking, or on consuming anything that will loosen my grip over myself and my surroundings, not unless it's for a special occasion. But one taste of a margarita, and all that sense and control goes down the drain. Or rather, my throat.

"I see you're still a book of random historical facts."

Patton smirks. "Well, I can't coast through life on just a pretty face."

I laugh, even though a part of me hates that he still knows how to pull that so easily from me. "I'm pretty sure you actually could."

Patton smiles, and I marvel at the faint color that rises to his cheeks. Even after all the fame and celebrity—literally being the face of billboards all over the world—he still doesn't quite know how to take a compliment. It's a glimpse into the man behind the actor, the unsure and unguarded boy I once knew.

"So," I say, chewing the last of my taco slowly. I've already finished off my second margarita and am feeling the effects. "Was this what you wanted? To seduce me with *Cheeky Mike's*, a spectacular view, and margaritas?"

Patton taps my knee with his, taking a sip of his drink. "Is it working?"

"No," I lie.

"Well, the night's still young. Maybe that'll change by margarita number three."

"Or maybe you'll just tell me where this is coming from, Patton. Especially after all this time."

He shrugs, balling up his taco wrapper and tossing it into the brown bag. He secures a corner of the brown bag under the cooler, stopping it from blowing away.

"Like I said, I've missed you, Neesh. You'd asked me never to contact you, never to come chasing after you, and I've respected your wishes. I've also been . . . working on myself." He looks out over the clearing, his brown hair sexily tousled from the wind. "I found out you were coming to town and decided to see if you'd give me a chance to talk to you. I wanted to see how you were doing." His eyes lock with mine again. "I wanted to see *you*."

My mouth opens to respond. I want to ask him what about himself he's been working on or who told him I was going to be here. But what comes out is, "I told you never to contact me, never to chase after me . . . and you just *listened*?"

Patton stares at me for a beat, seemingly flustered. I don't blame the guy, because I'm more than a little flustered at my indecisiveness. I literally told the guy I didn't want to rehash anything not even two hours ago, and here I am, asking him to do the very thing.

The thing is, I've always been the type of girl to say what I mean and mean what I say.

Always.

Except when it comes to Patton Pierce.

Back when we were together, I hadn't fully grown into this independent, take no prisoners and speaks her mind version of myself. I felt like an imposter in my own body, especially as it related to him, my up-and-coming Hollywood star husband. How could a gorgeous man like him, who had every woman begging to have a place on his arm, want *me*?

How could I ever compete with all those other women? How could I ever deserve him? Who was I anyway?

And then, when he started to climb that stardom ladder, and our time together was often either cut short or interrupted with phone calls from his agent, his director, his producer, or even a cast member, I started to believe that maybe all my insecurities *were* correct.

I started to believe that maybe I was the *before*—before the fame, before the red-carpet premieres, and before the award ceremonies.

In the end, I didn't just walk away because of that tragic night—a night I endured all alone for the second time—but because I truly believed I was alone, invisible beside the blinding light that was my husband.

Patton exhales slowly beside me. "I tried to chase you, Little Borealis. I called you every fucking day for a year."

He's not wrong. He did try to contact me for an entire year until I sent him one final text, asking him to give me space, then changed my number.

And when that finally stopped him, when he didn't try to find my new number through Piper, Sarina, or Dad, I told myself he'd moved on. That it was over.

And still, I was heartbroken that he had.

I know how irrational and contradictory that makes me sound. I'm the one who closed the door, yet I still wanted him to try to force it open.

"I even came to San Francisco to work it out, but at the time—"

"At the time, I was wrapped up in my grief, my loss—"

"*Our* grief," he interjects vehemently, in a tone that doesn't leave room for questions. "*Our* loss."

I swallow, tears pricking the corners of my eyes. It's one of the reasons I rarely drank, because it made me so emotional.

But he's right; he was grieving, too.

"I was so consumed by our loss that I didn't want to see anything from another angle." A tear escapes as I look at him. "It was the second time, Patton. Second time in two years. After everything my body had been through—"

"I know." He doesn't let me finish, cupping my face with his warm hands. "I know, baby. I'm so sorry."

I melt with his words as if they're the balm I'd been searching for.

Patton pulls me against him so I'm straddling his thighs. His thumb swipes my cheek as his fingers wrap around my neck. I lean into his touch, my hands fisting his shirt.

Our foreheads meet as our breaths entangle, heavy and out of rhythm. Something else, like electricity mixed with longing, charges the air between us. The temperature has dropped with the sun setting, but my skin burns everywhere he's touching me.

God, how long have I wanted this again? His touch, his words; my solace, my pain. He's the only man who's ever really known me, and likely the only man who ever will.

"Patton," I whisper or plead, I can't be sure.

"Shh, baby," he coos, eyes roaming my face, cataloging every change the last few years have carved into my skin. "Let me just look at you. I haven't seen you in so long, and I just—"

My lips press against his, swallowing the rest of his words as my fingers carve through his hair. For a short breath, neither of us moves. Maybe we're both stunned, weighing out the moment.

But then I start to explore, moving my lips over his, tasting him again like it's the first time. In some ways it feels like it is —like I'm meeting him all over again, but this time with the knowledge that he's my undoing.

He tastes like pineapples from the margarita, hints of the

tacos, and something completely him. It's intoxicating, and it has nothing to do with the alcohol I just consumed. It's pure Patton, and my body responds like it's been awaiting this exact taste for centuries.

As soon as my center rubs against him, feeling his hard length straining against his jeans, I let out a breathy moan that seems to snap something inside him. The sound hangs in the air between us, and I watch as Patton's pupils dilate and his resolve breaks.

In an instant, I'm lying flat on my back, my fingers fisting his hair and his forearms framed on either side of my head. He delves into my mouth, and our tongues tangle and duel, neither taking it easy, not after all this time.

His chest meets mine, and the weight of him—God, the delicious weight of him covering me—makes me feel both dizzy and alive. He's filled out over the years—harder, heavier, defined—and I feel every sculpted muscle under my fingertips.

His erection grazes my center, and even that friction, dulled through my jeans, makes me mewl against his mouth. Heat pools inside my panties, and I don't have to touch myself to know how wet I am for him. How ready and eager my body is for him after just one stolen moment.

His hand squeezes my left breast, tweaking and rolling my nipple until it's a stiff peak beneath the fabric of my shirt. His teeth nip my bottom lip, sucking and biting, causing my hips to lift of their own accord.

"Christ, Nisha. I feel like I've fallen off the wagon." He kisses me again before dragging his lips down to my neck, sucking until I whimper. "You still smell like pomegranates. Sweet, seductive." His lips brush mine again. "One fucking taste, and I'm an addict all over again."

My chest heaves, my body humming and alight. *God yes, I want this. I need this.*

And that's when something inside my brain comes back online.

An alarm I'd put on snooze.

Patton's fingers drag down to unbutton my jeans, his lips never parting from my skin. "Fuck, baby, I want you. I've always only wanted you—"

I swallow, hating myself for what I'm about to do.

"Patton?" My chest constricts as I cup his cheeks, lifting his lips off me, even as a huge part of me wants them exactly where they were.

Patton reluctantly finds my eyes, his breaths ragged.

"Where does this go?"

"What?" His breaths come out harsh against the word.

"Where does this go? What does this become? How does our situation change with this?"

"Nisha—"

"From what I read online, you took on a project that will have you filming in God knows where. For weeks, maybe months. The interview said you have no inclination to slow down; in fact, you're making more movies than almost any actor worldwide."

"Let me explain."

I place a hand over his heart, hearing his confirmation. "And that's okay. It's okay for you to have your career aspirations. You've worked hard to be where you are. I'd never want to come between that."

I shake my head, tears slipping from the corners of my eyes. "But I can't be a part of that again. I can't be on a flight every couple of weeks, flying to wherever you are to see you. I can't live with you being home only a few months a year, and that's if we're lucky and your multiple film schedules align."

I take a breath. "I don't want a partner who isn't there when I truly need him to be. I don't want to go through what

I went through that night, completely alone, calling your phone but getting nothing but your voicemail."

I remember it so clearly—sitting on my cold bathroom floor, tears streaming down my face, clutching my phone like it was my only lifeline. There were at least ten missed calls and a scared, teary voicemail begging him to call me back.

He didn't. Not for two days.

Not until I knew it was over.

Patton's eyes shutter, but not before I see the way my words tear at his soul. "I never meant for you to go through that alone, Nisha. I never meant for you to go through that at all."

"I know." I nod, my thumb grazing over his soft scruff. "And I believe you. I've never blamed you for it or the time before. But I also can't go through life following you while you chase your career. I can't be the shadow I felt like I was becoming . . . a shadow of myself."

I shift and Patton allows me to get up. Straightening myself up, I wipe the lingering tears off my face. The breeze hits my skin, and I wrap my arms around myself protectively, a gesture that feels both literal and metaphorical.

And that's when my brain slams that door shut, the one I'd left cracked open just for him. Because I have to pull my walls back up and remember the reasons I left.

He never denied his schedule and life *hadn't* changed. So starting to wish and dream again would only reopen the wounds I worked so hard to close.

No. I can't do that to myself again.

Patton Pierce belongs to the world, not me. And pretending otherwise will just lead me to the same heartache I felt all those years ago.

We might have been best friends, lovers, and spouses at one time. We may both still be wearing our friendship bracelets. But we're not those people anymore. Let me rephrase: *I'm* not the person I used to be anymore.

"I'm sorry, too, Patton," I say, sniffling. "And thank you for all of this." I wave to the blanket and the thoughtful gesture. "But nothing has changed for me after six years . . . yet everything has."

ten
patton

Seven Schlongs Hen Party

GARRETT MEYER

So, most of our wives came home well past the witching hour last night. What kind of intel are we dealing with? I'll share if you share.

DARIAN MEYER

I don't know much. Rani said there was a lot of alcohol and tissues involved.

DEAN MEYER

Alcohol and tissues? Makes me think of the last time Mala was mad at me. Spoiler alert: I didn't use the tissues to wipe my tears.

HUDSON CASE

Oh, for fuck's sake. What did we say about oversharing, Dean?

TROY WINTERS

Jesus. Some of us are trying to eat breakfast, jackass.

Pine For Me

DEAN MEYER

> What? It's just us girls here. Besides, I could have gone into WAY more detail about what I did with the alcohol.

DARIAN MEYER

> Yup. Definitely too early for this shit.

[**Darian Meyer** has left the chat]
[**Dean Meyer** has added **Darian Meyer** to the chat]

DEAN MEYER

> Oh, come on! Lighten up, little bro. Or did that hit too close to home? Are you upset because you still have to use alcohol and tissues since Rani's still considered a child-bride?

DARIAN MEYER

> She's NOT a child-bride, asshole.

GARRETT MEYER

> Can we get back to the topic of our wives before Dean traumatizes us all further?

DEV MENON

> I'm speaking for everyone when I say, yes. Piper didn't say much, but our liquor cabinet was a lot sparser this morning. She said there was "extensive discussion" about Patton.

PATTON PIERCE

> Wait, what? Sorry, just landed in Boston. Trying to catch up on messages. What do you mean, there was a discussion about me?

DEAN MEYER

Welcome to the Schlongs, Hollywood! The two things you need to know to get situated: 1.) We discuss everyone's business here, especially Hudson's, because he's old as fuck. 2.) Conversations about anal will trigger Darian. He is very much a "missionary, let's-make-love" kind of guy.

DARIAN MEYER

I'm not a—you know what? Never mind. I don't know why I even bother.

PATTON PIERCE

I've been in this chat for all of 30 seconds, and I'm already regretting it.

HUDSON CASE

Aside from Dean, we all are. Why are you in Boston this morning? Visiting your old stomping grounds or for the foster gala?

PATTON PIERCE

Yeah. The FosterBridges Foundation Gala. How did you know about that?

DEAN MEYER

Christ, Hudson. Do you get a push notification every time he takes a piss? I'm honestly a little concerned on your behalf, @Patton Pierce.

DEV MENON

That's rich coming from the man who wears pajamas with Troy's face on the crotch.

Pine For Me

DEAN MEYER

For the last time, IT'S NOT ON THE CROTCH! (Not for lack of trying, though. Mala was dead set against that design option for some reason).

TROY WINTERS

Thank God for Mala. I owe the woman a fruit basket.

HUDSON CASE

@Patton Pierce, saw an interview with you asking for donations to the program since you grew up in the foster system. I may have made a small contribution and gotten the same invite to the gala. Couldn't attend, though.

PATTON PIERCE

Thanks for the donation, man. That means a lot.

DEAN MEYER

Damn, Hollywood. My respect for you grows by the day. Cool of you to use your platform for something so meaningful.

TROY WINTERS

Does that mean your obsession with me is finally fading? I'd love to leave my house without worrying about you hiding in the bushes.

DEAN MEYER:

Let's not get hasty, my beautiful baseball god. I've gotten quite cozy in "your bushes".

TROY WINTERS

Yup, definitely going to be checking in on that restraining order again.

DEAN MEYER

Plus, Hudson's already claimed the "Patton fangirl" title. Remember how he wept into his brunch?

HUDSON CASE

I didn't weep! My eyes were just shiny because of allergies.

DEAN MEYER

Sure. Or cataracts.

HUDSON CASE

<middle finger emoji>

PATTON PIERCE

So, back to the ladies talking about me last night. Any details about that?

DEV MENON

Piper said it was something to do with what went down between you and Nisha last year.

GARRETT MEYER

Bella gave me a similar non-answer. So, what happened last year, @Patton Pierce? The girls know; don't leave us in the dark!

PATTON PIERCE

It's . . . complicated.

Pine For Me

DEAN MEYER

No shit, Sherlock. You're stalking your ex-wife from the house you bought across the street from her. We've all determined it's complicated.

TROY WINTERS

Come on, Pierce. We need details, not your Facebook relationship status.

PATTON PIERCE

As if you don't know. I'm sure my wife's twin has told you everything.

TROY WINTERS

Not everything. Sister code and all that shit.

DEV MENON

Piper said the same thing to me.

DEAN MEYER

Am I the only one who noticed he called her "my wife"?

HUDSON CASE

Definitely noticed it.

DEAN MEYER

Of course you did. I bet you're all breathing heavy over there, you creepy bastard.

HUDSON CASE

Eat shit.

GARRETT MEYER

Spill, @Patton Pierce. We told you about how Dean has a piece of gum Troy chewed six years ago enshrined in his house. You can tell us about you and Nisha.

DEAN MEYER

Firstly, we HADN'T told him about that, you jackass! And secondly, it's not enshrined. Do you take me for a lunatic? It's . . . PRESERVED. Under a UV lamp.

TROY WINTERS

So fucking disturbing.

DARIAN MEYER

Can we please get back to the subject at hand before Dean tells us he has Troy's toenail clippings, too? @Patton Pierce, what happened with Nisha last year?

DEAN MEYER

Oh, hey, Darian! Didn't know you were still here, little buddy! And for the record, I don't have his toenail clippings. That would be going a step too far.

Though, @Troy Winters, let's chat about your personal hygiene routine and the disposal methods later.

TROY WINTERS

Let's not.

PATTON PIERCE

Fine. We had dinner last year. I'd set up a private picnic. We started talking about the past, and things got hot and heavy. Except, one second I thought we were rekindling feelings, and the next, she was pushing away, saying we couldn't happen again.

GARRETT MEYER

Damn. That sucks, man.

Pine For Me

DEV MENON

And you still moved here to win her back? Do you even know how stubborn your ex-wife is? Once she decides something . . .

PATTON PIERCE

Trust me, I'm fucking aware. I've known the woman since we were teens. But for those few minutes, there was something there. She was letting me back in.

TROY WINTERS

Exactly why this combined bachelor/bachelorette party for me and Rina is going to be key. Nisha has no idea you're coming.

PATTON PIERCE

Does she know I'll be at your wedding in a couple of months?

TROY WINTERS

<wincing emoji> Not yet, but don't worry about that. We'll figure something out.

PATTON PIERCE

I don't know what you're planning, but she might castrate me for showing up unannounced again. She's still pissed I moved into her neighborhood.

DEAN MEYER

I could actually see Nisha going all Lorena Bobbitt. Not gonna lie, she kind of scares me.

HUDSON CASE

Let's add her to this group chat. Maybe if she were here, you'd finally shut up.

DEAN MEYER

I'm going to take a minute to be mildly offended.

DARIAN MEYER

Just a minute? You're going to need at least a week to process that level of disrespect. Feel free to leave the chat. Take all the time you need.

DEAN MEYER

Damn, look who just joined the ring. My little bro's growing up and throwing punches. I'm so proud.

<GIF of an old woman blowing her nose and wiping her tears with a handkerchief>

TROY WINTERS

Back to the subject at hand. Damn, the number of times this chat goes off-topic . . . @Patton Pierce, let me and Sarina handle Nisha. You just work on making that night count toward your long-term plan. Maybe wear a cup if you're so worried about your balls.

DEAN MEYER

Or don't, if you're into that kind of thing. We don't judge here. In fact, this is a great segue to share my newest dick piercing. It's called the Magic Cross . . .

```
[Darian Meyer has left the chat]
[Garrett Meyer has left the chat]
[Dev Menon has left the chat]
[Hudson Case has left the chat]
[Troy Winters has left the chat]
```

Pine For Me

PATTON PIERCE

Fuck, how do I exit this shit? I swear to God, Dean, if you share any dick pics here, I will have Nisha hunt you down and finish you!

DEAN MEYER

I knew you'd fit right in with us, Hollywood. Relax, I'll save this dick pic for Christmas. Maybe Mala and I will send it as our holiday cards this year.

eleven
nisha

The Spawn of Yoda And A
Mole Rat

The following Wednesday, I slip a needle into the next stitch and purl it tight, mimicking the knot in my throat. The seed stitch pattern I've been working on for Hector's sweater was supposed to look delicate and textured, but mine is pulled so taut, it's at risk of snapping.

Kind of like me.

My next client, a man I've never met named Henry Knox, texted the front desk saying he's running late, so I thought I'd squeeze in a few rows. And since Sarina and Piper are busy with their own clients, I figured I'd take the opportunity to watch something I never watch in front of them: a red-carpet gala on the *Style* channel.

One where my ex-husband just so happens to be in attendance.

On the large TV above a cabinet in my suite, Patton rises from his seat, wearing a tux that hugs his broad chest, thick biceps, and trim waist like it's doing God's work. Even on a screen, the man manages to look larger than life, like he knows how to make every head turn in his direction. And they all do.

Flashing a practiced smile at the camera, he's just about to head to the stage to accept his award for his work with the foster program he grew up in when Ursula stands up.

That's not actually her name. It's just what I've decided to call her in my head, since she reminds me of the villainous part-octopus sea witch from *The Little Mermaid*.

Every time the camera has panned to his table, she's been all over him: touching his hand, pretending to brush lint off his tux, and batting her fake lashes so hard, she's liable to create a windstorm.

My eyes take in her voluminous red hair and dainty features. A long leg peeks out from a slit so high on the side of her navy-blue dress, you'd think she was there to see her gynecologist. And her skin—a perfect blend of flawless and freckles—glows under the chandelier lighting, like she wears a permanent Instagram filter. It probably smells like it's been misted by fairies and rainbows, too.

Stupid heifer.

Placing a delicate hand—*tentacle*—on his shoulder, she leans over and whispers something into my ex-husband's ear before leaving a red kiss stain on his cheek and earning herself a smile.

When she dusts the lapel of his jacket *again*, I roll my eyes, muttering in a high-pitched voice I've decided sounds like her, "Oh, look, there's another piece of invisible lint on your hard and broad chest, Patton. Let me get that for you."

I tug at the yarn harder than I should. "What is she, a human lint roller? His personal groomer? And seriously, that dress? It's a charity event, not spring break in Cancun, Ursula! Have some decorum."

And the decency to keep your hands off men who don't belong to you.

Not that he belongs to me, either.

I watch as Patton frees himself from the red-haired octopus, making his way to the stage with long strides.

"I'm surprised the stage-five clinger isn't going up there with him," I mutter to myself, tugging another stitch with more force than necessary.

And that's when a prickle runs down my back. The kind you get when you're walking past a glass display case and the mannequin moves.

I freeze, mid-loop, feeling my pulse increase.

I know this feeling all too well . . . I've felt it several times in the past few days.

I slowly turn to look into the mirror at my styling station and, catching the reflection there, whip my head to the man standing at my doorway.

Ugh! Not again.

Seven years of radio silence—save for that time last year when I ran with my panties barely hanging on to the last shreds of my dignity—and now he's popping up everywhere like an overactive prairie dog.

With his arms crossed and a shoulder leaning against the frame, Patton stares back at me, trying and failing to wipe a grin off his face. Tufts of dark chestnut hair peek out from under his beige cap, and his eyes seem more piercing and focused today, like sunbeams intent on eviscerating their target through a magnifying glass.

His chin lifts and smug amusement dances in his eyes. "Didn't mean to interrupt your jealous roasting. Please, carry on. I was actually hoping you'd get to the part where the human lint-roller turns into actual lint and attaches herself to my suit sleeve."

I blink out of my stupor, my face hot. "I wasn't *jealous roasting*."

"Sure. Just providing colored commentary, then, of the green variety." He glances at the TV I've just hastily turned off before winking at me. "For what it's worth, I like that color on you."

"I'm not green because I'm jealous; I'm green because your inflated ego is making me nauseous."

"She's a producer's wife, by the way. Not even a blip on my radar, in case you were wondering."

"I wasn't."

But the word "blip" actually sends a sharp, metaphorically-green pang through my chest. How many "blips" have there been over the years? Have any stuck around long enough to be considered more?

From what I've read in the tabloids, there hasn't been anyone serious. But maybe he was good at keeping things hidden?

And why do I even care how many *blips* he's had? Anyone could argue that I was the one who left him. Do I even have the right to feel jealous?

Maybe, maybe not. But right or not, I still feel the raw burn every time he's pictured with someone else.

Because once upon a time, I was the one in those photos. I was the one who touched him, kissed him, and knew the real man behind the spotlight.

And now I'm the one secretly watching him on my salon TV like a sad cliché.

At his knowing smile, I huff. "How much did you hear?"

"Enough." He bites his bottom lip, but the mirth in his eyes only intensifies. "Especially the part about my *hard* and *broad* chest."

I throw my knitting supplies into a bag beside me like I'm teaching them a lesson, running an annoyed finger over my brow. "What are you doing here, Patton?"

My ex-husband pushes off the doorframe and strolls inside, each stride both lazy and confident, like they were designed to confuse my body . . . and my hammering heart.

He nudges the door closed behind him with a soft click before coming to a stand in front of me, hands tucked in his pockets, clouding my brain and better judgment with his intoxicating scent. "I have an appointment."

He's wearing dark gray shorts that draw attention to his muscular thighs and calves, along with camel-colored boat shoes. And as if his lower half wasn't already making my mouth water, a light blue button-down hugs his torso, the sleeves rolled up, showing off corded forearms I'd lick if it weren't considered socially inappropriate.

"No, you don't," I reply, taking a step back to give myself breathing room before picking up my trusty tablet. I scroll down to the name on my screen. "I'm expecting someone else."

"You mean, Henry Knox?" Patton raises a brow.

"Y-yes," I stammer. "How do you . . .? Wait. Are you Henry Knox?"

He shrugs. "He was quite the man back in the day. General in the American Revolution. Secretary of War under George Washington. Dude had quite an exciting life. Plus, he had a cool name. Very man-on-a-mission kinda vibe."

I glare at my stupidly attractive ex-husband. "Why not give your real name? You know *Haircuts and Heartthrobs* caters to famous, pompous, self-absorbed men such as yourself. Privacy is literally in our contract."

"Because if I had, you would have faked a power outage and shut down the salon."

I roll my eyes. "I forgot to mention, self-important."

"Tell me I'm wrong."

"You *are* wrong. Because what I would have done was hand you a free welcome-champagne and pawned you off to an apprentice, perhaps with hedge trimmers and a grudge against men. I'd have put you in the suite that still plays whale mating calls because no one can figure out how to fix the sound system."

"Champagne, whale sounds, and hedge trimmers. Don't

threaten me with a good time, sweetheart." He steps closer, erasing some of the space I'd freed for myself. "You've always known how to get me worked up."

I give him a deadpan look before crossing my arms. "You're forgetting your charms no longer work on me, Pierce."

He takes a step closer, backing me into my salon station and leaving zero oxygen in my vicinity. His fingertip trails down the side of my neck unhurriedly, sending a tremor through me.

"You sure about that? Because this throbbing pulse right here seems to say otherwise."

My fists tighten around the edge of the counter. "Don't flatter yourself. That's just my body figuring out whether to fight or flight."

His warm breath coasts over my ear. "Pretty sure you've tried both in the past. How did that work out for you?"

"I had years of peace until you showed back up."

He chuckles, and I swear to everything holy, my body locks up. My breaths come out as shallow pants, and something hot and sticky coats the inside of my panties. God, why do I become such a fumbling, lovesick ho around this man? It's like my brain is telling my body to get a grip, but it's literally doing the opposite.

His hand curves around the back of my neck, thumb tilting up my jaw. "Years of survival, sweetheart, not peace. You asked me for space; I gave you space. Don't confuse that with us being done, Little Borealis. We'll never be done."

My breath hitches, and my nipples harden to stiff peaks behind my thin shirt. Nipples, I know he can feel against his chest. Breathing he knows has become ragged.

His thumb slides over my bottom lip, and for a second, all I can see are those tiny freckles dusting the bridge of his nose that I used to trace with my fingers. "I'm not here for a haircut."

I swallow, my voice coming out as a ragged whisper. "Then, why . . . ?"

His eyes drop to my lips, his pupils dark and dilated. I'm not sure who moves first, but we're a hair's breadth away from a kiss I know will ruin me when Patton's eyes snap to the mirror behind me and his entire body goes rigid.

"Nisha, why is there a skinned chicken hanging in the corner behind me?"

My brows furrow, and I twist around Patton to get a better look.

There, upside-down and frozen, with his entire body aligned to the floor-to-ceiling climbing rope, is my hairless cat, Beaver. His stark white body is a mix of wrinkles and lean muscles as he grips the rope with all four paws, his piercing blue eyes trained on Patton with the intensity of a sniper.

He must have slipped inside while we were . . . distracted. His quiet stealth and his ability to turn doorknobs and open doors no longer surprises me. I've found him watching from inside cabinets he's pried open or perched in impossible spots, peering down at people like a porcelain gargoyle. His ninja-like grace can unnerve unsuspecting clients who aren't expecting a hairless, blue-eyed phantom to materialize out of nowhere.

Sarina, Piper, and I rescued Beaver and his sisters, Vajayjay and Snatch, from a bad situation a few years ago. At the time, they were three traumatized cats who had been abused so badly, they were scared of their own shadows. But once they started to trust us, something just clicked.

Interestingly, each cat chose one of us. Vajayjay chose Piper—though, she's probably more Dev's cat these days. Snatch immediately loved Sarina, and might be responsible for Troy's untimely demise at some point. And Beaver decided he was going to be my little protector.

Over the years, Beaver and I have developed an understanding based on love and shared quirks. For example, we're both quiet observers by nature, preferring to be in the shadows rather than taking center stage. We're also both strong and agile, sometimes using our bodies in ways that feel like we defy physics. And we both have a death glare that makes grown men cower.

"That's not a skinned chicken. That's my cat, Beaver."

"Your . . . cat," Patton says slowly, like he's testing out new vocabulary. "That *thing* is a cat?"

"Hey! Beaver is a highly sensitive and extremely intelligent Sphynx cat."

"He looks like the spawn of Yoda and a mole rat."

"He does not. And even so, he's still more sophisticated than the massive beast you brought over to ruin my rare plants."

"I'll have you know that Bob is also very sensitive. He always cries at the end of *Finding Nemo*. Besides, at least he has *fur*."

"Ah, yes. Because his fur makes up for his lack of bladder control." I place a hand on Patton's chest—mostly to stop myself from dragging him back into our almost-kiss—before moving past him toward my cat. "Beaver's always had a sixth sense for when I'm in trouble and in need of rescuing. And as always, he's right on time."

"And how do you think he'll rescue you? He looks frozen. Are you sure he's real? He hasn't blinked."

As if to prove how real he is, Beaver slides down the rope, landing on the floor like a ghost. His movements are so graceful, the rope barely sways. And like a predator having spotted his next victim, he prowls toward Patton with calculated steps.

The scene is all very *Animal Planet*.

Patton takes a hesitant step back. "Bro is giving axe-murderer in a horror film. You know I can't sleep for days after watching those. Should I lie down or run? I'm starting to see my life flash before my eyes."

I try not to laugh, watching my six-foot-one ex-husband, who's ridden on the hood of a car during a high-speed chase scene, squirm under the scrutiny of a twelve-pound cat.

"He's figuring out how fast he can get to your carotid artery. You should probably start making peace with God."

"Nisha—"

Tail flicking, Beaver slinks closer before coming to a stop in front of Patton. Then, finally breaking his eye contact, my cat opens his mouth and drops something small and dark directly on his shoe.

Patton looks down in horror. "Is that . . . a dead cricket?"

"Well, at least it's not a client's wallet like last week. That made for an interesting and awkward conversation."

Patton stares at Beaver, who is now sitting on his haunches, waiting expectantly. "What's . . . what does he want?"

I roll my eyes.

I remember Patton telling me a long time ago that he wasn't "a cat person," but watching this interaction between them has got to be the highlight of my day. And after what his ogre of a dog did to my Monstera, this just feels like poetic justice.

I sigh, crossing my arms at my traitorous cat. "He's showing you affection."

Patton chuckles darkly. "He and I have very different definitions of affection."

"Beaver's love language is gifts. If he decides he likes you, he will bring you things. Whether it's a stolen Rolex or the remains of a squirrel. He's a giver that way."

I can't help but smile at the adoration and curiosity on my cat's face. Patton may not be a cat lover, but my cat has decided he's a Patton lover, and I can see the determination in his eyes to change Patton's views.

Patton lifts his gaze from the dead bug on his shoe to me. "So, what you're telling me is, this is his version of a proposal?"

I nod. "I don't think he's going to take no for an answer."

Patton's eyes gleam, his words loaded with meaning. "At least he and I have that in common."

twelve
nisha

The Brain Eraser

My muscles release under the masseuse's warm touch on my back, a short groan escaping my lips when she presses the heel of her hand to a particularly tense spot.

My best friends and I are celebrating my sister's upcoming nuptials with Troy with a day of pampering at Hudson's sprawling ranch right outside of San Francisco. When he and Kavi offered their place for Sarina's bachelorette party, I thought we'd be hanging out in some rustic barn with horses and hay and make the best of it.

I should have known better, though. Because if they say Dev is richer than God, then Hudson is God's personal investment broker.

The man has more money than small countries, so it's no surprise that his "little ranch" comes with an indoor spa, complete with a hot tub, heated massage tables, personal masseuses, and a private chef who's preparing our lunch as we speak.

Yeah, we're really roughing it out here.

Later tonight, the converted barn will be packed with more of Sarina's friends—ladies from the salon, baseball wives, and whoever else made the cut for the evening's festivities. But for now, it's just the Clam Jam girls, getting massages, drinking mimosas, and chatting it up, all while I try to forget my ex-husband exists for the next few hours.

Which is why I specifically asked everyone not to mention him today.

It's been impossible to avoid him lately.

Just yesterday morning, from my kitchen window, I watched him try to walk his dog on our street. I say "try" because it mostly involved him stopping every few feet while Bob sniffed the ground with my bra dangling from his mouth while Patton's security detail trailed a half-block behind him, looking like the world's most awkward one-man parade.

Two mornings before that, I made the mistake of staring at his house while sitting in my driveway, my "Crying in the Car" playlist streaming through my speakers like it had for so many years. But as if he had a sixth sense for obliterating my peace, Patton emerged from his door in nothing but low-slung gray sweatpants and a backward cap, like one of those thirst traps you scroll past before guiltily backtracking to ogle.

His eyes locked on mine as he lifted his coffee cup in a lazy salute, a knowing smirk curving when he caught my gaze drifting to his bare chest. I slammed the accelerator and high-tailed it out of there so fast, I left skid marks on the pavement. But the damage was done. His stupid chest had burned itself into my retinas.

So yeah, this much-needed Patton-free spa date couldn't have come at a better time.

My best friends' husbands are here, too, spending the day with Troy doing "manly things," like horseback riding, fishing, and archery. Or maybe they're all scratching their balls and seeing who can spit the farthest. Who knows?

Anyway, the plan is to merge our groups later in the barn for a night of debauchery and drinks.

I'm just in the middle of groaning through another tender

spot when I catch movement outside. Through the spa's one-way window, I watch as the guys walk past wearing cowboy hats.

How cute. They're really getting into the whole scratching their balls thing with a whole getup and everything.

But then, the smile on my face falls as quickly as it bloomed, because . . .

Wait a fucking minute.

That can't be right.

My brows furrow, and I lift my head toward my friends chatting in the hot tub nearby, silently forcing the masseuse to pause. "Uh, why is Patton here with the guys?"

Bella and Rani eye each other, and Piper follows my line of sight to the window behind her. But it's my sister who speaks.

"Well, you did specifically ask us not to mention him."

My mouth hangs open in disbelief before I hiss, "Sarina 'Traitorous-Twin' Arora. You know damn well that is not what I meant."

"Hey! Don't you middle name me on my special day! And it's going to be Sarina 'Traitorous-Twin' Winters soon, so get it right."

I push myself onto my elbows, addressing all my friends, "How long have you guys known he was invited today?"

Kavi winces. "For a couple of days—"

"A couple of days?!" I shriek, making my masseuse stumble backward. Poor woman is probably wondering if her massage therapy license covers witnessing client homicides. "And you didn't think to tell me?"

That's it. I'm rescinding their friendship cards.

"Well, you did tell us not to mention him," Mala repeats Sarina's earlier words.

I glare at her, and then back at my sister and Piper, the two women who know everything about me and Patton. The two women who saw first-hand how everything went down. "Seriously?"

Piper raises her hands in surrender, making the water drip around her. "Look, yes, we should have told you. But, honestly, this is Troy's day, too."

"And he really wanted to invite Patton," Sarina adds. "They've all gotten close now that he's in the Schlongs chat."

"Unbelievable." I drop my head back onto the massage table with a thud. My massage therapist sensibly moves down to my legs, probably unsure how many more times I'll get activated. "First, he shows up in town under the guise of a new movie, then he pops up at my *dojang*, my doorstep, the salon on Wednesday, and now he's here? You'll probably tell me next that he's also invited to the wedding."

Sarina immediately looks guilty, shifting closer to the hot tub wall like she's hoping it'll swallow her whole.

"He showed up at the salon on Wednesday?" Piper asks. "I don't remember seeing him there, but I was probably with a client."

Ignoring her, I lift my head again and glare at my sister. *Bet the masseuse is happy she stayed south of all this drama happening in my head and neck.* "Tell me you're kidding."

The girls all shift awkwardly, avoiding eye contact with me.

"Troy really likes him," Sarina protests. "And you know I've always loved Patton like a brother."

That's when I feel a sharp pain cut through my chest.

"Look, babe," Piper starts as memories of the four of us laughing, chatting, and watching TV in Dad's living room flash in front of my eyes. "I know this has all been confusing and crazy for you—"

"Crazy? Yes. Confusing? No," I retort, snapping back to the present. "There's nothing confusing about my feelings for my husband."

"*Ex*-husband," Rani corrects.

I close my eyes for a beat. "Yes, my ex-husband. I'm not confused when it comes to him."

When silence stretches over us and I crack one eye open, they're all staring at me with similar expressions—part sympathy and part "denial is a river in Egypt".

I pull the blanket on my back over my head. "I hate all of you."

"Nisha, hon," Piper tries again. "Look, you know we're your ride-or-dies. Sarina and I literally cut off all ties with Patton when you guys split. And we'd do it all over again if we had to. But that doesn't mean we didn't love the kid we grew up with and the man he became."

"But we also hated how heartbroken you were when you left him," Sarina adds, as if finishing Piper's thoughts. "We knew that if we stayed in contact with him while you were trying to get over him, it would hurt you. But what happened between you two wasn't any one person's fault; it was just terrible circumstances."

My throat constricts, and I want to tell her I know that. I know it wasn't any one person's fault, and I know they cut Patton off because of me. He was like a protective and sweet brother to them.

And, God, I feel shitty about that. So fucking shitty.

Because even though I never made them choose explicitly, I knew they were doing it, anyway. For me.

I never thought about what the loss of their friendship might have felt like for him. How alone and abandoned he might have felt.

Especially when feeling alone and abandoned was something he never wanted to feel again. But I did that to him . . .

"Patton was always a good guy," my sister continues. "A good friend, a good brother-in-law, son-in-law—"

I pull the blanket off my head, making the girls gasp when

they see the tears streaking my cheeks. "But he wasn't a good husband . . . not when it counted."

Piper and Sarina make their way out of the hot tub first before the rest of the girls follow. And soon they've surrounded me, nudging my masseuse out of the circle.

I'm sure she's awkwardly standing in the corner, wondering if she should have called in sick today.

Sarina lowers herself, cupping my cheeks before wiping my tears with her thumbs. "Which is why you left him. But, babe, you're the only one in denial here. Because it's clear there is still something between you two. Something he wants to explore again."

"He's trying his damndest to get his wife back, Nish," Kavi adds. "I think what we all see is a man who is putting in the work—"

"Until his next movie. Until he's stuck on some fucking mountain with no connection to the real world and no clue that I need him." I sniffle, my voice hoarse.

"Maybe," Piper says, tucking a strand of my hair behind my ear. "But maybe not. Do you think he'd be back, immersing himself in your life like this if all he wanted was to show you more of the same?"

I swallow. "I don't know what I think anymore."

"You know what helps to reboot your brain sometimes?" Piper asks, a renewed gleam in her eyes suggesting it's time to get us all out of this funk. It's my sister's day, after all.

"What?" I ask, looking between them, knowing I'm going to regret the answer. Nonetheless, a smile still creeps up on my face, replacing the heartache and confusion there.

Piper saunters away toward a table near the sauna, coming back with a tray. And just like the night at her house with the green tea shots, when we toasted to "the tea" I spilled about me and Patton, there are seven shot glasses lined up with coffee-colored liquid.

"Oh, God. Not again," I groan.

"The Brain Eraser," Piper announces, handing us each a glass. "Because sometimes you just need to erase the past and start over. Down the hatch, ladies!"

The converted barn is more stunning than I could have imagined. There are string lights draped over exposed beams, high-top tables adorned with flickering candles lining the dance floor, and a stunning bar that's clearly stocked for a serious celebration.

Everywhere I look, faces both familiar and unfamiliar are laughing and chatting, celebrating the most important couple of the night—Sarina and Troy.

What I didn't expect was the discreet security positioned around the perimeter of the barn and scattered around the ranch. They're a little reminder that tonight's guests include a Hollywood A-lister, a well-known billionaire, and many high-profile ballplayers.

"Wow," I yell over the R&B music playing on the speakers to Kavi. "You and Hudson don't half-ass anything."

She giggles, lifting her glass to clink with mine, swaying before she winks at her husband seated at the bar next to Dev, Troy, and—

Ugh. The man I can't seem to avoid, outrun, or exorcise, no matter how much sage I've burned.

With dark denims hugging his long, muscular thighs, a white V-neck shirt showing off a thick neck I've french kissed like soft-serve ice cream in the summer sun, and a light-gray Versace blazer I remember gifting him on our second wedding anniversary, he's laughing at something Troy has said.

And though I can't hear the timbre of that laugh, I feel it

all the way down to my toes. Just like I feel his gaze when his head turns and our eyes collide.

It's not the first time I've caught him looking at me, but each time it happens, a thrill zips down my body, hollowing out my stomach, like the first drop on a roller coaster.

So, instead of giving him the satisfaction of dropping my gaze first, I flash him a toothy smile, sharp enough to draw blood, before turning around with my glass up in the air and bouncing to Tupac's *California Love* with my best friends and some of Sarina's baseball WAG friends.

My girlfriends and I arrived an hour ago, tipsy from day-drinking and dressed to kill. Sarina's in a mid-length white bodycon dress that hugs her curves, strappy white heels, and a sash that says "Gonna be Mrs. Troy Winters". Since her only request was for her best friends to wear either red or black, I chose black.

It is my go-to color after all—the color of my jaded heart.

My strapless leather dress contours around my medium-sized boobs, slender hips, and abs defined from years of martial arts training, hitting right above my knees. At five-feet-seven inches, I'm not short, but paired with my five-inch heels, I look Amazonian.

I've kept my makeup the way I always do—with winged eyeliner, making my black irises look like pools of obsidian, and a touch of lip gloss, the color and flavor of pomegranates.

The only jewelry I bothered with are the row of tiny star studs climbing up one ear and a single one in the other. And of course, the permanent bracelet that matches Patton's on my wrist.

Around each of our necks is a plastic gold necklace with a spinner pendant. It's tonight's entertainment, courtesy of Piper and her twisted brain.

Each spinner has four dares we have to complete throughout the night. Mine includes licking whipped cream off someone's finger, ordering a round of Mai Tais using charades, and—Sarina's personal favorite—faking an orgasm in front of a man.

But I'm a little annoyed. Because, while the rest of them have dares they can finish with their respective partners, I have to find a rando because . . . well, I don't have a man.

Did I mention there's also one that says, "Kiss a boy you used to love"?

Upon seeing it, I'd glared at my best friend so hard, I almost sent her to another planet. Yeah, *that was a little on the nose*, Piper. There's no question my spinner was rigged.

By her.

Probably by all of them.

I take a healthy sip of my pineapple margarita before dragging my tongue over my top lip to catch the salt crystals there. The Brain Erasers certainly helped me reset my emotional state, but it's the two drinks after that have really helped seal the deal. I'm feeling good—my arms and legs, nice and nimble, my body swaying on its own accord.

The energy is infectious as we move to the beat with our drinks in hand, laughing as they wait for me to spin my spinner for the next dare. I've already done two: order Mai Tais using charades and lick whipped cream off someone's finger.

For the first one, I'd pointed to myself and then to a man wearing a tie. I was happy to have gotten my point across to the bartender, but what I hadn't expected was tie-man's hand to find my ass.

And while I've always been more than capable of handling handsy men, I didn't miss the way Patton had white-knuckled his whiskey glass from across the bar, as if he were imagining it being tie-man's wrist.

He didn't have to fume long, though, because as quick as tie-man's hand had found my ass, I had it in mine. With a saccharine smile that would make any onlooker think we were just having a casual conversation, I bent his hand back until he tapped out at the bar.

For the whipped cream dare, I'd naturally chosen Piper. Of all my friends, she was the one who was both the most outrageous and the most sexual. I knew she'd play right along with what I had in mind.

So, I'd made sure to do it nice and slow, right in front of my ex-husband, licking and sucking her finger in a way that would remind him of something else he'd seen me suck . . .

I'd caught the flash in Patton's eyes—part desire and part warning. And for a moment, I wondered if it was the alcohol, the dare, or something more that was making me so bold.

Me, the woman who color-stacked her books and had alarms to water her plants, had sucked on my friend's finger like I was a fluffer on a porn set.

In front of my ex-husband. At my sister's bachelorette party.

God, my therapist was going to have a field day when she dove further into the depths of my crazy.

All my girlfriends also completed their dares with varying degrees of alcohol-fueled courage. However, the best so far was Sarina's.

She had to give Troy a lap dance in the middle of the dance floor. She'd kept it PG13, but it had made our friends whoop and laugh.

And Troy? The adoration, love, and protectiveness radiating from him said he was a goner. The way he looked at her made my heart burst for the two of them.

My sweet sister, who'd been such a strong and fierce single mom to my adorable nephew for so long, had finally found her happily-ever-after. And with an incredible single dad of the most adorable little girl. What more could I ask for?

The beat of the music thrums through me as I look down at my spinner.

Time for dare number three.

I give the spinner a flick and watch it land on . . . "kiss a boy you used to love."

Shit.

The chorus of laughs and gasps from my friends leaning in with obvious thrill weaves itself with the music and bodies dancing around us.

I shake my head, looking from Sarina to Piper, readying myself to tell them I'm not going to do it. But before I can, a chant of, "Do it. Do it. Do it," pulses through the group, urging me on.

My heart hammers in my ears as alcohol rushes through my veins.

A little voice in my head cautions me to think twice, but I ignore it. Because, as I have established before, my sensibilities subside whenever it comes to Patton Pierce.

So, it's no surprise that in the next moment I'm striding across the room toward the man leaning against the bar.

The air feels heavy, both in and out of my lungs, as my feet come to a halt in front of him.

Patton's brow lifts, and that's all the warning he gets before I grab the lapels of his blazer and yank him down to my lips.

The kiss is instant heat and hunger.

An instant rush, but surprisingly, not instant regret.

His hands capture my hips as if on instinct, dragging me closer, until there's no space between us. Until I feel his heart thud against my chest.

If he's stunned, it doesn't show by the way he takes control, parting my lips with his tongue and reclaiming what's always been his. The scent of bergamot and mint, along with the taste of whiskey, floods my senses, and all I want is to drown.

One moment we're surrounded by howls and gasps from our friends, and the next, all sound fades. There's no music or noise. No hammering inside my ears.

In that moment, there's just all-consuming tranquility, like nothing else exists.

Patton pulls back first, taking my breath with him. He drags his thumb over my still-tingling bottom lip, and I almost thank him for holding me upright.

His hand slides lower, discreetly brushing over the erect nipple behind my leather dress, before he lifts my spinner-pendant to read the last dare—*fake an orgasm in front of a man*.

The corner of his mouth quirks up, a daring glint in his eyes. Eyes I've looked into for hours on end. His warm breath coasts over the shell of my ear and my core constricts as his words register.

"Dare you to make it real."

thirteen
nisha

My Magic Bullet

My hands tremble as I unbuckle his belt.

Let's not even talk about the way my heart thrashes inside my chest or how my stomach flips like a fish out of water.

I feel possessed, crazed and frenetic. Like I've been body-snatched by an unhinged version of myself.

It's not the first time I've felt this deranged and out of control, either. No, my ex-husband has seen this side of me plenty of times, knowing exactly how to flip that switch inside me with his body, his words, and the kind of kiss that erases all common sense.

Forget Brain Eraser shots, this man is all I need to short-circuit.

And he knows it.

I'm not sure how we went from the party—still in full-force inside the barn—to the backseat of his private car, but we're here now, with the partition up and tinted windows cocooning us from the rest of the world.

With my legs straddled around his lap, my dress bunched up around my hips, and his warm hands on my ass, it's like everything and nothing I remember.

Familiar but new.

Safe but so fucking dangerous.

Patton makes a low, hungry sound against my neck as I roll my hips against his, feeling his erection at my core, separated only by the thin fabric of my panties and his jeans. Sometime between the barn and now, he'd discarded his blazer and I'd managed to unbutton his shirt, revealing the chest I've traced with my tongue more times than I can count.

Rocking my hips back, I unzip his pants and slide my hand over his straining hard-on, feeling the warmth of him through his boxers. The way he pulses against my palm makes me feel faint.

I swear just that feeling alone, with his length throbbing against my touch, his breath hot against my skin, and his fingers digging into my ass, has another rush of desire pooling between my thighs. If it wasn't for that tiny scrap of fabric there, his jeans would already be covered by the evidence of my want for him.

But he doesn't need that evidence to know how much my body craves him.

"Neesh," he rasps, breathing hard as his forehead drops to mine. "I'm going to hate myself for asking, but . . . are you sure about this?"

I still, even though my body feels like it's on fire. "Are you not sure? Do you not want it?"

His hands brush up my back, curling around my neck. His eyes bore into mine, intense and raw, stripped of the humor that's usually dancing on the surface.

"It's all I've wanted, every single day, for the last seven years. And while I'd imagined us in my bed instead of the back of my car, I know I won't regret a single fucking moment tomorrow." His thumbs trace along my jawline. "I just want to be sure you won't, either."

The fog of lust parts slightly as reality sinks back in—me

and him, alone and about to cross a line we won't come back from.

Our marriage. The trials and tribulations.

Our divorce. The aftermath.

All the carefully constructed walls I'd built over the years to safeguard my battered heart and protect myself from this man will likely crumble with this one decision.

One moment of weakness.

But the truth is, maybe this isn't a *moment* of weakness when I'm wholly weak where he's concerned. I'm a mess with him, but am I any better without him?

Looking into his eyes, sifting through the desire to find the truth and vulnerability there, I realize that I crossed that line the moment I kissed him in the barn. That I might have crossed the line well before that. Or hell, maybe I made up the line only to make myself feel better. Because maybe the line doesn't exist when it comes to him.

Because my ex-husband is my Achilles heel. The crack in my armor.

He's not just my war, but he's my white flag of surrender, too.

And if there's one thing I am sure of right now, it's that I can't fight this anymore. I can't guard my heart, my soul, or whatever the hell else the man wants, because he's determined to snatch them from me, no matter how much I resist. Hell, they might never have been mine to begin with.

"I can't be sure." My voice is a whisper as my hands fist the hair at the nape of his neck. "Not when it comes to you. And maybe we can talk about it tomorrow, but right now, I'm sure of one thing . . ." I trail off, kissing and sucking the column of his neck, rolling and grinding my hips over his need.

"And what's that?" he croaks.

"That I want you inside me. That I want you to fuck me like I'm still yours."

Pine For Me

A low, primal sound rumbles in his chest. It's all the warning I get before my world spins, and in one quick movement, he's flipped us so I'm beneath him, lying across the leather seat.

His body cages me in, hovering over me, as his lips crash down on mine with renewed hunger. Gone is the man who was asking for permission, and in his place is the man I'm familiar with, the man who's always known what he wants and how he plans to take it.

"You really think you ever stopped being mine?" he growls against my lips, hand sliding up my thigh to push up my dress and claim what was once his—still is. "You think some ink on paper could end us?"

I pant against him without a response, hearing him chuckle darkly. "No, baby. It would never be that easy."

His fingers find my center, shoving aside the fabric to glide up my heated slit. I gasp at the contact, my back bowing off the seat with just that first touch.

"Fuck, I've missed you," he murmurs, low and gritty. "Missed this body, this skin." His finger circles my entrance, making my empty core clench with need. "This pretty pussy."

"Yeah?" I ask, dragging my tongue over his bottom lip, catching it between my teeth. God, I'm so embarrassingly wet for him, I might combust if he doesn't go faster. "What else have you missed?"

The question gives away more than I mean to, revealing the cracks I rarely show. Why would he miss this—*my skin* and *my body*—when he's undoubtedly been with so many after me? Does he even remember us together? The way we fit from our very first time to the many breathless nights after?

I do. But that's because I've only been with two people after him—a forgettable one-night stand and Micah. And there's no need to rehash how disappointing both of those encounters were.

But I can't really blame those other men, either.

The truth is, no one has been able to get me out of my head. Not because they weren't trying, but because it takes a miracle and a thousand wishes to get me relaxed enough, wet enough, and lost enough to make me reach that peak, to actually make me come.

That, or the skilled hands and mouth of the man currently staring down at me like he wants to devour me whole. Patton's not just my Achilles heel, but he's my magic bullet, too.

"Your sounds," he answers, as the tip of his finger enters me, testing and prodding, deliberately slow. He's hovering over me on his forearm, staring down at me the way a lion would his prey. "From your loud moans to your delicate whimpers when I'm working this clit."

He flicks said clit to prove his point, his touch sending ripples and currents over my flesh, before pressing his finger fully inside me. The intrusion makes me buck against him, my body arching, my nipples grazing against the inside of my dress, begging to be touched and tweaked.

"Feel the way your pussy swallows my fingers, baby? It's like it's been waiting for me." He adds another finger, stretching me so deliciously, I mewl. "Feel the way you're clenching around me, pulling me deeper? Like you want me buried so deep inside you, I'll never find my way out."

He has no idea how deep he's already buried inside me.

The dim light coming through the windows casts shadows across his handsome face and the set of his jaw. It doesn't take much light to see how I'm affecting him, too, how enraptured he is with giving me pleasure.

My mouth goes slack when his fingers curl inside me, hitting that spot only he has ever been able to find, making my vision blur. I clutch his shoulders, nails digging into his skin as my hips rise and pleasure shoots through me like bolts of lightning.

"Patton," I gasp, slamming my eyes shut. "Oh, god!"

He makes little circles with the tips of his fingers inside me, his thumb finding my clit with practiced ease. I throw my head back, feeling my body tighten and a familiar flush rise over my skin.

"Look at me, Nisha," Patton commands, continuing to ease his fingers in and out of me, making my body do his bidding. "Let me see your eyes when I make you come."

I force my eyes open, meeting his intense gaze, so hungry and dark. The need between us crackles as he continues his assault, stroking me with expertise.

My breath hitches as my walls flutter around his fingers. "Patton!"

The corner of his lip curls, a smug smile blooming on his face, before he leans down to kiss me roughly. "That's it, baby," he whispers against my mouth. "Say my name. It's the only one you'll say from now on."

And with a final curl of his finger and a perfect circle of his thumb on my clit, I detonate like a collapsing star, pulling everything inward before shattering impossibly.

My head swims with lust and the remnants of the several drinks I consumed today. I'm not drunk though, I never was, though I can't deny that the alcohol gave me the courage to change the outcome of how this night might have ended—with me alone in my bed.

I'm still catching my breath, feeling my heart pound against my ribs, when Patton pulls his hand out from between my thighs and brings it to his mouth. Watching me, he sinfully licks each finger clean, like every drop of my arousal is quenching his thirst.

"And most of all, I missed this," he says, dragging his tongue over his lips.

My cheeks catch fire. "The taste of me?"

"Yes—fuck, yes—but not just that. I missed seeing you in

the aftermath. The way you radiate in your freshly-fucked glow."

I pull my bottom lip into my mouth, suppressing my smile and blush. "Technically, I haven't been fucked yet."

His mouth hovers over the shell of my ear. "Then, *technically*, we should change that."

My brow rises as I use my feet to maneuver his jeans down his body, taking his boxers with them. "Well, what are you waiting for, Pierce? A written invitation?"

How the fuck can I be wet again already?

But again, why am I even surprised, when I still have explicit memories of him giving me at least ten orgasms one night.

Chuckling, he nips my jaw before lining his erection at my entrance. But then his eyes come back to mine, and a flash of pain makes his smile falter. The pain we'd both stored away, hoping the hands of time would have softened its edges. And while that pain isn't as sharp as it once was, it's here now, raw and real, dancing between us.

His thumb brushes my temple, his throat bobbing before I see the question form on his lips. "Do you want me to use a condom?"

I shake my head. "Maybe not this time. Plus, you know the chances of . . ." The sentence doesn't need finishing, not with him. "I'm clean. Are you?"

The question makes me want to vomit. No, not the question, but his impending answer.

"I am."

"Good," I whisper, a mix of relief and something acidic warring inside my chest. I hate that we even had to have that exchange.

Patton searches my face for another moment. "Still sure about—"

I kiss him before he can finish, before we overthink. Before the baggage of our past can ruin this moment.

Maybe we'll unpack it tomorrow. But tonight? I just want to feel whole again after seven years of walking around with only half of me.

Our bodies writhe like muscle memory that never faded as the haze of desire drags us under again. My tongue tangles with his, desperate and persuasive, pulling a low groan from deep in his chest.

I pull back, breathless against his lips. "Finish what you started, Patton Pierce."

fourteen
patton

You Planning to Brand Me Next?

I thrust into the beautiful enigma that is my ex-wife.

Half my life knowing her, and I still can't anticipate her next move. She's as unpredictable in life as she is in a *dojang*, pushing me away with a snarky retort and pulling me closer with a searing kiss. Claiming to be unsure about everything between us one moment, and begging to be fucked the next.

To say I was shocked when she stomped her sweet ass over to me, dressed in black leather like my fantasy come to life, and pulled me into a kiss in front of everyone in the barn would be the understatement of the century. But fuck if I was going to let her second-guess it once she had.

After all, wasn't that the whole reason I was here—in her town, her neighborhood, and her circle? In every aspect of her life? To get her back and keep her this time?

She drives me insane.

And yet, she's the only thing that drives me at all. No woman has ever made me feel the way she does—like a glutton and a simp. Like I'm both the strongest and weakest version of myself where she's concerned.

I might have kept my distance physically for the past seven

years, but there wasn't a day she wasn't the force behind everything I did. Not a day I wasn't working through the damn crumpled list I found.

And when I sensed the crack in her facade during that kiss last year, I knew. Her "never again" had started to shift and "forever again" wasn't out of the realm of possibilities.

I won't pretend there haven't been others. A handful of models and actresses who scratched an itch the year after Nisha completely cut me off—fucking changed her number and explicitly asked for space. We'd finalized our divorce by then, and I was heartbroken and angry.

At her. At myself.

With the way she just gave up on us.

And the way I couldn't save us.

But like with anything real in this life, I quickly realized that once you've had a taste of it, it's hard to accept a substitute. Be it a Big Mac when you're accustomed to Wagyu beef, or boxed wine when the taste of a fifty-year-old Bordeaux still lingers on your tongue.

Not one of them made me laugh like she did, challenged me like she did. Not one made my pulse race or my skin heat with a mere upward tick of her lips.

Because not one was my ex-wife.

After that year, I gave up trying to satisfy the itch altogether. There was no use trying to quench my thirst with drops of water.

Sure, I'd take a date to an event here or there, and sometimes that would stir up tabloid buzz. But over the past five years, I haven't touched a woman besides her.

And since that evening on the cliff, with a kiss that scared her enough to run once again, I've been singularly focused on one thing and one thing only: getting my ex-wife back.

Because the truth is, no one else had ever made me forget. And, as I'd learned that day, she hadn't forgotten, either. Not with the way we came alive in each other's arms. Or the way we could die right then and there without regret.

Which is why I devised this crazy plan—to give her request to stay away the middle finger and win her back, or live the rest of my life trying.

Yes, I'd fucked up before. By not being there, coincidentally on the two times she needed me most. Like the universe had set out to sabotage my fucking life, I wasn't there when her heart—*our hearts*—was shattering to pieces. Because I was stuck on set with no way of getting back to her in time.

She'd forgiven me the first time, but the second had been her breaking point.

The damage was done, and maybe the repair has been a long time coming. But there's no denying it's coming.

Because I will repair us.

I will fix the heart I broke, even if I have to pick it up and glue it back together, piece by piece.

I look into Nisha's eyes before dropping my gaze to her lips. They're parted and swollen with my kisses, and I realize she's been rendered frozen, holding her breath ever since I thrust my cock inside her.

"Breathe, baby," I murmur, pressing my forehead to hers. "I've got you."

She exhales shakily, her body trembling beneath mine. "I forgot how big you are."

I pull out and pump back into her tight heat, feeling it strangle my cock like she's planning to choke it to death. Goddamn, she feels good, her wet arousal tightening around me like a vise.

I give her a moment to adjust to my size before pulling out once more and driving back in. "But look how you take every inch of me, welcoming me home like a good fucking girl. Your pussy remembers exactly who owns her, doesn't she?"

"Y-yes." Her throaty moan fills the car as she clenches around me.

Thank God I'd had the wherewithal to tell my security detail to scatter around my SUV, far enough away to not see it rocking like I'm sure it is.

Nisha's nails bite into my back as my cock pumps inside her. The fucker wants to dive so far deep, she'll feel him in her throat.

"Tell me, baby," I say, breathing harshly against her. "Did you miss this cock? Did you miss how hard I always fucked you, making your pussy weep for me?"

Nisha mumbles an incoherent response that sounds like a mix of "Yes" and "Mmmf," her eyes going from squeezing shut to opening wide.

Shifting my weight to one forearm, I use the other hand to pull down her strapless dress, revealing one perky nipple. Inside her, my dick hardens impossibly more as I lave her pebbled nipple with a flat tongue, making her hips lift in response.

Circling it with the tip of my tongue, I flick and suck it before I bite down on it hard, the way she's always loved.

Nisha moans, her fingers fisting my hair and her neck arching back to shove her chest further into me.

She's always loved having her nipples played with—not just teased or licked, but tugged and bitten, almost to the point of pain. It's something I learned early on that relaxed her and heightened her arousal.

She's never been easy to get off—needing my fingers, my mouth, and my cock to get her there after focused teasing and ministration—but if there's one thing I found that helped get her there faster, it was playing with her nipples.

I continue to roll her nipple in my mouth as I fuck her raw, pulling out to the tip before diving back to the hilt, pummeling her and making her gasp with each thrust.

I feel undone, like I'm a threadbare fabric coming apart at the seams. Like I've been timeworn or maybe I was never stitched right to begin with, and now I'm splitting open, one manic breath at a time.

"You look so fucking beautiful when you take my cock. When every drop of delicious juice from this pussy is for me." Popping off her nipple, I take a harsh breath. My heart hammers against my chest like it's digging a way out. "That's it, beautiful, suck me in deeper."

"Oh, God, Patton." She widens her legs, inviting me further. And like a toxin ready to flood her bloodstream, I drive in deeper, harder. "It feels so good."

Her body slides under me on the seat, our groins colliding in rhythmic slaps, creating obscene sounds that I'll probably use to get off to later when I'm alone.

But, fuck, I never want to be alone. Not after this.

"No, baby," I say roughly. "*It* doesn't feel good. *We* feel good."

"So good," she agrees when I hit a particular spot that makes her core flutter around me.

I chuckle, kissing her jaw. "So agreeable. Where does all that snark go when you're underneath me?"

As if I've willed said snark to resurface, she answers, "It makes an exception for a decent dick."

"Decent?" I nip her earlobe, making her jump under me. The movement makes my balls tighten, but I don't let myself come, pounding into her harder instead. "You're going to choke on this *decent* dick when it's ramming down the back of your throat."

She groans, and I swear her pussy gets slicker. "Promises, promises . . ."

I take her mouth with mine in a hungry, messy kiss, if only to shut her up. Our teeth clank as our tongues war. And just like the way I'm fucking her, there's nothing gentle about this kiss.

It's demanding and primal.

Unforgiving and chaotic.

Our mouths are merged, just like our bodies. Our breaths and our fucking souls, aligned in a way that feels both destined and inevitable. Like we were always meant to find our way back here.

And interestingly, reminiscent of the first time we had sex.

In the beat-up old truck I'd worked two jobs over two summers to pay for—my first car, held together by little more than duct tape and prayers.

We were just seventeen then, naïve and clueless. We might have been clumsy as hell, but even then we somehow seemed to move in-sync, like our instincts knew what our bodies had yet to experience.

We were each other's firsts.

And while she may not physically be my only anymore, she is in all the ways it matters.

But am I still hers?

The thought forms before I can stop it, buzzing between us like a goddamn mosquito. And it fucking kills me that I still wonder, that I still hope. Though, I know how hypocritical and unfair the thought is.

She had every right to have whoever she wanted in her bed. We were fucking divorced. And yet . . . I know I'll want to find and murder any guy who had the audacity to touch what was mine if I ever find out the motherfuckers' names.

One of them better not have been that beady-looking asshole, Michael. Or was it Micah? His name doesn't matter because I'll pummel him until he thinks he's Michael.

My jaw hardens as I break our kiss and fuck her even more ferociously before moving my lips down to her neck. I kiss and lick it, pulling a moan from her lips, before sucking hard enough to leave a mark.

I have no idea when she'll see fucking Michael again, but at least until I can get my ring back on her finger, he'll know she belongs to someone else.

Nisha's knowing eyes meet mine, her skin glistening in the dark. "You planning to brand me next?"

"It's crossed my mind a time or two . . . along with chaining you permanently to me and tattooing my name over your chest."

"Always threatening me with a good time, Hollywood."

This fucking girl and her mouth. It's like she always has a comeback at the ready. Maybe next time I'll stuff her mouth full of my dick so she really can't speak.

Lowering my mouth again, I take her other nipple between my lips, sucking and biting, rolling and teasing, before moving my hand down to her clit.

Nisha hisses at the contact and the change in angle as my dick moves inside her.

Using my middle two fingers, I start making steady, tight circles over her clit as I drag my cock through her walls.

"You've always been so responsive to my touch, haven't you, Little Borealis? Tell me," I ask, not able to stop the words from tumbling out of my mouth, "has anyone else ever made your body sing like this?"

She lets out a strangled moan, her back arching into my touch, fingernails scraping down my back. Her eyes meet mine, dark and unblinking. And just when I think she's going to hit me with another snarky response, those same eyes soften.

Her throat bobs with a swallow, and she shakes her head. "You ruined me for anyone else."

And that's when I turn into a madman, fucking her, fingering her, kissing her until she trembles around me. Until our brows bead with sweat and our breaths become one. Until her walls pulse around me and she comes with the sexiest moan I've ever heard.

Her thighs shake as she continues to milk my cock. My balls slap at her pussy, growing heavy as my body tightens and my spine tingles.

And then, almost as if I've been caught off-guard, I spill inside her sweet, slick heat in waves of euphoria.

Like I haven't in years.

Like I plan to for years to come.

When she's mine for good.

fifteen
nisha

I Don't Love the Idea of Darth
Vader Going Down on You

Sparks detonate on my skin as soft breath escapes my lips.
 No, not a breath. A pant. A request for more. A praise for the desire fluttering inside my core.

In my half-asleep, fully-turned-on haze, it takes me a second to recognize the sound as my own. But he does. Because he answers it with a groan, dragging the tip of his cock back and forth, from my entrance to my clit, coating himself with my juices.

Lying on our sides, he's positioned behind me with one arm under my neck. His other hand alternates between working his erection between my folds and tweaking my nipple. Instinctively, I wiggle my ass against him, hissing as I fist his sheets.

The morning sunlight trickles in through the gaps in his curtains, illuminating the evidence of our tryst last night—my dress falling off the arm of a chair in the corner, his blazer and jeans in a heap on the plush carpet . . . and is that my thong hanging from the dresser knob?

Wait . . . Why are they torn like that?
Oh, right.

Because as soon as we got to his house—ravenous and

ready for round two—he yanked them off me like a man possessed. I remember gasping as the sound of the lace tearing filled the room, along with his muttered promise to buy me a hundred more.

Now it's hanging there like a tiny flag, a reminder of all the lines we crossed and all the restraints we broke.

And while the careful, risk-averse, and still heartbroken part of me continues to ring warning bells inside my head, telling me this could be a big mistake, that I shouldn't walk back down this same path with a man who shattered me before, I tell the bitch we'll address her concerns later.

Because right now, enveloped in his arms and his touch, I can't think of the rights and wrongs, the shoulds and shouldn'ts, the past and the future.

I can only live in the present.

The present, where his lips and tongue are on my neck, his fingers are pressing inside me, making me buck, and I'm too far gone to care about the promises I made to myself over the past seven years.

My eyes squeeze shut as waves of electricity course down my spine, making me whimper and squirm under his touch. A touch that has woken me up just like this countless times in the past, knowing how much I love starting a new day with him buried between my legs.

"Patton . . . Oh, God! Yes . . ."

His erection slides in between my ass cheeks as his fingers work me. "Fuck, baby. Always so messy, so soaked and swollen for me."

My hand finds the back of his head, my fingers tightening in his hair as I whimper in response. I swear, my body feels like it's on fire.

"Tell me, Little Borealis, are you ready for my cock again?"

God. Every word out of his mouth is my undoing. The unraveling of my carefully reconstructed life and plans.

I'm sore in the best and worst of ways, but fuck if I'll admit that right now.

"Y-yes." My breathy whisper shamelessly confirms my need for him, not that he needs any more confirmation, given the way his fingers are dripping with my arousal.

And that's when I feel him slap my pussy, hard.

The sting and shock makes my body jolt, and I release a sound I've never heard before from my lips. And right when the tailspin he'd just sent my mind and body on starts to settle, he slaps it again, making me yelp.

The wetness that drips from between my thighs should have me mortified in embarrassment. And yet, I'm too far gone to care.

Patton's warm tongue drags up my neck before he nips at my earlobe. "You like that, sweetheart? You like having your pussy slapped? Me being rough with you?"

All I can do is nod because words seem to be escaping me at the moment.

And while this position—hell, almost every position between us—is familiar, *this* feels new. The rough edge in his voice and touch. The unabashed desire in his words. And the way my body craves more of it.

How is it possible that a man I thought couldn't be outdone, at least in the bedroom, has outdone himself?

He's changed. Not just in the way his body is more filled out and defined, but in the way he conducts himself, too. He now exudes a confidence that was always there beneath the surface but is out in plain sight now.

And perhaps it's because he's had years to find that on his own. Or perhaps someone else helped him find it.

As soon as that thought forms, and the unjustified rage threatens to course through my veins, I shove it away. Because whether this lasts a day, a month, or the year he claims he'll be here, I am where I want to be right this second.

And then what? It'll all be over?

Maybe, maybe not. But this time I'll be ready. Because I know I can't rely on a man who's always put his career first. But I also know I don't need him, that I *can* make it on my own.

I guess I've changed, too.

This? This physical connection drawn on by years of emotional longing? I haven't changed my mind about what it is. It's not a second chance or a new path to happily-ever-after.

It's a "fuck around and find out".

It's two people with a complicated past and too much heat between them to keep their hands off each other.

We may have changed, but that doesn't mean our broken history has. I'm no longer naïve enough to believe I can be a man's first priority, and he hasn't changed enough to make me believe otherwise.

Because despite his declaration that it was to chase me, I know he didn't move here for *me*. Otherwise, why would he admit he doesn't know how long he'll stay—a few months or a year?

No, Patton Pierce moved here for his first and true love— his job. Plain and simple. And I'd be a fool to believe anything different.

Patton shifts, reaching for the box of condoms behind him, bringing my thoughts back to the present.

We never discussed using them explicitly because that conversation was too heavy for the kind of night we both wanted to have. But despite what I said to him last night—that the chances are slim to nonexistent—it didn't need to be explicitly stated to know that the consequence would be too big.

I turn my head to watch him rip the wrapper with his teeth. I don't know why that small act always seems to turn me on. Perhaps it's the way the veins in his forearm tighten, or the flash of his perfect white teeth that nipped and bit me in the best of ways last night, but I'm practically shaking for him to get inside me.

God, the man is so beautiful. With his dark hair mussed from my fingers spearing it all night, his eyes the color of rain-soaked earth, and that perfectly-trimmed stubble, my ex-husband is temptation incarnate. If sin and seduction had a face, it would look like Patton Pierce—complete with that devastating smirk that says he knows I'm powerless when it comes to him.

He slides the head of his sheathed cock to the top of my slit, gathering my wetness and eliciting a gasp that feels like it comes from my soul.

"I'm not going to go easy, baby. It'll be hard and fast until the only thing you remember is who owns you, body and soul." His hot breath ghosts over the shell of my ear. "Me."

And then he's sliding inside me.

My breath hitches as my body tenses momentarily before relaxing enough to invite him in. He's long and thick, and his one movement seats him so far inside me, my brain temporarily glitches.

His body still curved behind me, Patton drags his hand up my stomach and over my breasts before he wraps it around my throat. He squeezes gently, heightening all my senses, before grabbing my jaw and turning my face.

His lips devour mine in a kiss that seems to slow time, the heat between us melting the polar icecaps. Somewhere, a penguin just lost his home, but I can't seem to care, not when he's kissing me like he's trying to convince me that gravity doesn't exist and the only thing keeping me tethered to earth is him.

I slide my hand down to my aching center while his cock drags in and out of me and his balls slap against my folds. It feels so fucking good, yet still not enough.

I need more. So much more.

God, why don't we have more hands?

Because I need his hands tweaking my nipples, gripping my neck, and playing with my clit. Oh, and fisting my hair and yanking it just the way I like. *Is that too much to ask?*

He bites my bottom lip, and I cry out when the crown of his cock hits that sensitive spot deep inside me. "Patton!"

"Fuck." His hand tightens around my throat as he plunges inside me again and again, panting like a savage beast. "Fuck, baby, you feel so good. So tight and hot. So mine."

I whimper, circling my clit with my fingers, my mouth falling open as my body revs up.

Patton's tongue drags over my swollen lip and whether it's the fact that he knows I've always needed a lot to get me off or he's just reading my mind, he says, "Want to take that vibrator for a spin?"

My brows furrow. "What?"

"I saw it in your gift bag last night," he pants, nodding to the little bag on the nightstand—the one full of the various gag gifts my girlfriends and I all got during Sarina's party.

I follow his gaze, then glance back at him, my lips twitching. "Okay."

He reaches over me, arm brushing my nipples, before grabbing the bag. Fumbling through the crinkling tissue paper, he takes out a sleek, black vibrator wand with Darth Vader's helmeted head on one end and several silver buttons marching down the body.

Patton stares at Darth Vibrator like it might start doing the heavy breathing thing from the movies. "I saw this in the box that day when your mail was delivered to me. Not going to lie, it terrified me."

I roll my eyes. "Piper's strange sense of humor. I was in charge of gift bags, and she suggested I order a bunch from this website that sells Star Wars-themed sex toys."

"Why Star Wars-themed?"

I wince, not wanting to think about my sister and her fiancé at the moment. "Something to do with the first time Troy and Sarina had sex. Though, I believe there was an alien-shaped condom involved, too." At Patton's raised brow, I quickly say, "Never mind."

Patton's thumb brushes over one of the buttons, making the wand vibrate in his hand. With a sly smile, he drags the buzzing helmet down my stomach to the top of my slit, making my skin come alive under the vibration.

He pauses with a frown. "I don't love the idea of Darth Vader going down on you."

"Jealous? He does have a commanding presence."

Patton doesn't miss a beat. Still spooning me, he thrusts back inside me in one deliberate stroke, stealing the breath from my lungs. "Pretty sure I'm doing just fine in the 'commanding presence' department."

He lowers the vibrator to my clit, and my entire body arches as waves of current run down my legs, curling my toes. My fingers fist the sheets as Patton starts moving again, increasing his rhythm and fucking me with such hard and fast strokes, I lose my breath.

His other hand roams over my chest, finding my nipple, twisting and pinching until I'm trembling in his arms. My pleasure mounts with every low groan I wrench from his throat and the rough drag of his breath against my skin.

Our moans mix with the sounds of our bodies colliding and the hum of the vibrator like a wild symphony, each note clashing in the most perfectly erotic tempo. The room is a cacophony of chaotic sounds, lustful sighs, and breathless gasps.

Filthy pleasure and unbridled need.

My orgasm looms right within reach as Patton rolls the

vibrator over my clit, creating a hurricane inside my core as he continues to pound into me with a quickened pace.

He wasn't kidding when he said he wouldn't take it easy on me.

He pulls out almost all the way before slamming back in so hard, I cry out again. "Oh my God. Oh, God, Patton. Please don't stop. I'm so clo—"

"I am your father."

My climax comes to a screeching halt as the words die on my tongue. My eyes fly open.

What. The. Fuck?

I turn to glance over my shoulder at Patton, who looks like a deer in headlights. "Did you . . . ? Did you just say that?"

"No, of course I didn't." He jerks the toy in his hand. "It was this—"

"That's it. Don't underestimate the power of the Dark Side."

An incredulous laugh bubbles out of me. "Oh my God. It talks?!"

"I knew there was a reason it terrified me." He holds the thing out like it's trying to bite him before pressing what looks like a mute button.

"The Force is strong with you."

I'm shaking with laughter now, watching Patton frantically push the button over and over, only for the wand to buzz louder.

"Who knew Vader's dirty talk was so on point." I wheeze.

Patton scowls at me before his dark brows pinch, looking at the tool in his hand. "What the fuck is wrong with this thing?" He hits the power button, but instead of turning off, the toy only gets louder, like it's feeding off our panic. "How does it turn off?"

"Together, we can rule the galaxy."

Patton fumbles with the buttons again before twisting

Darth Vader's head like he's hoping to rip it clean off his body. "Die, you piece of shit!"

"I must obey my master!"

I'm in full-body hysterics, tears leaking down to my temple, as I watch my ex-husband rage at the dildo in his hand before he hurls it to the floor. Darth Vader lands with a *thud* on the carpet, finally going silent.

Still giggling, I try to catch my breath. But one look at Patton's clenched jaw, and I spiral all over again.

Patton grabs my jaw, turning me to face him, clearly trying to get back some semblance of control. "Fucking Darth Vader is a bigger asshole than I thought."

Another laugh bubbles up through me, but I try to control it by cupping my ex-husband's head in my hands and bringing his lips to mine. My lips tremble with laughter, earning me an annoyed groan.

We're finally back to reclaiming the spark we almost lost, with his fingers rubbing circles over my clit and our tongues dueling in another heated kiss when—

"You have failed me for the last time."

"When I left you, I was but the learner. Now I'm the master."

That's when I double over once again, wheezing so hard my ribs ache and my shoulders shake.

Patton groans into the pillow. "I think we can safely say this is the end of our Star Wars kink era."

I'm in stitches, holding my side. "Pretty sure the Force wants nothing to do with us."

"That's it." Patton swings his legs over the side of the bed, his hair mussed and still looking like the beautiful naked Greek god he is. "I'm throwing this asshole into the garbage. He'll see what the real Dark Side looks like."

He's just reaching for the still-vibrating toy when the

bedroom door swings open and in lumbers his giant bloodhound, ears swinging like curtains and eyes permanently mournful.

Both Patton and I watch, frozen in place, as Bob pads into the room like a detective on a case.

He'd come bounding toward me last night when Patton and I entered his house, wagging his tail and sniffing every inch of me like he was on duty before Patton snuck us into his room without letting Bob in.

But somehow, the dog figured out how to open his door.

He's still got my flowery bra in his mouth—the blush-colored one with the soft lace that I looked for so many times after I left Patton's home in L.A.

Bob takes a quick account of us on the bed before sniffing the toy beneath him. I try not to die of mortification that he can probably smell *me* on Darth Vader's helmet.

"Bob, leave it," Patton warns, half-rising from his spot.

But it's too late. Because Bob makes a faster decision in that moment, discarding my bra and picking up the vibrator in his jowls.

With a wag of his tail and one glance over his shoulder at us, he walks out like he's gotten exactly what he came for.

When he disappears down the hall, we hear, *"You have failed me for the last time,"* sending me into another fit of giggles, though I try to cover my mouth with my hand.

"Great." Patton drags his hand over his face. "My dog has bonded with a Sith Lord sex toy. Probably because it smells like you."

His words melt more of the ice that's been thawing for quite some time now, and I know, even though I haven't spent much time with his sweet dog, that I'm going to fall hard and fast for him.

"I told people the bra was just a phase. And now . . . this."

I shrug, trying to keep my mouth from fidgeting. "I mean, at least he's consistent. Clearly, he's got a type."

Patton's eyes roam down my body, heating as he speaks. "Yeah. You."

sixteen
nisha

The Clam Jam

PIPER MENON

@Nisha Arora, did you finish your dare last night? We demand answers! You left with Hollywood, and if my spidey sense is correct, there was no FAKING IT involved. You got dicked, didn't you?

SARINA ARORA

Don't think for one second that I believed your "I'm tipsy and have a headache" excuse. Tipsy or not, you were doing that thing when you're lying—where you look at my left ear when you speak.

NISHA ARORA

I do not do that. And I WAS tipsy!

MALA MEYER

Oh, is that why you kissed him in front of everyone and nearly caused a barn fire with all that sexual tension? Because you were TIPSY?

SARINA ARORA

Girl is lying to no one but herself.

Swati M.H.

RANI MEYER

I literally got wet watching that kiss. Went home and took it out on Darian. He woke up happy this morning.

PIPER MENON

Pretty sure we all got the D last night just from being in the proximity of that kiss. My vagina was clapping like she was sensing a sister in heat.

NISHA ARORA

OMG. You all are deeply disturbed.

BELLA MEYER

Interestingly though, I don't hear you denying it. You slept with him, didn't you?

SARINA ARORA

Why else would someone walking by Patton's car say it was ROCKING? For twenty minutes.

NISHA ARORA

Shut up. No one said that.

Wait . . . did someone seriously say that?

PIPER MENON

Now if that isn't an admission of guilt. TBH, I'm shocked it only took twenty minutes to resurrect your pussy from the dead.

NISHA ARORA

God, I hate you so much.

KAVI CASE

Tell us NOW, Neesh. You know we will keep at this until you fold.

Pine For Me

NISHA ARORA

Fine! MAYBE we did.

SARINA ARORA

I KNEW IT!

MALA MEYER

Details NOW, Neesh! Was it filthy or sweet?

PIPER MENON

Did he whisper your name like a prayer or choke you while he made your clam squeak?

NISHA ARORA

I honestly don't understand why we're friends.

KAVI CASE

SPILL!!!

NISHA ARORA

Fine. Yes to all. Happy now?? Jesus.

RANI MEYER

[GIF of woman thrusting hips and dancing] SCREECHING!

PIPER MENON

The fucking smile stretched over my face right now. I swear, I look like a lunatic. YES, I'm fucking happy now!

SARINA ARORA

Same! GAH, sis! So happy!

Swati M.H.

BELLA MEYER

> You were lethal in that leather dress, Nisha. But we still need more details. Did you spend the night? Was it like everything you remembered or better?

NISHA ARORA

> [GIF of woman covering her face with both hands]

> God, it was the same but so much better, too. I can't explain it. But you guys, don't get so excited. This doesn't mean we're back together.

MALA MEYER

> Not going to lie, it's hard NOT to be excited, especially knowing how you feel about him.

NISHA ARORA

> It doesn't matter how I feel. He made it clear he didn't know how long he was going to stay, and I'm not doing the whole waiting around thing again.

> Whatever this is, however long it lasts, I'm not pretending it's something it's not. I've learned the hard way that feeling good in Patton's arms doesn't mean I'm safe there.

SARINA ARORA

> We get it, babe. You're protecting your heart, as you should. Especially since it bled over him before.

KAVI CASE

> And just so you know, you never have to pretend with us. But you also don't have to downplay what it meant to you, either.

Pine For Me

BELLA MEYER

You don't owe us a label. Whatever happened last night, whether it was a one-night thing or if it turns into more, it's yours. We just love seeing a little light on your face again. And there's no denying that you've been glowing ever since he came back.

PIPER MENON

Exactly. And if that glow is caused by running into his dick repeatedly without labeling it as anything more, then so be it. We just want each and every filthy and orgasmic detail.

SARINA ARORA

Let's do brunch after my dress fitting this weekend and get more details on my sister's sexcapade.

NISHA ARORA

Let's not.

SARINA ARORA:

Two words: Helium balloons. <balloons emoji>

NISHA ARORA

Four words: You're dead to me.

PIPER MENON

Too bad. Brunch is booked and you're coming, before or after you've come on Patton's face. Your choice.

RANI MEYER

I am bringing my whiteboard titled "The Great Re-Dicking" to flowchart this vaginal awakening and discuss important positions and such.

Swati M.H.

NISHA ARORA

I will literally light myself on fire.

MALA MEYER

No worries. I'll bring marshmallows.

NISHA ARORA

You are all the actual worst. Fine. I'll be there. Now stop texting me. I've reached my daily quota of your idiocy.

KAVI CASE

You can't get rid of us, no matter how much you want to.

NISHA ARORA

Sort of like a yeast infection.

PIPER MENON

That's right. We're persistent, irritating, and unforgettable.

NISHA ARORA

Ugh. See you at brunch.

seventeen
nisha

This Will Be A Day Long Remembered

Five Weeks Later

"Remind me again why this mutant beast has a dildo in his mouth." Cradling his dog, Sapphire, in his arms like he would a newborn, my dad flicks a bangled hand condescendingly at Bob, who's currently parading through Dad's living room with my talking Darth Vader vibrator clutched between his massive jaws like a stick.

"Give yourself to the Dark Side."

My face flames. "He . . . found it."

"Mom, what's a dildo?" My eight-year-old nephew, Rome, squints in Bob's direction.

He's seated beside me at the dining table, where my sister is serving him Dad's famous *samosas*. Usually, Troy and his daughter, Pearl, also join what has now become monthly get-togethers at Dad's house, but she just recently started swimming lessons, so Troy took her there.

Sarina swivels a glare at me as if I'm responsible for the impromptu sex-ed talk. I mean, technically, we got the damn things for *her* bachelorette party. And technically, it was Piper's idea. But sure, blame me for graciously accepting a gift.

Seated across from Rome, Piper snorts before breaking off a piece of *naan* to hand to her almost one-year-old daughter, Ariana, who happily accepts the offering from her highchair.

With her dark hair and eyes and fair skin, she is the perfect combination of Piper and Dev. He also couldn't make it today because, apparently, even on Sundays, billion-dollar empires don't run themselves. But the sass and the non-stop babbling? Those are all Piper.

"Want to expand on that story, Neesh?" Piper asks, taking a forkful of her *samosa* and dipping it into the tamarind chutney Dad made. "*How*, pray tell, would Patton's dog have found and claimed *your* dildo? Oh, and while you're at it, why don't you also explain how that dildo replaced the previous item he used to walk around with . . . your bra."

If looks could kill, my eyes would have shot her dead. But I'm not able to hold my aim long because Bob chooses that moment to shake his head, like he's trying to strangle the damn vibrator to death, making Vader wheeze out his signature heavy breathing.

"Hhhhooo. Haaahhhaaa."

And just like that, I wish I hadn't accepted this lunch invitation or Patton's request to help him take care of his lunatic dog while he left town for a day to tape *The Tonight Show*.

My dad, never one to let a moment to embarrass his daughters go to shame, pretends to clutch his pearls. "Is there something you haven't told me yet, daughter? Are you keeping me in the dark?!"

"Dad—" I start, hoping to thwart the inevitable emotional blackmail.

"I had heard my ex-son-in-law was in town filming a new movie with the help of my to-be son-in-law, but that you would be bedding him and not tell me . . ." He wipes a fake tear from the corner of his eye. "Well, that's just hurtful." He eyes Bob, who is now rolling the toy across the rug, with mock horror. "And unhygienic, if I'm being perfectly honest. I just deep-cleaned that rug."

God, how is this my life?

"First of all, I wasn't purposely keeping you in the dark." I point a forkful of *samosa* at him before placing it back on my plate. The scent, which is usually mouthwatering, has me feeling queasy. Lately, anything fried has been hitting me weird. "You and Emanuel have been cruising the damn world for the past two months—"

"My phone worked perfectly fine on the cruise," Dad argues, to which his boyfriend Emanuel nods in agreement.

Dad and Emanuel have been together for about two years. It's the longest relationship my dad has had since Mom died from a random aneurysm when Sarina and I were fifteen. And though Emanuel looks like the human version of a freight train, he's nothing but gentle and adoring with Dad. It's exactly what my beautiful soul of a father deserves, even if he can be a diva at times.

"Well, it's not like this was an emergency."

"It was absolutely an emergency! If one of my daughters is bedding a man—"

Piper and Sarina groan in unison, with Sarina cutting him off, *thank God*, "Dad, will you stop calling it 'bedding'?" She flicks a glance at her son, who is thankfully distracted with a book about space. "This is not 1792."

I take a calming breath. "And second, I honestly don't know that there's much to say. Yes, we've been . . . you know?" I purse my lips and swivel my eyes, indicating my meaning without words so that little ears don't hear. "But we haven't put any labels on it, nor do I want to."

Not for lack of Patton's trying, though.

We've been "seeing" each other—code for banging each other's brains out—regularly for the past several weeks. But every time he tries to look beyond the present or give whatever is happening between us a name, I redirect him. Hell, I straight up change the subject and do the whole "Squirrel!" thing while pointing out a covered window.

Dad starts to speak when Bob, having finished rolling around on the rug, comes over to inspect—ahem, sniff—Sapphire's butt. She yelps in disgust and scrambles onto Emanuel's lap like a damsel in distress. She eyes Bob warily from her perch on Emanuel's trunk-like thigh with a warning growl.

"Oh, absolutely not, sir!" Dad scolds, waving a flowery napkin at him like a finish-line flag. "Get all thoughts of defiling my little princess out of your meaty head. She is a lady. A refined lady who eats pastured chicken and receives daily massages. She has no interest in boys from the other side of the tracks."

Bob, completely unbothered and possibly having lost interest already, flops onto the floor and lets out a long sigh that makes his jowls flutter around the dildo between them.

"Obi-Wan has taught you well."

I pinch the bridge of my nose. "Oh, for god's sake."

"Anyway," Dad continues, turning toward me. "So, this not-labeled thing between you two has been going on for several weeks, then?"

"Five or so."

"And you think, what? That not labeling it will protect you from future heartbreak? From getting attached again? Or from rekindling what you had?"

He reaches for the jug of mango lassi, pouring himself a glass before eyeing me for an answer. And it's not just him. All pairs of eyes, aside from the kids at the table, are on me expectantly.

I swallow. "I don't know. I just . . . I just don't want to go down the same path we were on again."

"Then don't." Dad's eyes soften. "Choose a different path,

a new path. But don't be in denial, sweetheart. You have always loved him, and deep down, you know you always will."

I don't argue. There's no point doing so when the people who know you to your core are all sitting around one table.

Dad takes Emanuel's hand in his, squeezing it before looking at me. "I lost your mom almost seventeen years ago. Like Patton was for you, she was my best friend, too. I still remember the day, about a year before she died, when I came out to her."

His eyes gloss over, and his throat bobs with emotion. And though we were all laughing and joking just minutes ago, the shift in the room is clear now, the void left by the most important woman in many of our lives still lingers between us cavernously.

My chest aches, and in my peripheral vision, I see Sarina dab at the corner of her eye with a napkin.

"She was so gracious, so kind and understanding," Dad continues. "We didn't know what that meant for our future, but we knew one thing—that no matter what, we would love each other. No matter what, that love would never die. And it didn't, even when she did." Reaching across the table, he places his hand over mine. "Love like that doesn't just disappear, sweetheart."

I shift in my seat uncomfortably.

The truth is, the past five weeks have been . . . unexpected.

As reluctant as I was to sleep with him after the night of Sarina's bachelorette party, the man, with his lethal charm and persistence, wore me down.

He showed up at my door with breakfast every morning for a week. And not just any breakfast, but my kryptonite—French toast. I have no idea if he made food runs himself or sent an assistant, but each meal was from a different restaurant. Each better than the last. Each a love letter sprinkled with powdered sugar and cinnamon.

So, after another week of fighting it, I found myself inviting him in and letting him do all the filthy things I'd pretended for seven years that I didn't still dream about.

Between his film schedule and PR events and my hours at the salon and *dojang*, we've both been busy. There have been days we've only had a handful of minutes together, but we've made them count.

An hour curled up on his couch, talking and staring into each other's eyes, while Bob slept at our feet, Darth Vader providing the background noise in our conversation. A quick dinner he'd picked up on his way back home. Or a kiss that lingered until we were both breathless and ready to rip each other's clothes off when he visited me at the salon.

And there have been other days—lazy Sundays and late August nights—where whispered pillow talk and ravenous lovemaking made me feel like we spoke a language we created ourselves. One no one else could understand.

So, yeah, I haven't labeled it, but I can't deny it's *something*. And that terrifies me more than I can put into words.

Piper's voice pulls me out of my thoughts, and I realize I'd been moving the same piece of *samosa* around in the chutney with my fork. "It's what we've been saying in our group chat. We're not encouraging you to dive back into the deep end, but maybe just stop worrying that you're going to drown if you get close."

I'm just thinking about their words when Dad asks, "Why haven't you eaten anything? It's been twenty minutes, and you've been rolling the same bite around your plate."

My stomach does that turning thing it's been doing lately. "I don't think I'm very hungry. Sorry, Dad. I'm sure it's delicious, but—"

The back of Dad's fingers brushing my forehead cuts off the rest of my words. His bangles jingle as he moves the backs of his fingers to my neck. "Sweetie, are you sick?"

I shake my head. "No, just haven't felt like eating deep-fried food lately—"

A gasp across the table has me looking at my sister, her saucer eyes taking me in as if they're seeing me after years.

I look from her to Piper and then Dad. Even Emanuel seems to be clued in on something I'm not. "What?"

Sarina's mouth opens and closes, her eyes flicking between my plate to my face. "Neesh, when was your last period?"

The question makes my heart thud against my chest. "What? No . . . it's not what you think—"

"Babe." Piper leans over the table like she's about to whisper a national secret. "Are you sure? Remember how you hated kiwis the last—"

I shake my head assertively as a pang hits me square between the ribs. "No, it's not that. It's not even possible. I've always had irregular periods with my polycystic ovaries."

"Still, sweetie." Dad squeezes my hand again. "It *could* be. The doctor didn't say never; she just said the chances were naturally low."

"This will be a day long remembered. Hhhhooo. Haaahhhaaa."

Fucking Vader and his impeccable timing.

I shoot up from my chair, the scrape of wood on wood making both Bob and Sapphire jump. Even Ariana pauses, mid-eating, and Rome finally looks up from his book, their eyes wide in question, wondering what the hell got into their aunt.

No. This can't be.

It simply can't.

Yes, the doctor said the chances were naturally low, extremely low. Which is why Patton and I had gone through several rounds of in vitro fertilization to get pregnant all those years ago when treatments to induce regular ovulation didn't work for me. So, how could it be possible now? We've been so careful, having used protection every time after that first time...

But we didn't use it that very first time...

God. Please tell me this isn't happening.

"I'm... I need to—" I mumble what I think is a sentence but couldn't repeat it if I tried.

"Call it a coincidence or intuition," Piper says, reaching into her cavernous Hermes purse, "but I have two pregnancy tests in here."

"What?" The question is echoed by multiple people around the table, including me.

Piper flicks a nonchalant wrist in our direction, pulling out a pink and white box. "Dev and I aren't *trying*, trying"—she brushes her hand over Ariana's short hair, smiling when she coos—"but it's not like we aren't trying, either, you know what I mean?"

At her wink, I eye the box in her hand like it's about to detonate. "But—"

She shoves it in my direction and tips her chin toward the bathroom. "You'll know for sure in less than five minutes."

And I do.

Because five minutes later, everything changes.

eighteen
nisha

The Woman on Patton
Pierce's Arm

Seven Years Ago

"Yesss," I hiss, my hips rising off the bed, my breaths becoming more unsteady.

Patton makes his way down my bare chest, taking one of my stiff peaks into his mouth. He flicks the tip, scraping his teeth over the sensitive bud before tugging it.

"Ahh. Oh, God," I mumble, pulling my bottom lip between my teeth.

Most women would probably find the pinching, biting, and rough sucking to be too much. But Patton has always known how much pressure I need, exactly how I like it. A little rough and painful.

Though, he's been more careful and controlled lately.

It makes sense given the rounds of IVF it took to get to this point. We're both a little protective of our miracle.

He moves to the other side, dragging his stubble across my skin, teasing my other nipple with his tongue. Each time he tugs and nibbles it, my back arches higher, my moans echoing inside our room.

"So goddamn responsive," he murmurs, plucking and

sucking my scorching bud before kissing his way down to my navel.

He lingers there, leaving a hundred kisses reverently, speaking to the life growing inside me. "I can't wait to meet you, little one."

My chest warms, tears stinging my eyes at his gentle, reverent voice. It's been ten weeks—more than the time we had the first time.

About a year ago, I miscarried six weeks into the pregnancy, after two rounds of IVF. Patton had flown out and was filming a commercial across the country, and I'd gone to the clinic alone, expecting a routine checkup.

But the moment the tech's smile dropped, I knew.

I knew we'd never meet him or her.

It was as if the sunlight streaming in through the window had vanished all at once, like someone had pulled a blackout curtain across it. And instead of my husband's reassuring arms, it was the tech's—a virtual stranger's—who'd held me as the tears streaked down my face.

It wasn't his fault—of course it wasn't. And though I'd heard his heartbreak over the phone, I couldn't help but feel like I was all alone.

I shove aside the thoughts, scraping my fingers through his hair, watching as he rests his cheek on my belly. He stays there for a moment before continuing his descent.

My stomach tightens when he reaches the apex between my thighs, glancing up to find my eyes. He knows he doesn't need my concession, not when the heat in my eyes gives him that in spades.

Dragging his flat tongue over my center, bottom to top, Patton tastes me like I'm a confection melting in the sun.

"You're so delicious, baby." His low voice ripples over my wet heat before he drags his nose down the same path, rubbing it up and down my slit like he can't get enough. "The way you taste . . . the way you smell. Fuck me, you're intoxicating."

"Mmm," I mumble at a loss for coherent words.

My chest rises and falls as I lock eyes with him again. His usually warm browns are blazing, alight with unbridled desire. It's the type that could swallow me whole and leave nothing but ashes behind.

I writhe, silently begging for more, making him smile.

He doesn't make me wait too long, though, giving me another long and torturous swipe, tasting me so thoroughly, a sheen of sweat sparkles over my skin. His tongue wedges between my lips as he continues to lick from my entrance to the top of my clit, circling it until my toes curl.

"Oh, m–my G–God," I stutter, my hand tightening in his hair, my eyes rolling to the back of my head. "That feels so good."

Like I'm soaring and plummeting.

Living and dying.

Pulling my legs apart, he sucks on my clit, plunging two fingers inside. I bow off the bed, shoving my needy pussy against his mouth, feeling myself drip around him.

"Mmmph. Plea—Gah." More indecipherable words tumble out from my lips as my husband eats me like I'm his favorite meal and he'll never be full.

"That's it, baby," he says, softly tugging one of my lips between his teeth. "I want all your sounds. Fuck my fingers with this tight little pussy."

Licking me with more speed and flicking my clit back and forth, Patton's fingers brush that spot buried deep inside me, the one he always seems to find.

My body tightens, and I fist the sheets as I throw my head back, only barely registering his voice when he asks, "Whose pussy is this, sweetheart? Who's the only one who gets to eat it? Fuck it?"

He nibbles my other lip when I don't answer, giving it a soft warning bite.

"Yours," I heave. "Only yours."

I feel his satisfied grin as he continues to massage my clit with his tongue, sucking harder as his fingers thrust deeper.

My moans become all-out war cries when quakes erupt inside me, forcing my knees to bend and my thighs to shake until I'm practically shoving his head further between my legs.

And then, with the impact of a meteor crashing against the earth, I climax. Patton continues to lick at my folds, humming as he laps up my release.

God, his hums, the vibrato of his voice against my slick skin. They say more than words ever could.

Giving me one last lick, he slows the tempo, gently pulling out his fingers. Kissing up my body again, he comes to a stop, hovering over me.

"Oh, my God, Patton," I breathe, reaching up to kiss him, tasting myself on his lips. "That was . . . life changing."

His chuckle rumbles against my body, his hard cock nudging at my entrance. I open my legs before reaching down to guide him into me, and we both groan as our bodies come together, lock and key.

"Fuuuck, you're so wet." His nostrils flare as his forehead meets mine. "So beautiful. So perfect."

Even though he's fully seated inside me, I can feel him holding himself back, like he does so often now. He's been careful, tender and terrified, ever since he saw the flicker on the screen.

Reaching up, I rake my fingers through his hair and kiss him again. "You won't break me, baby. I promise."

His eyes bounce between mine for a moment, but he must find what he's looking for because a second later, he starts to move. Not reckless, but deliberate and sure. His body curves over mine in a perfect fit.

"Fuck," he groans against the shell of my ear.

My legs widen, inviting him in further, keeping him there like it's where he belongs. My core tightens around him with each thrust, drawing him closer.

This feeling of being loved by him—with him inside me, his weight above me, and his scent surrounding me—is unlike anything else in this entire world. It's dizzying. Even now, after years of being married to him, I still can't believe he's mine.

Gently pulling me with him, he lifts me off the bed so he's sitting on his knees with me straddling his thighs. His hands hold steady on my hips as he guides me over his length, the fullness of him making me gasp. My breasts press against his chest, my hands grasping his shoulders as I take him into my body with each slow, fluid motion.

"Patton!" I cry out, my voice catching on a moan as my head tips back and my pussy clenches around him. "God, that feels amazing."

Beads of sweat form over our brows, the heat between us threatening to cause a fire, as we lock eyes. I rise and fall over his lap, my pussy savoring every inch, every shiver and quake. When I rotate my hips slowly around his cock, a rush of satisfaction rolls through me, listening to him groan against my neck.

"Goddamn, Nisha," he whispers, his voice thick with emotion. "You're everything, baby."

I continue to rock my hips back and forth as I find his lips, kissing him until we're clinging to each other, both out of breath.

His hands guide me with reverence, and when he takes over, lifting into me from beneath, his thrusts are powerful but controlled, each one laden with feeling rather than force.

Just when my pussy starts to convulse, telling him in no uncertain terms how close I am, he changes our position, edging my impending orgasm. Because he knows me, my body, and exactly how to make this last.

Laying me back against the pillow, he hovers over me. I widen my legs to give him access as he guides himself to my entrance. Wrapping his hand around the back of my thigh and pushing it toward my chest, he plunges inside me again.

Looking into each other's eyes, we moan in unison, the change of position sending goosebumps over my body.

With every stroke, I feel him deeper, marking his name on every cell inside my body. And when he uses his fingers to massage my clit, I swear I see stars.

"You ready to come, Little Borealis?"

I nod, biting my lip as my eyes roll back into my head.

Patton rolls his hips, each deep stroke making me breathless. "I need you to say it, baby. You're stuffed full of my cock, now beg me to let you come."

God. And here I was thinking I couldn't get any wetter.

"Please," I pant. "Please let me come, Patton."

He buries himself with slow, purposeful strokes, like he's memorizing my body all over again. And when he finds that spot, he coaxes the pleasure from me with each brush of his tip until I'm screaming in ecstasy.

My climax swells like a tidal wave, my hips bucking against him. My body tightens like the string on a bow, ready to snap with even the slightest tug. "Oh god! I'm coming. Patton, I'm . . ."

I fist the sheets, squeezing my eyes shut, shoving my head into the pillow. Words hiss past my lips. "I'm coming so hard."

And as soon as my orgasm crests, I feel him shoot his load inside me with a strangled roar. "Gahh! Holy fuck."

Our heavy breaths turn to shallow pants as he pulls out from inside me. Rising to his knees, he opens my legs and watches his cum drip from my center. And doing what I've seen him do so many times before, he drags his fingers through it, trying to catch every drop before stuffing it inside me again.

My shoulders shake with a giggle. "I can't get more pregnant, you crazy man."

He joins me on the bed, pulling my back to his chest before placing a gentle hand over my belly protectively. "If it were up to me, I'd have a whole baseball team with you. But your body's been through enough to give us this little miracle."

"Baseball team?" I look back at him. "Are you saying my uterus just *narrowly* escaped becoming a team bus?"

"Pretty much." His lips brush my cheek, the subtle notes of his familiar bergamot and minty scent making me nuzzle further into him. "It chose to be the Rolls-Royce of reproductive power instead. Exclusive and one-of-a-kind, just like its owner."

"You really do know how to charm a girl's reproductive system."

He runs the tip of his nose along my neck. "Well, that's a good thing, considering I'm about to upset you."

My heart sinks. Even without him saying the words aloud, I already have an inkling of what they'll be.

I turn, finding his eyes. "What is it?"

He takes a long breath. "Tony's asking me to fly out tonight. He wants to film a few scenes for *Credit Card Millionaire* before the monsoons start in Thailand."

"But you just got home two days ago. You said we'd have two full weeks before you had to fly out again."

God, I *hate* sounding so needy. I've never been this way, truly. But whether it's the lack of seeing him over the past few years, aside from a few days here or there, or these pregnancy hormones, or simply just feeling lonely in this city, I've been a mess lately.

Not to mention, it's been hard to have a normal relationship—giving him updates about the baby—with Patton being in all sorts of different time zones so many weeks of the year. Just this past year alone, he's filmed two major films and squeezed in several small passion projects between press tours.

"I know." His voice is contrite as he tucks a strand of hair behind my ear. "I promise, I'll be here for your birthday."

"Patton, that's almost six weeks away."

"Babe, this movie is expected to become a worldwide blockbuster—"

I pull out of his arms, my after-sex glow feeling more like a bad sunburn. Getting off the bed, I rise to my feet and pull on the white button-down he'd discarded on the rug before our lovemaking.

"Neesh—"

"What about in a few months when this baby is here, Patton? Will you be around then, or am I signing up to become a single parent?"

He scoots to the edge of the bed before getting to his feet and pulling on his boxers. Even disheveled, with his dark hair sticking up around his head and his neck and cheeks still flushed, he looks every bit the gorgeous man who's displayed across the billboard on Sunset Boulevard.

Sauntering forward, he closes the distance between us in two strides. His hands try to find purchase on my hips, but I take a step back before they can.

"You wanted this baby as much as I did. You knew I would have trouble conceiving, and you said you didn't want to wait until we were in our thirties—"

"I know I said that. Of course I want this baby—"

"Then why do I feel like you want your career more?"

He stares at me incredulously. "A—that's not fair. And B—it's simply not true."

My hands lock on my hips. "Did you ask me before you

signed on for those projects? Knowing we were trying to have a family, did you even consider the time commitment for so many movies? It's more than you've ever taken on in a single year."

I pace to our dresser, then turn around and amble toward him again. "Yes, we moved across the country for your career, but have you considered the impact that's had on my life? I have no one here—"

"What about Sarina and Rome? Plus, I thought you liked working at the salon?"

"You know I barely see my sister. Her asshole pro-golfer husband drags her and my nephew all over the world so much, it's like they don't even live here."

Patton knows how much I miss my sister and seeing my two-year-old nephew, because I've complained often about how much I dislike her husband, Jamie. Ever since she married him, it's like I don't recognize her anymore. She's a shell of the person I've known since the womb.

"And as for the salon—yes, I do like working there, but when I come home, it's to an empty house. Day in and day out, for weeks."

"What about volunteering in the foster program? I thought you said you had made a few friends there?"

"I have, but it's still new."

The foster system is something both Patton and I are passionate about, given he lived it first-hand and I saw it through his eyes.

After his mom was sent to jail for dealing drugs when Patton was six, Patton was thrown into the system, bouncing around before he found some stability with a great family in the same Boston neighborhood I grew up in. It's the reason we went to the same high school and even found each other in the same *dojang*. And though he's never forgiven his mom for both her decisions and for never having found him, even after she got out, he's always been grateful for how his life turned out.

"So come with me," he says, moving to me again, cupping my face with his hands.

I lean into his touch, but still feel frustrated with his lack of understanding.

Or maybe it's me. Maybe I just don't know how to explain it to him. Maybe I don't even know what I want.

Didn't I agree to be here, supporting him while he lived out his dreams? Didn't I realize that *this* was what I was signing up for when we came here after he got his first break?

I guess I never realized how that stardom was going to become his lifestyle—*his whole life*. How it wasn't just about filming, but marketing, publicizing, and so much more, even as an actor. That, at some point, he'd become public property, not just his talent, but his time and presence. That every dinner would be cut short by "a quick phone call".

I didn't realize when we were just newlywed twenty-one-year-olds, dreaming about him "making it" and me using my business degree to open up a salon, that his dream would grow while mine shrank.

Somewhere between his rising stardom and our move to L.A., the life I'd imagined has taken me by surprise. Like expecting to catch a ball headed your way but misjudging the speed, so that when it hits your hands, the impact sends a throb up your arms.

I've attended five red-carpet events over the past four years. To be honest, they were four too many to have gotten an understanding of things. Things I don't really want to invest my time on, like figuring out what to wear so I don't end up on someone's worst-dressed list or smiling through conversations with people who asked what I did but didn't give a shit about my answer.

Everything feels performative—friendships, compliments,

even laughter. Everyone's always "on"—for the cameras, for their next role, or maybe because they've forgotten who they really are. And honestly, I get it; it's part of their job.

But it's not mine. It's not what I signed up for.

Because I signed up for *him*.

And even though I've accepted being in the background or even being known only as "Patton's wife" or "Patton's plus-one," I can't deny there are times I wish I had something that was mine. An identity of my own.

God, look at me. Don't I sound like a privileged asshole? How many women out there would kill to be me, the woman on Patton Pierce's arm?

I shake my head, encircling his wrists with my hands. "Patton, I can barely make it through a drive across town to the salon without throwing up. You want me to get on a fifteen-hour flight to Thailand? Plus, I want to stay close to my doctors here, in case something happens—"

His hand tightens around my jaw. "Nothing is going to happen. You're further along this time."

"I hope not," my voice is quieter now, "but I don't want to risk anything. And anyway, what about after the baby's here? What, do we just follow you around the globe, hopping from set to set with a diaper bag and a car seat in tow?"

His hands drop from my face.

"I know you want me with you. That you love me. I love you, too, Patton. But I don't know if—"

My words are cut off when his phone vibrates on the nightstand, and he goes to check who it is. From just the way his shoulders sag, I know he has to take the call.

No, he doesn't *have* to take the call, but I know he will. Because that's who we've become—a couple on Hollywood's schedule.

I make my way to our bedroom door, my heart somewhere in the pit of my stomach.

He's stuck between a rock and a hard place. I get that. He's chased this dream for as long as I've known him. From our high school stage to the silver screen, he's worked his ass off to get here.

I know how much he loves me, I do. So, I get that this can't be easy for him, either.

And yet, I still feel a little deprioritized. Like I'm a piece of mail he's told himself he'll open later when he has more time, energy, and bandwidth.

Knowing this conversation isn't going to be resolved today —not when he's made the decision to leave tonight—I decide to let him off the hook. *Again*.

I'll just make it easier on him, letting him know I understand, even if understanding doesn't make it hurt any less.

I give him a reassuring smile over my shoulder, hoping it reaches my eyes. "I'm going to make myself some tea."

nineteen
nisha

The Color of War

Seven Years Ago

"Oof."

I groan when another cramp registers, yanking me awake like claws around my stomach. I blink in the dark, but it's so heavy and consuming, it doesn't feel much different from having my eyes closed.

Under the covers, my hand drags down to my belly as another wave rolls through me. It's a tightness so painful that it leaves me breathless and sweaty.

My mind travels to what I ate for dinner tonight—homemade ramen and a bowl of fruit. That couldn't be it, could it? I've had bouts of nausea and bloating for weeks, but this . . . ? It feels different and wrong, like my organs are folding in on themselves, contracting and crying out.

My hand stretches toward the other side of the bed, desperately trying to find Patton, my heart plummeting when all I feel is cool sheets. You'd think I'd have remembered after three weeks . . .

It's been three weeks since he left for Thailand. Three weeks since I felt his warm body next to mine, his arms here to surround me in times like this. The loneliness, the fact that there's no one here to hear my cries, hits me almost as hard as the physical pain.

Another sharp stab pierces my lower abdomen, and I pull into a sitting position, my breath catching, eyes pricking with fear.

Something is happening. Something that will leave me broken.

And then it catches again when my hand brushes over the damp sheets.

No, not damp. Wet. Sticky.

Oh, God. No. Please, God, not again...

But even as I form the desperate prayer, another cramp has me doubling over, instinctively bringing my knees to my chest as a sob ripples up my chest and tears from my throat.

It's not until I swing my legs over the side of the bed, my heart pounding against my ribs, and rise to my feet that panic really settles in. With sweat beading over my brows, my head tilts down as my eyes imagine the color of the liquid I can feel trailing down my legs.

Maybe it's not what I think. Maybe I just wet myself.

I did drink a lot of water before going to sleep...

But that's the thing about hope. It's the tiny flame we keep burning in our hearts before reality snuffs it out.

Fingers brushing the wall, the feel of textured paint reminding me that I'm awake and that this is not a dream, I slowly trek toward the bathroom. It feels a thousand miles away.

My hand fumbles for the light switch, trembling so violently I can barely flip it on. And when I finally do, the harsh fluorescent light assaults my vision like needles jabbing my eyes. I squeeze them shut, giving myself a chance to prolong the inevitability of reopening them and facing my worst fear.

Pine For Me

And my world tilts when I finally do.

Red.

So much red.

Bright, thick, and so, so very wrong.

It's soaked through my pajama pants. They're the ones Patton brought me last Christmas, with pale yellow daffodils and sunflowers that reminded me of the bouquet I held when I walked down the aisle toward him four years ago, the same flowers woven into my hair.

We knew we were young and inexperienced, but God, there wasn't anything we wanted more than each other. It didn't matter that his foster parents were skeptical, or that my dad was reluctant, asking me if I was really ready to get married so young.

I knew.

I'd found my person—my best friend apart from my sister—and no one on this earth could have deterred me from being with him.

I blink as the memories fade behind the color now saturating all others.

"No," I whisper, the word barely audible over the ringing in my ears. My nose tingles and my eyes blur as the full weight of what I'm looking at crashes over me. Then louder, like saying it with more authority might undo what's clearly being taken away from me. "No!"

Another cramp seizes me as I grasp the doorframe, my other hand wrapping protectively around my abdomen, as if I can physically keep my womb intact.

I shake my head, repeating the only word I can seem to speak. My back hits the wall, and the weight of the moment drags me down to the cold marble. I stare down at the blood-soaked fabric, watching it seep and spread, much like the ache unfurling in my chest, devouring the sunny color.

Leaving only the color of war behind.

The cramping intensifies, forcing me to pull my knees to my chest. I wrap my arms around them, rocking as tears soak my cheeks.

Thirteen weeks.

A life we fought to have, to bring into the world, gone in thirteen weeks. A baby we wanted and imagined every day for thirteen weeks...

All the plans and dreams, hopes for our future little family, are now bleeding out of me on the cold bathroom floor.

"Please," I whisper to the empty room, to God and the universe, to anyone listening. "Please don't take this away from me... not again."

But despite my pleading, it's happening.

The life I was carrying, protecting, and loving—the one my body went through immeasurable pain to create and hold, the one I constantly prayed for—is slipping away like the fuzzy afterthoughts of a dream.

I reach for my phone—I hadn't realized I'd carried it with me—calling for the only voice I want to hear right now. The only voice who'll understand.

Because he's lost this, too, even if he doesn't know it yet.

My first call goes straight to Patton's voicemail.

I try again and again, each ring feeling endless, each trip to voicemail as painful as the cramps wracking my body and crushing my soul.

A voice in the back of my head reminds me that he said he'd be unreachable for the next few days, on a set in some remote part of Thailand with spotty phone service. Still, each failed attempt hurls me deeper into a despair that's swallowing me whole. A despair, as thick as tar, that I can't see past or swim through.

On the fifth try, my hands can barely hold the phone, my shaky whisper hoarse and unfamiliar to my own ears. "Please, Patton, pick up. Please... I need you."

But he doesn't.

And who knows when he finally will. In a day? A week? Definitely when this is all over and there's nothing left to talk about.

Nothing left to save.

Thirteen weeks. A baby I've been whispering and singing to for thirteen weeks.

"I'm sorry," I whisper, my voice gurgling past my tears as I run a hand down my throbbing abdomen. "I'm so sorry, sweetheart. So sorry that I couldn't keep you, couldn't be your mommy."

My voice breaks around the gravel in my throat. "I'm s-so sorry I couldn't hold you. Kiss you. Show you how much I l-love y-you."

Tears stream down my face, soaking the collar of my tank top, as I continue to shake my head against the wall, my words a chant against the reality I'm having to face alone. "I'm so sorry . . . So sorry I failed you."

How much longer can I keep watching my body fail to do what so many other women do so easily? So naturally.

My sister got pregnant without even trying, and she carried my nephew to term without a single complication. The women at my salon chatter about how hard it's been to lose the pregnancy weight, not how hard it was to get pregnant; how hard it was to stay pregnant.

And the look in my boss's eyes when I told her I needed to adjust my schedule around some of my treatments. Her eyes spoke the words her decorum didn't afford her lips—*"Poor thing. So young. How could you need treatments to get pregnant?"*

What would her eyes say watching this—my body, barely past one trimester and already giving up? Again.

How much longer can I endure going through this alone, without him?

I can't. I just fucking can't anymore.

The anger hits me suddenly, white-hot and all-consuming, like the explosion of a star. I'm furious at my body for forsaking me, furious at Patton for not being here when I need him again, and furious at God for not giving me the *one thing* I've wanted more than anything else in my life.

But mostly, I'm furious at myself for getting so excited so quickly. For thinking that this time would be different because I passed the first trimester date. I'm furious at myself for allowing hope to settle in my heart, for allowing myself to daydream about the future.

My breaths come out faster, ragged and shallow, as if each gulp of air is trying to fill the emptiness my womb just created. The cramping is getting worse, and I know what this means.

I need to get to the ER.

But I sit a little longer, clutching the phone in my trembling hands, willing it to ring. Willing him to see the missed calls, to sense that I need him. To realize through some telepathic connection that our real world is crumbling while he's on set creating a fictional world for others.

Except all I get is silence.

And in that deafening silence, I come to terms with more than just what my body wasn't able to hold.

I come to terms with the distance that's grown between us, not in the past few weeks, but over the past four years. A distance accumulating like mold inside walls, slowly and silently, until one day the structure decays from within.

I come to terms with the lonely nights, the missed calls, and the conversations interrupted by more important phone calls.

I come to terms with the fact that love alone, even as immense as an ocean, isn't enough to keep two people from drifting apart.

twenty
nisha

What to Expect When You Weren't Expecting

"Wow, that's turning out to be quite the sweater," I say, eyeing the mostly-complete black cable-knit in Abby's hands. "I've never made anything quite as intricate before—just simple sweaters, or beanies and scarves."

I smile, watching my fingers work through the last loops on the beanie I'm making for Rome, knowing he's going to love the Saturn appliqué I stitched on. Instead of the usual planet, the center is a baseball—his favorite sport—between Saturn's rings.

"Thank you," Abby murmurs softly, her green eyes gifting me with the smile her lips rarely do.

Sounds of trays being placed on tables and the hum of lunch conversations filter into my closet-sized, make-shift salon tucked into the shelter. I'm in the salon chair, waiting for Janice to come in for her haircut as soon as she finishes her lunch, while Abby sits by the sink.

Over the past several weeks, I've somehow managed to coerce Abby a little further out of her shell. Okay, so maybe that's an overstatement. But she's started saying more than a handful of words to me, a feat compared to how tight-lipped she was when I first met her.

In that time, I've learned that she's a skilled knitter and has found a temporary job working as a bagger for the Safeway in Almaden, but she doesn't love it. I also noticed little things about her, like how she pulls on her sleeves or chews her nails when nervous.

She once told me she moved to San Jose searching for something. I still don't know what that something is, but I haven't pushed. She'll tell me when she's ready, or maybe she won't. Either way, for reasons I can't quite explain, I like having her around.

Perhaps it's her quiet presence or this feeling I have that she's seen things I couldn't begin to imagine. Or perhaps it's her veiled strength, the kind that shows up in people who don't know when they'll get their next meal or where they'll sleep that night, but continue to fight. Continue to rebuild and restitch.

There's a lingering sorrow in her eyes, and maybe it's that which my soul connects with.

"When did you learn to knit?" I ask, because somehow, I can't seem to keep my mouth shut around the woman.

Her gaze flicks around my closet-sized make-shift salon. "More than thirty years ago. I started knitting when I was pregnant."

Her words stir in my chest, and though I want to ask more, I get the feeling she wouldn't tell me. I get it. Some scars are better left alone, as even touching them poses a risk of reopening them.

"Me, too," I respond, keeping my eyes on the yarn in my hands. "I made these sea-foam-colored booties the first time." My smile wobbles, recalling how proud I was when I'd finished them. "But I never got to use them."

Abby's fingers still mid-stitch, and when I glance up, her gaze is already on mine. "Perhaps they'll get used this time around?"

My heart slams into my ribs, my mouth dropping open. I'm not even six weeks along, and definitely not showing. I haven't told a single soul besides the ones who were there this past Sunday at Dad's house.

I haven't even told Patton.

I know she posed it as a question, but it didn't sound like one.

"How . . ." I lick my lips, feeling my brows pinch. "How did you know?"

She shrugs almost imperceptibly. "You looked like you were going to be sick when Hector stopped by to offer you his onion rings earlier. And I saw you looking in the mirror, running a hand over your stomach when you thought no one was watching."

I blink at her, perturbed by the calm and certainty in her voice. For someone who barely speaks above a whisper and hopes to blend into the background, she doesn't miss anything.

"I . . ." I clear my throat. "I haven't told anyone."

She nods, fingers threading yarn. "I understand."

"Hold up," Piper says, reclining in my styling chair, gesturing in the general area of my torso with a half-eaten protein bar. "So this Abby lady just knew about your uterus drama when you hadn't shared it with her?" She raises a perfect brow. "I don't know if that's just some serious women's intuition or a HIPAA violation."

"Yeah. Isn't that strange?" I ask, laying my clean shears perfectly in line next to the combs, which are, of course, arranged by size. "Like, am I just walking around with a neon sign that says, *'Knocked up and fucking panicking!'*"

"Maybe it's the glow," Sarina says, helping Snatch get her

little bald head through the neck of a sweater, before glancing back at me from the doorway. "You look radiant."

Snatch wiggles out of Sarina's hold, having had enough fashion torture for the day, and lands on the floor soundlessly. Of the three cats, Snatch is definitely the best dressed, not by choice, of course. My sister just thinks her cat needs more "layers" to keep her warm, but I swear that cat has a bigger closet than I do.

Tail flicking in obvious annoyance, Snatch prowls over to the cat tree to join Beaver, who is currently standing on his hind legs, as still as a piece of creepy taxidermy, except for the occasional twitch of his right ear.

He does this often, just standing there unmoving like a weirdo. It freaks people out. We've had clients—tech bros worth eight figures—yelp like little girls when they realize he's not just a white statue.

Once, this hipster twenty-something millionaire dropped his craft matcha, and Beaver didn't even blink. I bet he was internally saying, "Gotcha, sucker!"

Is it weird that we have cats in the salon? Yes. But they're part of our family here and part of the contract our clients have to sign. Literally. I believe it says something like, "This salon is co-managed by three emotionally complex felines. Enter at your own risk."

They're well cared for, too. Each night, they're tucked into the cozy backroom just for them, and if the salon ever closes for an extended period of time, one of us takes them home like the pampered royalty they are.

"Definitely radiant," Piper agrees, taking another bite of her bar. "Plus, your boobs look phenomenal. Bet Patton's having a field day with those."

I roll my eyes at her wagging brow before moving around my suite, fluffing throw pillows unnecessarily. "He's not because I haven't seen him yet."

Pine For Me

I straighten the magazines on the small table, even though they haven't been touched since I last straightened them three hours ago.

Some people journal; others scream into pillows. Me? I organize things with the precision of a museum curator and the nervous energy of a squirrel on espresso.

Basically, when things feel like they're out of control, I like to keep my hands busy and pretend everything is fine.

But everything is *not* fine. Not even kinda.

I don't need to look at my sister and best friend to know they just exchanged a glance. We've been slammed with clients and conflicting schedules. Ever since I took the test at Dad's house four days ago, I really haven't had a chance to speak to either of them, aside from a couple of texts they both sent me asking how I was feeling.

I suppose my vague, "I'm fine," replies are now catching up to me, and they've staged this intervention between their appointments.

"Haven't seen him because he's out of town or because you're avoiding him?" Sarina asks, leaning against the doorway with crossed arms.

Have I mentioned how annoying it is to have people who know you this well?

"Look, I just need a minute, okay?"

And maybe another minute to Google *"what to expect when you weren't expecting."*

I pull a broom from the hidden area behind a tall shelf and start to sweep nonexistent hair into the built-in suction-thingy on the floor.

"I need a little time to process the fact that there's a human growing inside me, *again*."

Beaver chooses that moment to unfreeze himself and drop a ring at my feet. I pick it up to take a closer look. "Oh, my

God, Beaver. This is someone's wedding ring. He's probably looking for it."

I place it in Sarina's outstretched hand. She's dealt with this kind of thing before with my cat and will figure out how to get it to its rightful owner.

"Seriously, your cat is going to get himself on the FBI's Most Wanted list," Piper says, watching Beaver sit back on his haunches, looking proud of himself.

I pinch my brows at my mischievous but adorable cat, hoping to look admonishing. "Buddy, you can't go around robbing people! This is a respectable establishment."

Picking him up, I put him back in the cat tree to hang out with Snatch before going back to the task of sweeping my already-clean room.

Dropping the empty protein bar wrapper into a nearby garbage bin, Piper rises from her chair, taking the broom from my hands. "Babe, we know you have a lot to process. And knowing you, you're scared shitless but too stubborn to admit it."

"It's okay to admit you're scared, Neesh," my sister says, walking inside and pulling my hand in hers. "The way you always hold yourself together is admirable, but you don't have to with us. I can imagine what you're thinking, given what happened before..."

My shoulders deflate like the rest of my body as they pull me into an embrace I didn't think I needed.

These two have seen me at my worst, but I also hate burdening them—or anyone—with my problems. Between Piper becoming a new mom, and Sarina still in the throes of last-minute wedding planning, they shouldn't have to worry about me.

"I just . . ." I pad over to the styling chair Piper had vacated, sinking into it with a sigh. "Since the moment I found out, it's like I'm bracing for impact at every turn. Like I'm expecting to wake up cramping, or go to the bathroom and see blood, or God, feel that soul-deep emptiness that I felt when . . ."

I don't finish the rest of my sentence, but I don't have to. They're identical expressions of empathy and sorrow tell me they understand.

"I literally thought this was never going to be in the cards for me again," I whisper. "And I'd made peace with that. But now that it's happening, I feel like I'm waiting for my body to betray me. For this hope to be crushed again before I've even had a chance to process everything."

Piper leans on the broomstick clutched in her hands. "I know you're scared, honey, but it's not a bad thing to hope again. Hope isn't the enemy here, fear is."

"Hope didn't get me too far the first two times," I retort, my mind shoving away images of bloodied pajamas and the fluorescent lights of the ER.

"Isn't *hope* the reason you went through all those IVF treatments?" Piper asks, her voice trying to pierce my fears and doubts. "Isn't it the reason you even let Patton back into your life recently? Don't even try to deny it. Even your stubborn ass has hoped and prayed for a way back to that man since you left him."

"And the universe has made that happen," Sarina says, her eyes softening. "Sis, it's clear you both still love each other. Is telling him about this pregnancy going to change that? Because I bet he'll be over the moon."

I press my temples with my fingers, squeezing my eyes shut. "Yeah, sure. He'll be over the moon. *Temporarily*. He'll be over the moon until he has to fucking leave for the moon because there's a new movie he wants to chase there. Or a mini-series. Or a documentary about hut building. Because there's always something more pressing."

Always something more important *than me*.

And this time, I don't know if I'll survive another goodbye.

"And what if this time is different?" I ask, wiping a traitorous tear that has the audacity to slip from the corner of my eye. "What if I *actually* have this baby? What then?"

What if my body *actually* cooperates and does what it's supposed to, and I make it to the third trimester?

"Wouldn't that be a good thing?" Sarina frowns.

"Of course it would be a good thing! But Patton and I still haven't defined anything between us. Not when he already told me he was only here temporarily. Over the past five weeks, we've been circling each other like confused planets, avoiding talking about the past and just focusing on whatever this is for now."

I start to get up to find something else to organize, but Piper pushes me back down on the leather seat. "Stay. Sit. Talk, Neesh. Stop trying to hide from this."

I wrap my arms around myself defensively. "Patton's career will always call. And guess where that will leave me? Alone, doing two A.M. feedings by myself."

And this time, I won't even be able to fall apart.

"Jesus, babe," Piper says, shaking her head. "You're already planning your abandonment, and the guy doesn't even know you're pregnant yet."

"Because he'll leave! It's what he does. I'll always be second to his career."

"That was seven years ago," Sarina says gently. "Do you honestly think Patton still hasn't realized his mistakes? That he'd leave you or the baby when you both need him?"

I shrug. "Who knows? But I can't pin my future on the hope that he's changed."

"Yes, but you also can't move forward holding so much resentment from the past," Piper argues. "Give the man a real chance."

"And don't forget," Sarina says, tucking a wisp of her curly hair behind her ear. "You left him, too."

Wow. Leave it to a twin to show you the mirror.

Her words hit their mark, because any other argument dies on my lips, leaving me feeling like shit.

She's right.

I left him, too—a man who was abandoned by his own mother because of the choices she made. A man who grew up bouncing around from one foster home to another, not knowing when he'd have to pack his bags.

And I just left him. With a letter.

It's not that I've been oblivious to that until now—I knew what I was doing then, too. I just chose my grief over his trauma.

"God, I feel like such an asshole," I whisper, my throat feeling dry. "I've spent the past seven years telling myself I was justified because he wasn't there. But I wasn't there for him, either."

Piper crouches next to me, intertwining our fingers. "Which is why I think you both need to get all these things out on the table—unpack previous hurts, future plans. All of it. And I'll tell you what else helps in situations like these—"

"Your go-to solution of taking shots isn't going to work in this case," I deadpan. "I'm pregnant, remember?"

A smile plays on her lips, and I know it's her way of diffusing the tension. "I wasn't going to suggest shots . . . I was going to suggest some good old-fashioned fucking."

I snort. "Why am I not surprised?"

"Dev and I had an argument last night about whether we should allow the rabbits to sleep in our bed. I was for, and he was against, because he's a total square sometimes. Well, one thing led to another, and though we never came to a resolution, we did *come* . . . many, many times."

Sarina pinches the bridge of her nose, shaking her head.

Piper shrugs. "Nothing clears the air like a good dicking. Believe me, it's a tried-and-true method."

I groan but can't help laughing. This conversation has clearly devolved, but if there's anyone who can get a laugh out of me, it's my crazy pants best friend. "I'll keep that in mind."

"So, you'll tell him?" she asks.

"Has he been trying to get in touch with you?" Sarina adds.

"Yes," I say, recalling his multiple texts, asking if everything is okay since I haven't opened my door to him whenever he's come by. "He's even left French toast at my door every morning like some sort of breakfast fairy."

They both say "aww" like we're back in high school.

"Fine!" I raise my hands, letting them fall on my lap. "I'll tell him soon. Let me just talk to my doctor and confirm everything. It's not like I was planning to have a secret baby situation where he'd run into his kid twelve years later and recognize her as his because they have the same mole on their face. I was always going to tell him. I just . . . needed a little nudge to do it sooner. And I will."

"That's our girl," Sarina says, walking over to me.

The girls embrace me once more, and I'm just about to tell them that I have another client coming in soon—some Silicon Valley hotshot by the name of Alex Fleming, whom I haven't met before—when there's a knock at the door. That must be him.

I walk over to answer, the girls in tow behind me. Usually, our receptionist, Joshua, guides clients to the suites, but he must be helping someone else.

Except when I swing the door open, I'm greeted by a very different guest.

My brows knit as I step out of my suite. "Micah? What brings you here?"

Sarina and Piper excuse themselves—Snatch following

Pine For Me

Sarina out—slipping past Micah with a polite wave before heading to their respective suites. Though I don't miss the way Sarina lifts a brow at me over her shoulder before disappearing into her room. She's clearly curious about why Micah is here.

Me, too.

Micah's hands slide into his pockets as he examines me like one would an abandoned suitcase at the airport, looking for signs of threat.

"You texted the *dojang* group chat and said you wouldn't be coming in anymore," he says, articulating the vowels with the kind of precision only the British seem genetically programmed for. "No reason, no date for when you'd return. Nothing."

I tilt my chin up, rubbing my lips together. "That's right."

His face tilts like he thinks I've lost my marbles, and honestly, he's not far off. I did lose my lunch earlier, a perfect egg salad sandwich with mustard. Turns out this baby has quite a list of opinions, and mustard is an act of violence.

It's going to be a real doozy when I tell my sister, because the woman treats spicy Dijon like it's a food group. No joke, I recently saw her drizzle it over pita and hummus like it was chocolate syrup on a sundae.

Yup, gross. I'm still baffled that we shared a womb.

"Nisha, what do you mean, *'that's right'*? Why won't you be coming to the *dojang* anymore? You're an essential part of the instructing team."

I shift my weight from one foot to another, aware that I'm blocking the doorway. "I've just . . . had something come up." *Not untrue.* "I can tell you more about it later, once things are a bit more . . . settled. But for now, I need to take a leave from teaching."

I know my text caught him off guard. I've been a part of the *dojang* for years and have rarely taken days off. I'm close to our students, too, especially Sydney. I'd texted her separately to say I'd explain more soon, and she'd taken it well. Micah, however, not so much.

"A leave?" he repeats, baffled. "But you love teaching. Oh, my God. Are you—" His hand cups my shoulder gently as he bends to meet my eyes with his concerned ones. "Are you sick?"

"What—"

But before I can say more, his hands cradle my face, gently, reverently. Like we're lovers about to say a lengthy goodbye at the train station in a black-and-white film set in 1942. I can practically hear the violin swell and see the flock of doves being released into the sky in slow motion.

But I'm too startled to move. It's not like he's being handsy—just tragically wrong.

Perfect timing for my best friends to have disappeared.

"God, Nisha. I'm so sorry. I had no clue."

No clue about what? I think with my face smooshed into his very firm, very confused chest.

Oh, God, does he think I have cancer? I mean, morning sickness has been no joke lately, and this baby clearly wants me to survive on toast and boiled peas, but do I really look that bad?

Micah's enormous hand covers the side of my head, squishing my mouth so that even if I tried to speak, I'd sound like I just had a tooth pulled. Meanwhile, he continues to whisper heartfelt condolences, stroking my back like I'm about to ascend.

It's finally then that I decide enough is enough. Pregnant or not, I'm plenty capable of getting the man's hands off me.

I'm just about to knee him in the balls and threaten him with additional bodily harm when a throat clears behind us.

Loud and annoyed.

The kind of throat-clear that sounds like it could have been made by an angry bear.

We both freeze. More accurately, my eyes get stuck looking

like large saucers, my mouth probably still looks like a fish trying to speak, and my brain goes through a mental Rolodex, trying to place that deep tenor.

And when Micah and I finally turn, that Rolodex clicks into place: Patton.

Except this time, he's not sporting his usual Hollywood billboard smile.

No, this Patton's jaw is clenched tighter than a pickle jar, his eyes like murderous storm clouds locked on Micah's hands, and his biceps are bulging around his crossed arms like he's restraining his inner gladiator.

And then, as if things could get any worse, they do.

Beaver, my cat who's hellbent on converting Patton from a dog person to a cat person, launches out of the drawer where I keep my purse.

I'm just wondering how he got in there when he stalks forward, shooting Micah a judgmental glare before slinking past us to drop something at Patton's feet.

My positive pregnancy test.

Oh.

Shit.

Cue the doves scattering. Cue the dramatic violins. Cue me awkward-laughing while hoping the floorboards open up and swallow me whole.

twenty-one
patton

The Eyes of a Serial Killer

At first, the tips of my ears feel hot, the collar of my Henley feels like a noose, and my knuckles feel like they'll break with how hard I'm fisting my hands.

That fucker *Michael* has his hands on my wife.

My. Fucking. Wife.

I swear on everything holy as I stalk toward them that I will tear the limbs off the asshole who fucking dares to touch what's mine.

Mine.

My breaths feel ragged as I come to a stop in front of them, taking in the scene. Nisha's face is flush against his chest, his hand stroking down her back while the other keeps her head secured. He's murmuring shit—sweet nothings, probably—his lips moving against her hair. As if he has any fucking right to hold her and talk to her that way.

Instinct compels me to grab the fucker by the throat and haul him against the nearest wall, punching his perfect nose out of shape.

Instead, I clear my throat. Loudly. With a warning that hangs in the air.

They both freeze like deer in headlights before turning to

face me. The look on Nisha's face, a progression from shock to panic to guilt, barrels into my chest.

I know my ex-wife, and she isn't one to panic quickly. Sure, she might have a few nervous tics that compel her to organize every cupboard and drawer, but those are also the times she thinks, plans, and prepares.

So, given the look that just passed over her face, paired with the fact that she hasn't answered my texts or calls, I know something is wrong. And let's not forget she still looks guilty as she detaches herself from Michael's arms.

Michael's eyes widen in surprise as he takes me in. And just when Nisha's mouth opens, probably to explain, her cat appears out of nowhere with something in his mouth.

Over the past few weeks, the weird little fucker has grown on me. And not only because he's always bringing me shit, like he's trying to court me with gifts, but because he's . . . kind of cute in his own big-eyed, hairless alien sort of way.

A couple of weeks ago, he brought me Johnny Depp's wallet. Thankfully, Johnny and I know each other, and he took the whole thing lightly, so it wasn't too awkward, but yeah, it could have been worse.

With his tail standing straight up in the air like an antenna, Beaver's eyes stay on me as he prowls forward. Coming to a stop, he drops the item at my feet and sits back on his hind legs like he's waiting for applause.

A gasp leaves Nisha's lips as my eyes take in the item, narrowing when my brain registers what it is.

A . . . pregnancy test.

Mixed with the sound of blood rushing through my ears, I hear Michael mumble a "Holy shit," as I bend down to retrieve the stick.

"Patton." Nisha's voice sounds far away as my brain tries to come to terms with what I'm looking at.

Two pink lines stare back at me, clear as the early

September afternoon outside. For a moment, my lungs can't remember how to operate.

I can't breathe. Can't think...

Is this...? Is this for real?

The emotion that slams into me is so intense, so substantial, that it physically moves me. I take a step back, my other hand running through my hair. Pure joy and elation, mixed with a hint of terror and shock, makes my legs feel weak, like I'm standing on stilts.

She's pregnant.

She's fucking pregnant with my baby.

Again.

I look up, having momentarily forgotten that I'm still standing in front of them, to find both Nisha and the asshole next to her staring at me with varying degrees of bewilderment.

Michael's eyes flit from the pregnancy test in my hand to Nisha's face, some unspoken exchange passing between them, raising my hackles.

Wait... why did he give her that look?

Is... *oh, God.*

Is the baby not mine?

We haven't really talked about exclusivity, but I didn't think we needed to. She's the only woman I've been with in years, but maybe that's not the case for her?

With the test still clutched in my hand and my eyes locked on my ex-wife, I speak with deadly calm despite the thunderous way my heart is hammering and the million directions my thoughts are spinning. "Is it mine?"

Something like hurt flits across Nisha's face before it hardens and a dangerous glint flashes in her eyes. It's the same one that generally precedes a roundhouse-kick to the head when she's on the mat.

Pine For Me

She takes a step forward, her mouth opening to respond when Michael speaks.

"Blimey, are you . . . are you *Patton Pierce*?" His head swivels between me to Nisha and then back again like it's trying to unscrew itself. "Nisha, is he Patton Pierce?"

Neither of us answers, locked in an eye-war.

Michael uses the time to continue being a motormouth. "Wow. I honestly can't believe it. I'm Micah, by the way. And, clearly, there's a lot to unpack here"—his eyes dart between the test in my hand to both Nisha's and my face—"but I'm a huge fan. You're actually shorter than I expected . . . not that you're short! Just, you look seven-foot-tall in your movies. And your work on *Pilots of the Pacific* was—"

"Answer the question, Nisha," I say, ignoring the idiot. My jaw is granite as I look down at my ex-wife. *"Is. It. Mine?"*

Her eyes spit fire, the pointed ends of her eyeliner looking like weapons. "Whose else would it be, you arrogant dick?"

My gaze flicks to Michael—Micah, *whatever*—giving her my answer.

She takes the test from my hands, slipping it inside the pocket of her black dress. The low-cut V-neck shows off just a sliver of the tops of her breasts, and even though I'm pissed and confused and still reeling from this pregnancy bombshell, my body reacts to her like it always does.

"Are you suggesting I cheated on you?" Her finger jabs between my ribs, her deathly glare telling me she won't hesitate to pierce my chest if needed. "That I could be carrying his baby while I've been sleeping with *you*?" She flicks a thumb behind him. "How fucking dare you."

Christ, even furious, she's the hottest, most captivating woman I've ever seen.

"You've been sleeping with him? Also, don't sound so disgusted, love," Micah says in an offended tone. "We did have quite the romp—"

My hand fists his collar before he's even finished his sentence, my snarl causing his hands to rise in surrender.

The sudden movement causes Beaver to hiss at the asshole, his body arching, canines exposed and eyes murderous. But then, he goes so still, you'd think he was frozen. And that vision in itself is really fucking creepy.

Micah's gaze flicks from Beaver to me. "Whoa. Now, hold on a second. Firstly, Nisha, your cat is weird as fuck. Secondly, Patton, mate, I understand you're famous and all, but I'm an fifth *dan* black belt in taekwondo. I don't want to hurt—"

In one quick sweep with my feet, I have him sprawled out on his back, my hand around his throat. Micah's breath whooshes out of him in a strained "Oof" as he stares up in wide-eyed shock.

I lean down to his ear, my voice deadly. "And I'm a sixth *dan*, Michael. Say one more thing about my wife . . . hell, dare to touch her or even *think* about her, and—"

"It's Micah. And what do you mean, your *wife*?"

Someone places a hand on my shoulder, and I turn to see that it's one of the guys from my security detail. I'd asked them to wait in the reception area, but they must have heard the commotion. "Sir, we can take it from here."

I shake my head, and he releases me.

Sarina and Piper stand behind him, both gawking at the scene in front of them. They must have come out of their suites, having heard the commotion, too.

We've been talking a bit more lately. Last week, the girls even came to the stadium to watch me film, right along with Troy and Dev. I won't say we're as close as we were in high school, but with time, I could see us all getting there again.

"What in the *Great British Bake Off* is happening here?" Piper squeaks, taking in the scene.

"Looks like Patton is introducing himself to Micah," Sarina quips.

"Patton Luca Pierce." Nisha's shrill voice pulls me out of my haze. "*Let him go*. This is my place of business, not a back-alley fight club. Thank God we don't have other clients here right now."

"What do you mean, your wife?" Micah blurts again from his position on the floor, sending a stunned look toward Nisha. "You're *married*?"

Nisha releases a frustrated breath. "Oh, for God's sake! I'm this loon's ex-wife, and probably soon-to-be ex-girlfriend, too, if he doesn't get his head out of his ass."

Girlfriend?

I'm not opposed to the word—as ass-backwards as it is—but beggars can't be choosers. If she's finally acknowledging a relationship between us, giving us a label other than exes after seven years, then I'll fucking take it.

Her glare turns to me. "And yes, Micah and I"—she waves her hand as if that's enough to explain it—"'dated' a couple of years ago, but it never went anywhere. You know why? Because I wasn't over you, you jealous prick!"

My heart hammers as I rise to my feet, closing the distance between us.

For the sake of my fucking sanity, I shove aside her admission of "dating" the douchebag on the floor. As furious as I am that he ever had his hands on her, I'm not angry with her. We were divorced—as much as I hated that we were, that was the fact—and therefore, she had a right to be with whoever she wanted.

It still doesn't make me want to murder him any less, though.

"And this baby," she says, her hand resting on her stomach, "is *yours*. I want to throat-punch you for even *thinking* it was anyone else's when I've spent the past five weeks with you."

I place my hand over hers, the other diving into her hair and pulling on it so she's forced to look up at me. "It's mine?"

"Yes, you idiot."

My chest constricts as her words wrap around my insides, taking root in abandoned places.

It's mine. The child she's carrying is mine.

The thought sends another jolt of primal possessiveness through me.

"Then why have you been avoiding me?" I ask, my chest rising and falling against her from both the adrenaline and this completely unexpected news.

"Because I needed a chance to process!" Her hand grasps mine before she pulls me toward her suite. "Let's just talk inside. I'm assuming you're *Alex Fleming*, since he hasn't shown up?"

I smile, following her in. "Did you know he was the scientist who discovered penicillin?"

"I do now."

"I debated going with Michael Faraday, the creator of the helium balloon, but given your aversion . . ."

She glares at me, and I drop my smile. Pregnant or not, it would take point-two seconds for my ex-wife to have me sprawled out on the floor like the other idiot.

"Anyway, if I'd given my real name, you know you would have found a way to cancel."

She rolls her eyes, but says nothing, probably because she knows I'm right.

"Give me a second," she says, heading toward the half-bath connected to her suite. "I need to pee. Be right back."

I turn to close the suite door when the sight in the hall makes me freeze.

All three cats—Beaver, Snatch, and Vajayjay—are starting to circle Micah as he tries to stand, tails in the air like bullwhips and alien-eyes locked on him like they're about to do a human sacrifice.

Micah flaps a hand at them. "Shoo. Go on now. Move."

The cats just hiss at him in response, causing him to pull his hand back quickly like it's been bitten. I can't help the smile that tugs at my face. Mr. Fifth *dan* is losing his shit because of three house cats.

Vajayjay, the most "talkative" of the three siblings, breaks the formation to press one of the buttons against the wall, making it speak in a robotic voice. *"I'm hungry."*

Since they adopted the cats, Piper, Sarina, and Nisha have been training them to use communication buttons to announce their needs. And while his siblings love using the buttons, Beaver is more of a silent-type. According to Nisha, he prefers to communicate through unnerving stares and random gifts.

But two weeks ago, when I'd dropped by to see Nisha after she left my bed without giving me my usual good-morning kiss, Beaver shocked everyone. Right as I was leaving, having gotten more than a kiss when I took my girl up against the wall in her suite, Beaver rushed to press the "Stay with me" and "I love you" buttons.

Not going to lie, it was that day I knew the hairless hellion had wormed his way under my skin. I still won't call myself a cat person, but Beaver is the exception.

"I'm hungry." Vajayjay presses the button again, staring straight at Micah before hitting the "Go away" button.

"Uh, Nisha?" Micah calls out, trying to take a step out of their circle, only for Snatch to block his path, tail swishing like a sword. "Anyone? Bloody hell, are these hellhounds about to attack?"

"Patton? What's going on out there?" Nisha's concerned voice resounds behind me.

My grin widens. "Looks like the cats are vetting your friend."

She makes her way to the door, taking in the scene. A gasp falls from her lips when she sees Micah is now back on the floor with Beaver sitting on top of his chest like a triumphant hunter over a kill.

"Christ, can someone please take this demonic cat off me?" Micah wheezes.

And right when Beaver raises a paw, claws twitching, about to bop Micah in the face, Nisha's voice cuts through. "Beaver, no!"

Beaver freezes mid-strike while the other cats flee the scene like the little criminals they are.

Nisha swings her glare onto me. "Seriously? You just stood here, watching them torture him?"

"Torture is such a strong word. They were . . . interviewing him." I rub my jaw, wincing dramatically. "Doesn't look like he passed."

Giving me an exasperated shake of her head, Nisha steps into the hall. She scoops up her cat, murmuring something to him in a soft but admonishing tone, before turning to Micah. "I am so sorry about that, Micah. I don't know what's gotten into the cats. They don't usually act like this."

"Don't usually act like this?!" Micah struggles to his feet, combing his hand through his hair. "I should hope not! Your cats were circling me like bloody vultures! And that one"—he points to Beaver, still in Nisha's hands—"has the eyes of a serial killer."

Nisha opens her mouth, likely to apologize again, when Micah lifts a hand, cutting her off.

"It's fine. But between your ex-husband or current boyfriend, or whatever the hell he is, nearly taking off my head, getting mauled by your bald four-legged mafia, and finding out you're pregnant, it's about as much as I can take. I'm going to leave before someone actually kills me."

He straightens his collar, shooting me a glare.

I throw him a salute. "Thanks for the housecall, *Michael*, but as you can see, Beaver and I have my wife handled."

Micah's jaw ticks, and my ex-wife shoots me a glare that makes my dick stir, but I give them both my most charming smile.

~

"You're a caveman, you know that?"

My arm wraps around her stomach, my palm splaying over the place our baby is growing. I lean in to brush a kiss on the curve of her neck. "I do, and I won't apologize for it . . . not when it comes to you."

We're sitting in a leather recliner in her suite. Nisha's on my lap with her back against my chest. The scent of her pomegranate shampoo mingles with something uniquely her, drawing my nose into her hair. Fuck, she always smells so good, like home and desire.

Like heaven in my arms.

My lips brush the shell of her ear, lined with the tiny diamond stars she's worn ever since I gave her that nickname in high school. "You've always been the most beautiful woman I've seen, Neesh. But pregnant with my baby?" I press a kiss to the sensitive spot below her ear, feeling her shiver against me. "You're stunning."

Nisha shifts in my arms, turning to cradle my face. "I need to go to the doctor first and confirm everything, Patton." Her eyes bounce between mine in a plea, her fear barely contained behind her dark irises. "Don't get too excited. You know what happened last—"

I press a finger to her lips. It won't be like last time; I refuse to believe it'll be anything like last time. "This time will be different."

"How can you be so sure?"

"Aside from the fact that this"—I lay my palm on her

belly, holding the two most precious things in my arms—"happened naturally, we're different."

Our eyes hold, and I know she's remembering all those grueling months when her body was a battlefield of hormones and hope. When making love became a clinical necessity rather than an act of passion and desire.

"Are we?" Her voice is small and uncertain. "Different, I mean. Because while I know I've changed, I don't really know how much you have." Her fingers drop to my chest, her eyes following as they trace patterns on my shirt. "From what I can tell, you're still just as busy."

"How so?"

"Aren't you?" Her eyes flick back up to meet mine. "You're filming the movie here, but you told *Vanity Fair* last year that you had no reason to slow down. From what I read, you've committed to several movies over the next couple of years. And that's okay," she adds quickly, her hand pressing firmly against my chest as if underscoring her words. "I know how much you love your job, and I'm not asking you to justify anything."

"Don't believe everything you read, baby." I capture her hand, bringing it up to kiss the inside of her wrist, where she's still wearing our friendship bracelet. "Aside from the handful of overnight trips I've made for press tours and the one day I flew out for that foster charity event, have you seen me go anywhere?"

She hesitates, her brows furrowing. "Well, no. But I thought that's just because filming the movie here is taking up your time. You said you'd leave as soon as you were done."

"I said that when I didn't know if things would ever change between us. I was hellbent on trying to knock down the walls you'd built over the years, but I didn't know if I'd *actually* be able to."

"And now?"

I grasp her face in my hands, my thumbs tracing the tops of her cheeks. "Don't you fucking get it, Little Borealis? I'm here *for* you, *because* of you. Nothing in this goddamn world is as important to me as you. I'm not fucking going anywhere."

"But—"

"And, no, it didn't take me seven years to figure that out, sweetheart. I knew it the moment I came back home and saw you'd left."

"Patton, I'm . . ." Her glistening eyes meet mine. "I'm so sorry."

I shake my head. "No, baby. *I'm* sorry. I'm so fucking sorry you had to go through that"—my voice cracks, the words shredding my insides—"all on your own. You shouldn't have had to, not once and definitely not twice. I should have been there."

A sob bubbles out of her as her body collapses against mine. Our arms fold around each other as our hearts mourn every loss we've ever suffered—our children, our marriage, our friendship. My chest burns as her tears soak my shirt.

My eyes prick as I hold her, brushing my fingers through her hair as she cries into my neck. I kiss her temple, her jaw, anywhere I can reach until her sobs turn to shuddering breaths.

When she lifts her head, I wipe her cheeks with my thumbs, wishing for the millionth time over the past seven years that I'd been there to wipe her cheeks that night when she endured everything all on her own.

"When I told *Vanity Fair* I had no reason to slow down, I hadn't found my way back to you again." I swallow past the barbed wire inside my throat. "I was still working on myself, trying to find the best version of myself."

"What do you mean?"

"Soon after you left, I started going to therapy to work through some of my trauma from my childhood, like the unsafe environment I was in before I went into the foster system and the abandonment I felt after my mom was taken away. I had significant things I needed to address before I could heal from them. Apart from therapy, I also raised awareness and volunteered at various foster organizations and kept up with my taekwondo training."

Her eyes bounce between mine in surprise. "I didn't know that."

"And then one day I was watching a Bay Area Blazers game on TV. Their star pitcher had made this incredible comeback from a potentially career-ending injury, but that's not what caught my eye. It was Sarina in the stands, fighting to get to him. The camera panned to her making a scene, trying to get to Troy. And when he finally saw her, he ran over and pulled her into a kiss."

"Oh, my God. Yeah." A small smile tugs at her lips. "It was when she realized how much she loved him and couldn't wait to tell him." Her smile fades, confusion clouding her features. "But what does that have to do with you being here?"

"That's when I realized I had a path back to you." I lean my forehead against hers. "I pitched a comeback story of a baseball star to my producer, told him I needed to interview Troy for research. But really, I was working toward getting the biggest role of my life, the role I'd lost." My voice drops to a whisper. "Being your husband."

Her eyes shimmer with fresh tears. "Patton . . ."

"I have worked for seven years to be with you again, Little Borealis. And I'll work seventy more if I have to. All those projects and films you've read about? I pulled out of them months ago."

"But you've worked hard for your career, and I'd never want you to abandon your dreams. My problem wasn't that you loved your job; it was that I felt left behind. I spent more nights alone than with you. We'd go weeks without having a meaningful conversation while you were on set, and even when you were home, our conversations were constantly interrupted with work calls. I just felt like we'd lost all balance, like I always came second."

The pain in her voice cuts through me like a thousand razor blades, and I close my eyes, letting the weight of my failures slam against my heart. "Fuck, that was my fault, Neesh. All my fault."

When I open my eyes, I make sure she can see the sincerity inside them, the regret I've carried for so long. "I just kept chasing the next high, thinking 'one more movie,' and then I'd take a break. 'One more big production,' and then I'd finally be home with my wife. But the more I took on, the more opportunities came my way that I felt like I couldn't refuse. I should have, though. Because in the end, I lost the most important thing in my life." My voice breaks. "I lost you . . . and I won't do that again."

"But what about your career? Your fans? You love what you do."

"I'll continue to make films, maybe get into producing. But I'll never take on so many projects again." I lay my hand on her stomach. "Not when I have so much more to fill my heart."

"What if we're not enough?" she whispers. "I want you to feel fulfilled, too."

"You're more than enough, baby. You always have been. I was just too blind to see it. I could give every minute of every day to this industry, and it would still demand more." I shake my head. "What I realized was I needed to create boundaries, a work-life balance. I never want to give it so much again, certainly not at the cost of my happiness."

"But—"

"None of the fame, no premier mattered without you by my side. No Oscar filled the hole you left. The spotlight was dark and lonely. So when I realized you really weren't coming back, I decided to work on myself to become the man you wished for."

"What do you mean?" She leans back slightly, studying my face.

"I found your list."

"What list? I didn't leave you a list. Just a letter."

A small smile plays on my lips. "I'll give you a clue. It was aptly titled 'Ten Things I Wish About You'."

A sharp gasp leaves her lips as recognition dawns. "You found that?"

I shift, tugging my wallet out of my pocket and taking out the crumpled paper with words I have memorized by heart. "I did."

twenty-two
patton

Ten Things I Wish
About You

Seven Years Ago

I push through the door of our penthouse apartment, clicking it shut behind me, noting how my desperate voice echoes louder than usual today. "Neesh!"

I haphazardly leave my luggage in the empty foyer, the sound carrying through the space that feels too vast. It's the same spot Nisha usually greets me in, with that smile that makes me forget the weeks I've been away, and eyes that speak louder than the words she always whispers in my arms. *"God, I missed you, husband."*

My feet carry me forward, toward our spacious living room, looking for signs of my wife. My eyes skim the multitude of perfectly fluffed throw pillows on our sectional before I turn to walk down the long hall toward our bedroom, past the gallery wall of black and white photographs of our wedding—my hands cradling my gorgeous bride's face with my lips against hers. The two of us with her dad, sister, and Piper. The two of us with my foster parents, Joe and Molly.

Each frame seems to follow me as I pass, the people from those happy moments staring back a little vacantly today.

"Nisha?" I repeat, looking around the room as if she'll pop out from behind our bed. But it stands uninhabited, the white duvet cover pulled tight and pastel-colored throw-pillows arranged neatly.

Except, today our bed doesn't feel so inviting—not the way it usually feels when I get back home, pulling her into it before we've even exchanged a single word. No real conversation, no exchanged pleasantries, just needing to be inside her more than I need my next breath.

I turn my gaze toward the window seat she likes so much, looking for her knitting supplies, but find it empty, too.

I stride toward the adjoining bathroom, my heart pounding as I rap my knuckles on the door. "Nisha? You in there?"

Silence. No sound of a running shower or her humming.

I turn the knob, pushing the door open to step onto the marble tile. But the bathroom is empty.

Not just empty.

Different. Wrong.

It takes me a moment to understand why, like trying to visualize a puzzle with the center pieces missing.

Her robe—the wine-red one that always hangs next to the walk-in shower—is missing. The counter, with her caddy of neatly organized skincare products, makeup brushes, and the perfume she loves, is bare, save for the pump dispenser of hand soap. Even her electric toothbrush is gone from its charging station near the sink.

My heart stutters, my lungs feeling like they're too small to capture any air.

The missed calls I found, the broken and pleading voicemail she left me three days ago, had me rushing to the airport and taking the first flight back home, knowing something was dreadfully wrong.

"Please, Patton, pick up. Please . . . I need you."

We've been through so much to get pregnant again; what if something happened to Nisha or the baby? But she would have told me. Even if it was through a text or in a voicemail, she would have told me.

Wouldn't she?

I know my wife.

Her strength, her fortitude to withstand more than almost anyone on the planet, and her pride. Even with the disappointment she expressed the night I left, telling me how lonely she'd been feeling, how blindsided she felt when I told her I was leaving, she held it together.

I knew I was breaking her heart, pushing her beyond her limits and asking her to accept my choices without her input, but she never told me not to go.

Maybe she'd already reached her limit?

Maybe she'd already decided enough was enough?

I move toward her closet, flipping on the switch, and the sight nearly brings me to my knees.

It's empty, save for the small trashcan in the corner and a price tag lying next to it, like she was trying to throw it in there but didn't bother in her rush to get out. It's completely devoid of her clothes, her fifty shades of black shoes, and the little jewelry boxes she'd collected over the years.

Where is she?

Where did she go?

The stagnant air still holds a trace of her pomegranate shampoo, the scent I was looking forward to burying my face in for the past three weeks. But even that seems to fade with every inhale I take.

With my hand trembling around my phone and my breaths colliding against one another on their way out, I call her. Without thinking, I step on the small pedal of the trashcan, needing something to do while I wait for her to pick up.

The phone rings three times before her voicemail picks up.

I call her again, bending to pick up the crumpled lined paper inside the bin. This time my call goes straight to voicemail.

My hands shake as I unfold the paper as if it contains the answers I'm looking for. It's probably nothing—a grocery list or supplies for the nursery—so I can't quite understand what compels me to smooth it out and read the title at the top written in her familiar clear-cursive slant. *Ten Things I Wish About You.*

My eyes dart down the list, but the words seem to swim on the page, refusing to register—something about phone calls and being best friends.

I can't process this right now. Not when all I want to do is search for her in every room and closet in the apartment, hoping this is just her torturing me for leaving so spontaneously.

I admit that springing my departure on her right after we'd made love was a little underhanded. I thought she'd be in a better mood to handle the news if I'd shown her how much I loved her, but maybe that wasn't right.

Okay, it definitely wasn't right. But she wouldn't leave because of that, would she?

No. We'd talked after that; several times over the last three weeks, save for the past few days that I was on set in a remote location.

But I'd told her I'd be reachable soon; I told her I'd talk to her as soon as filming was over. And I made sure that if there was an emergency, she had the landline number for the makeshift production office. Someone would have tracked me down if she needed me sooner.

So, why wouldn't she wait?

My mind filters through our recent conversations—mainly Nisha telling me that her morning sickness was getting worse by the day, that she could barely keep anything down. Unfortunately, with my insane schedule and the time difference, it was hard for us to have lengthy conversations. But I'd tried to be there for her emotionally the best I could, hadn't I?

Our last time together, she'd admitted how lonely she felt here. She wasn't happy with how many projects I'd taken on, but I thought she understood that this was the "growing phase".

Actors waited their entire lives for the roles I was getting. I was still early in my career, and rejecting opportunities at this time would kill the momentum we'd worked so hard for me to build. I thought she knew that. I thought she believed in it . . . believed in me.

Crumbling the piece of paper again, I stuff it into my pocket and slam the back of my head against the wall in her closet, questions running rampant inside my mind.

"Fuck!"

My eyes prick as my brain works, trying to comprehend what's happening.

This morning I got back to the mainland in Thailand and turned on my phone as soon as I had reception. My stomach dropped when I heard the panicked voicemail she left three days ago.

I tried calling her, to no avail, before packing my things and getting the hell out of there to get to her. Her broken words echoed inside my head the entire flight, and I fought to keep my thoughts from taking a dark turn. Because I knew that when I got to her, we would work it out.

Nothing was insurmountable when we were together.

It's been that way since we were sixteen, since the week I moved in with Joe and Molly and met the most beautiful girl in school. At first, I thought my luck had peaked when they assigned me a locker next to hers. Then she actually talked to me, introduced me to her sister and her best friend, and encouraged me to join the theater class. Luck would have it that we even ended up in the same *dojang*, learning taekwondo together.

Soon, she was unveiling little pieces of herself, telling me things she only told a few others. Because while the girl had befriended me, she was a quiet enigma, preferring to be the listener rather than the talker, the calm rather than the chaos.

I learned that her mom had died the year before, and Nisha used the mats in our *dojang* to quiet some of the grief, practicing for hours on end. It was also because of her mom that her family was fluent in sign language, given her mom was deaf.

I learned the first thing she wanted to do when she turned eighteen was get her arm inked with vines of stars and flowers, that French toast was the answer for every meal, and that she had an inexplicable fear of helium balloons.

The last one dated back to when she and her twin had turned five. Apparently, she'd wandered into the dark hallway for the bedroom and found their birthday balloons floating near the ceiling. In her half-asleep mind, they'd turned into looming ghosts. Instead of making it to the bathroom, she'd peed her pants, and the fear embedded deep into her psyche.

Even now, Nisha couldn't look at a helium balloon without trembling. And my wife—my fierce, indomitable wife—trembled at nothing.

With my thumb over another phone number, I rush out of the bathroom. I wait as the ring goes through to Sarina's phone. When she doesn't answer, I call Piper.

Again, no answer.

What the fuck?

Standing in the living room, I send off several text messages to Nisha, urging her to call me. But when I don't receive her normal Read receipt after several minutes, I call her dad.

After Nisha and I moved to L.A., and Sarina married her

pro-golfer husband, Suraj found a tech job that brought him from Boston to San Francisco to be closer to his daughters.

Relief washes over me when he answers, and I cut him off mid-hello.

"Suraj, hi. Sorry to call you out of the blue, but I'm wondering if you've heard from Nisha today? She left me a . . . strange voicemail a few days ago." I skip the part about it worrying the hell out of me. "I just heard it this morning since I was unreachable on set."

I also leave out the part about taking the first flight home because of the voicemail, or that I got home to find her stuff missing. No point worrying him until I know more.

"Patton, good to hear from you." My father-in-law's usually boisterous voice sounds uncharacteristically subdued. "Actually . . . yes. I flew back with Nisha last night. She said she'll be staying with me for a little while."

The relief I just felt after hearing his voice evaporates instantly. "She's with you? Why? Is she okay?"

There's a pause, and I can hear some rustling in the background before a door slides open and shut. The faint sound of traffic comes through the line, indicating he's stepped outside.

"Son . . ." His voice is gentle, as if he's unsure how to deliver the rest of the message. "Did you read the note she left for you? She pinned it to your fridge."

I immediately find the note—a piece of the same lined paper that's crumpled inside my pocket—stuck to the fridge.

Suraj takes a long breath. "Son, she's been through a lot over the past few days . . . Something no one should have to go through."

"W-what do you mean? What has she been through?" I stutter out the questions even as my gut tells me that I already know.

The baby. Something happened to the baby.

The baby her body took on so much to create and house.

The baby we've talked about so often ever since she got pregnant again. The baby we both have wanted for so long.

"I believe you'll find your answers in the note—"

"Suraj, I'll read the note, but can you please put my wife on the phone? I need to speak to her. Whatever she's going through, we can get through it together."

"She just laid down for a nap. But, Patton, I spoke to her. I even tried to convince her to talk to you. But she says she's not ready."

"Can you just tell me what happened? Did something happen to her, to the baby? Is this about me leaving for Thailand? I can get out of the contract if that's what she wants. I can figure out a way to stop working so much—"

"Patton, I don't know if this is about what she wants. It's a question of what she needs. I think at some point you'll both need to do some soul searching and figure out if your wants and needs align anymore."

What? What does that mean? What does he mean, we'll need to figure out if our wants align? Of course, they align.

"Suraj—"

"Give her time, Patton. She's . . . not herself right now. When she's ready to talk, I'm sure she will."

The hollow in my chest threatens to take over my body while the same thought keeps circling inside my brain. *How can this be happening?*

"How long?" I ask, choking on the words. "How long does she need?"

"I don't know . . . I'm sorry, son."

∽

Sitting on the kitchen floor, with my back against the cabinets, something dies inside me as I read the letter my wife left me.

The moment feels surreal, like a nightmare I can't wake myself up from.

> Patton,
> Here are my truths.
> The first truth is that I love you. I will always love you.
> The second is that I lost our baby three nights ago.

My breath halts inside my lungs, my vision going blurry as the words fuse together on the page. I read them again, slowly this time, as if they'll make more sense, but they don't.

> I know that news will break you the same way it broke me, sitting alone on our bathroom floor in the middle of the night, watching my body fail at the one thing it was made to do.
>
> You'll say it's not my fault, and maybe you're right. But right now, I can't stop blaming myself.

My stomach twists as bile threatens to rise. The fact that she had to endure all that... God, Nisha...

No, baby, it's absolutely not your fault.

> I know you'll blame yourself, too—for not being here, for missing my calls, and for somehow not knowing that I needed you. But this is not

about blame anymore. It's about two people who want the best for each other but can't seem to give the other what they need.

She's wrong. It is about blame, and all of it lies with me.

I lost our baby alone. I drove myself to the hospital alone. I answered the doctor's questions alone. I came back to our empty bed and grieved alone.
And in all that aloneness, I realized I've felt that way for a long time. Not just these past weeks, but for months . . . maybe even years.

I realized that this is the future I signed up for, with or without kids. Because it's clear what comes first for you, and, unfortunately, it's not me. Not us.

The letter trembles in my grip, each "alone" like a blade tearing at my skin. She's right about all of it, except for one thing. She's never been second place to anything—not my career and not my aspirations. I just never proved it when it mattered.

I feel guilty even as I write this. I know why you left. The opportunities you're getting are the ones you've always dreamed of, and you absolutely deserve them. But somewhere along the way, your dreams became our dreams, and mine got forgotten in the midst of goodbyes and hellos.

I never asked you to choose between me and your career. I never wanted to be that kind of wife—the kind who begs and pleads, clings and cries, only for you to resent me one day.

I could never fucking resent her. Never. She should have asked. She should have made me see.

A voice inside my head reminds me that she tried, with every frown when I had to leave soon after I came home and every protest when I had to miss another anniversary or Christmas.

But I can't be this kind of wife, either—the one who quietly accepts the loneliness every time it's handed to her. The one who loses herself, little by little, until there's nothing left.

So, here's another truth: I love you, but love isn't closing the distance that's growing between us.

I'm leaving. Not to punish you or to make you come after me, but to find myself again. You might think I'm being cruel, but staying until my love turns bitter, until every plea turns into a fight would be crueler.

The air feels thin. No, not thin . . . more like noxious gas.

I know you think we can work this out, and maybe one day we can. But right now, I need time to grieve, space to heal, and distance to remember who I am when I'm not Patton Pierce's wife.

I can't stop you from calling or trying to find me, but I'm not ready.. I don't know if or when I'll be.

But here's my last truth, the one I have to believe: if we're meant to find our way back to each other, we will.

Love,
Nisha

I wipe the tear that rolls down my cheek, slumping against the cabinet as if I've been stabbed by a thousand daggers. The letter falls from my hand like it suddenly weighs a thousand pounds.

So, that's it?
She's gone?
Our baby is gone?
My world, as I know it, is gone?

It's a sucker-punch stronger than anything I've felt before. Even stronger than the confused heartbreak I felt as a six-year-old boy, seeing my mother get arrested and taken away right in front of me. My world collapsed then, but it's completely shattered now.

She left me . . . just like my mother did.

And the part that's killing me is that she's right about all of it. About me not being here enough, about her being alone.

God, she lost our baby, and I wasn't fucking here. I can't begin to imagine what she went through that night, and when she needed me the most—to hold her, to rock her in my arms—I wasn't here.

She was alone all the time anyway, so of course she would leave. Who the hell wouldn't? But to not take my calls or want to talk to me . . .? How am I supposed to survive that?

Something crinkles inside my pocket, and I remember the crumpled paper I stuffed inside. My fingers shake as I pull it out to read through the list again since I never comprehended it the first time.

Ten Things I Wish About You:

1. I wish I had more of you than anyone else does.

2. I wish you'd stop promising "soon" when we both know you mean "never".

3. I wish you could be present in all our big moments. I wish you could be present in the small ones, too.

4. I wish I didn't have to face my fears alone.

5. I wish you'd make me laugh until I cry, not cry because you're gone again.

6. I wish you remembered that you married your best friend, not your job.

7. I wish you'd believe that you're more than the boy who got left behind—you're the man I chose.

8. I wish you knew that my silence isn't acceptance, it's heartbreak. It's exhaustion.
9. I wish you'd remember that I matter more than any phone call.
10. I wish you'd see that I'm drowning.

The last line blurs, echoing inside my head like a gavel in a courtroom.

I wish you'd see that I'm drowning.

How could I not have seen? How could I have missed it behind her sad smiles and slumped shoulders?

Despite the tears still falling, I fold the list into a small square, placing it inside my wallet and making a vow to read it every day to remind myself of my failures, of everything I lost.

And that's exactly what happens.

For years, I stay true to my vow, reading her list on planes, in lonely hotel rooms, between takes, and on breaks. The paper starts to soften and crease. And though the ink starts to fade, it burns bright inside my mind, her heartbroken wishes etched inside my soul.

It's my punishment and my penance, a reminder of all she wanted and everything I didn't give her. Maybe one day it would be my redemption.

Though, what I don't realize then is that the list won't just be a plan for *if* I ever get her back; it'll be the commandments I'll live by for *when* I have her again in my arms.

For the next year, I'll call her like the hope of hearing her voice is the only thing keeping me alive. I'll even fly to San Francisco and beg her to talk to me.

Until one day, when she sends me a final text, begging me to let go, before changing her number.

So I do. I let her go. Not because I want to, but because she's left me no choice.

Pine For Me

I let her go and spend the next years working on myself, to face the parts of me I'd ignored to one day become someone worthy of her again.

Except, what I don't know then—*what I can't possibly know*—is that six years from now, she'll be standing in front of me. And when I finally have her mouth on mine, I'll realize that she never really let go, despite what she'd asked me to do.

That, like me, she never really moved on, either.

And this time, I'll make sure she never wants to.

twenty-three
patton

Seven Schlongs Hen Party

TROY WINTERS

Not to start rumors, but @Patton Pierce, bro, what happened at Haircuts and Heartthrobs yesterday? Sarina said she came out of her suite and saw you strangling a dude.

DEAN MEYER

Ooh, kinky. Can I ask what his safeword was?

HUDSON CASE

@Patton Pierce, are you alright? I'm sure the asshole deserved it, but what the hell happened!?

DEAN MEYER

Love how you're asking if Patton is alright when he was the one doing the strangling. Seriously, Patton could commit homicide and you'd call it philanthropy.

PATTON PIERCE

I'd hardly call it strangling. Just needed him to keep his hands off what's mine.

Pine For Me

GARRETT MEYER

Keep his hands off what's yours? Wait, does this have something to do with Nisha?

DEAN MEYER

That's the only reason I can think of that would make Patton go all aggro. Deets, Hollywood! Did some asshole try to motorboat your woman?

DARIAN MEYER

Dean, not every fight is about boobs.

DEAN MEYER

That's true. Some are about honor and food . . . but mostly about boobs.

PATTON PIERCE

He's a colleague from her dojang. Apparently, they "dated," which should be reason enough to strangle him. The fact that I had any restraint . . .

Anyway, he was asking why she couldn't teach taekwondo anymore, then assumed she was sick. Next thing I know, he had his hands all over her.

I kept it together until he said something about sleeping with her. That's when I lost it. Anyway, it's resolved. My team slapped him with an NDA and paid him off to keep his mouth shut.

DARIAN MEYER

Why can't Nisha teach taekwondo anymore?

TROY WINTERS

Interesting. Sarina never told me Nisha is taking time off from the dojang.

Swati M.H.

PATTON PIERCE
Just for a few months. It's no big deal.

DEV MENON
No big deal? She almost didn't come to my and Piper's wedding because it happened to coincide with some big event at the dojang. There's no way she would take time off. Unless . . .

DEAN MEYER
Unless what? What the fuck? Don't leave us hanging, Dev!

TROY WINTERS
Holy shit. But Sarina would have told me if . . .

GARRETT MEYER
If what?

PATTON PIERCE
If nothing. Can we forget I said anything?

HUDSON CASE
You want us to forget that you accidentally spilled the beans on Nisha being pregnant? The Dumb and Dumber twins on this chat can't figure it out, but it's pretty obvious that's what it is.

DEAN MEYER
Holy. Fucking. Shit.

GARRETT MEYER
WHAT? Dude! @Patton Pierce, is Hudson correct? Is Nisha pregnant??

Pine For Me

PATTON PIERCE

> Sorry, guys, I'm running late for something. Talk later.

[**Patton Pierce** has left the chat]
[**Dean Meyer** has added **Patton Pierce** to the chat]

DEAN MEYER

> Oh, hell no. You're one of the schlongs, bro. And we never leave another schlong hanging.

HUDSON CASE

> There's a visual I wasn't planning to have this early in the morning.

DEAN MEYER

> What can I say? I'm a giver. @Patton Pierce, get your ass back in this conversation. You can't ghost us like some basic bitch on Tinder.

PATTON PIERCE

> Fuck. Fine. Yes, she's pregnant. But it's still really early, so you guys can't say anything. I'm a dead man if she finds out I said anything.

DEAN MEYER

> I've seen her spar. One of her precision kicks and you'd be done. So, yeah, I actually believe you.

TROY WINTERS

> Shit. Sorry, bro. I already sent off a text to Sarina.

DEV MENON

> Fuck, same. I messaged Piper to ask.

Swati M.H.

PATTON PIERCE

> Tell me you guys are kidding.

DEV MENON

> I wish I was. But honestly, Piper would smell it a mile away if I was keeping a secret like this.

DEAN MEYER

> At least it wasn't me for once with the extreme premature ejaculation of the mouth.

DARIAN MEYER

> There are so many other ways you could have phrased that, but of course that's what you went with.

DEAN MEYER

> You're right, little brother. Let me rephrase: at least I didn't BLOW MY LOAD of information this time.

HUDSON CASE

> [Gif of Harvey Specter pinching the bridge of his nose] This is why I drink.

DEAN MEYER

> You've been drinking since Prohibition. Calm down.

TROY WINTERS

> There's no way our girls didn't know, @Dev Menon. That means they've been keeping it from us.

DEV MENON

> Yeah? And what are we going to do about it?

Pine For Me

DEAN MEYER

Nothing. Unless you two are willing to have your dicks go into hibernation for the foreseeable future. Because that's exactly what will happen if you accuse them of keeping secrets.

TROY WINTERS

And given I'm getting married to my girl in a matter of weeks, fuck no, I'm not willing to do that.

DARIAN MEYER

Sorry @Patton Pierce. I'm going to have to tell Rani, too. I've never been able to keep anything from her.

DEAN MEYER

Christ, Dar. Grow a spine, brother. It's embarrassing.

GARRETT MEYER

Says the guy who asked his wife which brand of underwear she usually buys him.

DEAN MEYER

Yeah, well, some of us need reinforced stitching and extra room. Don't be bitter because we're twins, yet you got ripped off.

GARRETT MEYER

Ripped off? The only thing you got more of is hot air and ass hair.

DEAN MEYER

Listen, Mala has never once complained about having something to hold on to. Plus, I'm hung like a Shire horse, while you're hung like a Shetland pony.

GARRETT MEYER

A Shire horse? Bro, the only horse you're hung like is a My Little Pony.

DARIAN MEYER

Christ. Can I eat one meal without hearing about your dicks?

DEAN MEYER

Relax, bro. We're not leaving you out. You can be the miniature donkey—short, stubborn, and the kind no one wants to ride.

[**Darian Meyer** has left the chat]
[**Dean Meyer** has added **Darian Meyer** to the chat]

DEAN MEYER

Jesus. So sensitive.

HUDSON CASE

Can we table the Meyer brothers' dick-measuring contest and get back to the bomb Patton dropped on us? @Patton Pierce, I'm assuming the baby is yours and not dojang douche's?

TROY WINTERS

What's the dude's name? I remember Sarina telling me a while ago. Mikey? Miguel? Michelangelo?

PATTON PIERCE

Michael. And, fuck yeah, it's mine. But she's only five weeks along, so we're being tight-lipped. Or, we WERE before I screwed up.

Pine For Me

TROY WINTERS

Hmm. Michael seems too pedestrian. Could have sworn it was one of those "I peaked in high school" kind of names, like Mick or Mac.

DEV MENON

Congrats, Patton! That's amazing news.

DEAN MEYER

Wait, five weeks?! Wasn't Troy and Sarina's combined parties five weeks ago? You saying our plan for you to win her back actually worked??

PATTON PIERCE

Something like that. We're . . . still figuring it out.

GARRETT MEYER

You guys hooked up and are having a baby together. Clearly, there are still feelings there. What's there to figure out?

PATTON PIERCE

Honestly, I'm just trying not to fuck things up again. I want to show her I've changed and that she and the baby come first. Don't want her to write me off before I've even had a real chance.

DEV MENON

She won't. It's obvious to everyone that she still has feelings for you.

PATTON PIERCE

Feelings were never our problem. But getting Nisha's trust back for real? That's like trying to move a brick wall by asking nicely.

Swati M.H.

GARRETT MEYER

Not to pry, but if feelings were never the problem, what was?

PATTON PIERCE

In a nutshell? Me. I chased my career hard, always on the road. Nisha put up with it . . . until the night she miscarried for the second time. I wasn't there. She went through all of it on her own. After that, she realized she didn't want to keep living that way anymore. So, she left and never looked back.

We've been down this road before, and I'm terrified I'm going to screw it up again.

DARIAN MEYER

Shit, man. I'm sorry to hear about that.

HUDSON CASE

You won't screw it up. This time will be different because you'll be there every step of the way.

DEV MENON

Speaking of, I know you're still filming the baseball movie, but with this news, does this mean you're staying for good?

PATTON PIERCE

Fuck, yeah. If she'll have me.

TROY WINTERS

She will. But I feel you, man. Sarina made me work for every inch of progress. If stubbornness were an Olympic sport, the Arora sisters would win medals.

Pine For Me

DEAN MEYER

And when you say "every inch," how many are you referring to? Seven? Eight?

HUDSON CASE

Of course we couldn't go a day without Dean inquiring about Troy's dick.

TROY WINTERS

Wait, he inquires about my dick daily?

DEV MENON

And twice on Sundays.

TROY WINTERS

The fuck?

[Troy Winters has left the chat]
[Dean Meyers has added Troy Winters to the chat]

DEAN MEYER

Dude! Of course it's not DAILY! Jesus, what do you take me for? A fucking creeper?

HUDSON CASE

Yes.

DARIAN MENON

Yes.

PATTON PIERCE

Fuck. Nisha just texted me with a very detailed account of how she plans to rip my spleen from my body. [Gif of Chris Pratt running a hand down his face]

TROY WINTERS

Shit. Sarina must have messaged her as soon as I texted.

DEV MENON

I swear, these women have a faster network than the fucking CIA.

DEAN MEYER

@Patton Pierce, I wouldn't blame you if you hid in your house like a scared little bitch. I have half a mind to do the same every time I see your ex-wife. She's fucking intimidating, bro.

GARRETT MEYER

She lives right in front of you. There's no way you can just hide out in your house.

PATTON PIERCE

You're right. How do you think Ecuador is this time of year? I could move there and change my name.

DEV MENON

You could move to Neptune, and Nisha would track you down with nothing but her hair clipper and sheer rage.

DEAN MEYER

Facts. She once side-eyed me from across the room during a party, and I swear, my balls retracted into my body. In fact, my body started treating them like kidneys, processing my urine and shit. Well, not my actual shit because my colon still did that but, you get the idea.

HUDSON CASE

For fuck's sake, Dean. Have you ever considered just stopping at the funny part?

Pine For Me

DEAN MEYER

No, because stopping is for quitters and geriatrics like you.

HUDSON CASE

At least my balls still function as balls.

DEAN MEYER

They haven't been tested since the Reagan administration, so who the fuck knows?

PATTON PIERCE

As riveting as this is, I should really go and grovel to my wife.

GARRETT MEYER

You mean your pregnant, homicidal EX-wife?

PATTON PIERCE

Pregnant, homicidal, and hot-as-fuck, yup. I just hope she doesn't actually mean what she said about my spleen. Wish me luck, brothers.

TROY WINTERS

We're pooling our money to send flowers to your funeral.

PATTON PIERCE

Thanks for the vote of confidence, assholes.

TROY WINTERS

Anytime.

twenty-four
nisha

The Clam Jam

RANI MEYER

HOLD THE LINE! @Nisha Arora, what is this I'm hearing from Darian? You're PREGNANT?!

MALA MEYER

Wait, what??

RANI MEYER

Dean hasn't told you? The guys found out in their group chat.

MALA MEYER

Not yet. I think he was just called out to a house fire. Either that, or he got distracted taking dick pics to send me.

RANI MEYER

Ugh, gross. I swear, your husband needs an intervention. With garlic and a bat.

KAVI CASE

The man's permanent setting is "unhinged". Also, Nisha! You're pregnant?!

Pine For Me

RANI MEYER

Seriously @Nisha Arora. You have fifteen seconds to get on this chat and come clean. Why were we not informed earlier?

NISHA ARORA

Literally sharpening my knitting needles right now. I am going to MURDER Patton.

SARINA ARORA

Troy texted me asking about it, BTW.

PIPER MENON

Dev texted me the same thing. But seriously, since when did our men become bigger gossips than wine moms? I didn't tell Dev because I didn't want him to say anything to Patton until you were ready, Neesh.

RANI MEYER

So it's true? You ARE pregnant? And you didn't think to tell the rest of us?? What are we, chopped liver?

BELLA MEYER

OMG, congrats, Nisha! But also, say bye to those pineapple margaritas!

NISHA ARORA

Ugh, don't remind me. And it's not like that, Rani. I just found out, and I'm only five weeks along. Neither me nor Patton want to get excited too early, since you guys already know what happened the last two times.

Anyway, this isn't how I meant for everyone to find out. I was going to tell you all properly once I was a little further along and not puking up my guts anymore.

Swati M.H.

RANI MEYER

> Ugh, you played the "what happened last time" card, and now I can't be mad anymore. Fine, I get it. But GAH, I can't help being excited!

MALA MEYER

> Oh my gosh! This is the best news I've heard all week! Not the puking part, but the pregnant part.

KAVI CASE

> Wait, did you say five weeks? As in, the weekend of the joint parties?

PIPER MENON

> As in, the night she came in looking like a dominatrix in all that black leather. <wink emoji> <fire emoji>

RANI MEYER

> I mean, I don't blame Patton AT ALL. I almost switched teams that night after seeing our girl in that dress.

BELLA MEYER

> I have to ask, and feel free to tell me I'm crossing the line, Neesh, but . . . didn't you guys go through rounds of IVF to get pregnant last time? And this just happened naturally?

MALA MEYER

> Exactly, that's the surprising part. The "pregnant" part, not so much.

Pine For Me

NISHA ARORA

What do you mean, "the pregnant part, not so much"?! Did you guys see this in my master plan binder somewhere? Because I didn't.

KAVI CASE

Clearly, the whole section titled "How to Avoid Getting Knocked Up by Your Ex" in your master plan binder needed work. <shrug emoji>

MALA MEYER

But with the way you two have been hooking up, we all knew SOMETHING was bound to happen. I just figured you'd get back together for real first. Apparently, your uterus decided to bypass all that drama!

NISHA ARORA

"For real first" as in, getting married again??

MALA MEYER

No, not necessarily. But I don't think anyone in this beautiful bitch brigade has ruled that out as a possibility for you guys.

NISHA ARORA

Marriage again? BAHAH! Yeah, no.

SARINA ARORA

Didn't you literally call yourself his girlfriend yesterday? But sure, marriage is a stretch. Keep lying to yourself, sis.

> **NISHA ARORA**
>
> Marriage ISN'T a stretch when it happens the first time. But a second time with the same person?? That IS a stretch. My uterus might have gotten a jump start, but I'm not insane.

SARINA ARORA

> Is it insanity to believe that people can change? That they can grow and learn from their mistakes? I've said this before, he's not the same man you left.

PIPER MENON

> Also, let's not pretend you're not still in love with him. Because your browser history of his name over the years would prove otherwise.

BELLA MEYER

> Wait, before we go further, @Nisha Arora, can I ask how he took the news when you told him?

KAVI CASE

> Yeah, did he seem happy?

> **NISHA ARORA**
>
> He's . . . really happy. Even though part of me wanted him to hold back a little. But he said things I wasn't expecting.

MALA MEYER

> Like what? Don't leave us hanging, girl!

Pine For Me

NISHA ARORA

> That he moved here for me. That he's cutting back on work for us and for his own happiness. That fame meant nothing without me. That over the past seven years, he's been working on becoming the man I deserve.

> And that he plans to stay.

RANI MEYER

> [Gif of a woman fainting] Lord. With his husky voice and those fuck-me eyes, bet he had your vagina wanting to jump on and make a twin. <wink emoji>

KAVI CASE

> [Gif of woman trying to solve a hard math problem] Pretty sure that's not how it works, babe, but I'm all for Nisha trying.

BELLA MEYER

> But also, he MOVED HERE FOR YOU?! He PLANS TO STAY?! Nisha, isn't that exactly what you wanted?

PIPER MENON

> Can we all acknowledge how I predicted this? I told you he'd be dusting out your girl parts, and boom! Pregnant! Honestly, I need to hit some tables in Vegas.

NISHA ARORA

> Look, I'm not saying all that wasn't great to hear. It's exactly what I've wanted him to say. But SAYING and DOING are very different things.

Swati M.H.

> We're having a baby <crossed fingers emoji> <prayer hands emoji>, but that doesn't mean I have forgotten that he let me down before. Who's to say he won't again?

SARINA ARORA

> Okay, you're scared. Totally valid. No one knows how you feel better than me, given how standoffish I was with Troy for so long. But being scared doesn't mean you refuse to see that the man has ACTUALLY changed.

RANI MEYER

> Exactly! He moved across the street for you. He's scaling back on work. He surprises you with French toast from that restaurant you love. Those are all ACTIONS!

PIPER MENON

> Let's not forget that he dicks you whenever and wherever you please!

BELLA MEYER

> It's okay to be cautious, Neesh, but be cautiously optimistic. Because the longer you wait, the more you're just denying your chance at something real.

PIPER MENON

> Translation: stop being a pussy about this pussy situation.

NISHA ARORA

> FINE! Maybe he's actually changed, and maybe there's hope of a second chance for us. But don't start looking for bridesmaids dresses yet. I'm not promising marriage just because he knocked me up with his pussy-duster dick!

Pine For Me

PIPER MENON

BAHAH! Pussy-duster! I'm dead! That's going straight into my vocab for describing a good dick.

SARINA ARORA

Baby steps. Ooh, and a baby, too! <wink emoji> Gah! I can't believe I'm going to be an aunt!

NISHA ARORA

What did I say about getting too excited?

PIPER MENON

Does that mean we can't even throw you a baby shower later?

NISHA ARORA

That's exactly what that means. No celebrations until I have this baby in my arms.

SARINA ARORA

Ugh, fine. We get it. But once that baby is here, we're not holding back!

Since we're on the topic, are you still good to keep Rome and Pearl this weekend? Troy and I are meeting the wedding planner in Cabo San Lucas to check out the wedding venue in person.

NISHA ARORA

Of course! Patton is actually bringing Bob over, and we've got a whole day planned with them.

Swati M.H.

SARINA ARORA

> They are already pumped about spending time with their aunt Nisha, but when I tell them Uncle Patton and Bob will be there, too . . . they're going to go nuts.

KAVI CASE

> OMG, is Bob still using your Darth Vader vibrator as his chew toy?

NISHA ARORA

> Worse. He broke it, so now it repeats, "I am your father," every few minutes. Which is deeply disturbing on multiple levels, especially since we have a baby on the way.

RANI MEYER

> I just snorted coffee through my nose.

PIPER MENON

> Or maybe this is a sign from the universe to call your baby Luke.

NISHA ARORA

> Yeah, that's exactly how I want to explain my kid's name origin. "Well, sweetie, you see, Mommy's dildo chose your name for us."

MALA MEYER

> HAHAH! Since we're on the subject of adorable kids and making babies, @Sarina Arora, when is the next baby Winters coming?

SARINA ARORA

> Let's get through the wedding at the end of the month before you even think about asking me that question.

Pine For Me

MALA MEYER

So, if I'm reading between the lines correctly, you're saying Troy's swimmers are on standby until the honeymoon?

SARINA ARORA

No, if you're reading between the lines correctly, I'm saying that I need to focus on the wedding before I let him knock me up.

PIPER MENON

"Let him"? Girl, we've seen the way you look at him. You're going to be begging for Troy's baby gravy before the cake-cutting.

NISHA ARORA

Here comes another bout of morning sickness . . .

SARINA ARORA

Ew. Please refrain from calling my fiancé's sperm "baby gravy".

KAVI CASE

Seconding that. Piper, I'll Venmo you ten bucks if you promise to retire "baby gravy" from your vocabulary.

PIPER MENON

No worries. We'll stick to Troy's penis pudding, then.

[**Nisha Arora** has left the chat]
[**Piper Menon** has added **Nisha Arora** to the chat]

RANI MEYER

OH MY GOD. <Holding back vomit emoji>

Swati M.H.

KAVI CASE

[Gif of woman screaming, "My eyes! My eyes!"]

PIPER MENON

Okay, fine! I promise to use only wholesome phrases like "mouthwash" and "love juice" from now on.

[**Nisha Arora** has left the chat]

PIPER MENON

Sigh. I'm not bringing her back. She'd just leave again once I suggested "throat yogurt".

[**Sarina Arora** has left the chat]
[**Bella Meyer** has left the chat]
[**Kavi Case** has left the chat]
[**Mala Meyer** has left the chat]

PIPER MENON

Rani? You still riding this out with me?

RANI MEYER

Figured I'd see how many more you had.

PIPER MENON

Oh, I could go on. Vanilla ice cream, banana juice, albino tadpoles, poor man's custard, baby shower, grandma's hair gel.

RANI MEYER

Okay, I'm tapping out.

PIPER MENON

Penis colada, protein punch, cock snot.

[**Rani Meyer** has left the chat]

twenty-five
nisha

Hollywood Heartthrobs In
Frilly Aprons

Pearl giggles as Bob sniffs her from head to toe, her little hand jutting out to pet his ears. *"He's so big, Aunt Nisha,"* she signs. *"And his ears are so long."*

I smile from my place behind the kitchen island, where I have several tomatoes and an onion laying on a cutting board. I had intended to slice them, but I'm too engrossed in watching Pearl and Rome interact with Bob.

It's not the first time they've met, but Bob's theatrics never fail to entertain them.

"Where's his toy?" Rome speaks while he signs for Pearl's benefit before crouching down to scratch Bob's chin. "You know, the mini baseball bat that looks like Darth Vader?"

I roll my lips together. Clearly, my nine-year-old nephew has come up with his own definition of my vibrator since no one has explained to him what it really is. We've all just stuck with calling it "Bob's special toy". And really, from some angles, it does look like a talking baseball bat stuck on repeat.

I'm just about to answer when we hear a muffled mechanical voice from somewhere between my couch cushions. *"I'm your father. I'm your father."*

Bob, who was melting into the affection from the kids—

his hind leg twitching with happiness—immediately perks up at the sound and hobbles over to the couch. Bob must have buried his toy there this morning while Patton and I were "preoccupied".

What? It was the only time we knew we'd get for a while since the kids were due to arrive an hour later to spend the weekend with us while Troy and Sarina were in Mexico.

Speaking of, I can't wait to catch up with my sister to find out how she liked the venue. They're doing a small wedding with just their closest family and friends, but no matter the size, planning a wedding is stressful.

Needless to say, we're all looking forward to being a part of their big day. And now, it seems I, Sarina's maid of honor, will have a date to take to it.

Bob emerges with my dildo clutched between his jowls before parading it around the living room like a show pony. I'm just glad he's obsessed with the dildo instead of my houseplants. I still have PTSD from watching him "water" my Thai Constellation Monstera that first time.

But I will reluctantly admit, the beast has grown on me.

Whether he's sensing the baby or because we've grown closer over the last few weeks, he's been even more attentive, shoving his head under my palm until I give in, or keeping his eyes glued on me from across the room like one of those creepy illusion paintings.

Plus, he's a complete goofball with antics that rival a Victorian damsel. Just the sight of a butterfly can send him into a dramatic floor flop as if he's been shot. Let's just say, it makes our evening walks very entertaining.

Pearl laughs again, her long red hair swinging around her waist. She's almost five but tall for her age, with the same shade of hazel eyes as her famous baseball player dad.

For three years, Troy raised Pearl as a single dad while being the star pitcher for the Blazers. It's no small feat with a deaf daughter who needed special attention and communication, especially when he was often on the road.

But after his elbow injury sidelined him a little over a year and a half ago, something changed. I think taking care of Pearl at home made him realize what he'd been missing. And though he'd returned for another season post-recovery, his heart wasn't with baseball anymore.

It didn't hurt that he'd also fallen hard for my sister—who'd been divorced from her douchey ex-husband for years—and seamlessly stepped into a father role for Rome, too. Now, they're the epitome of a perfect blended family with Rome learning baseball from one of the best in the league while Pearl communicates effortlessly with Sarina.

Our mother was deaf, so both my sister and I learned sign language almost before we could speak. But what's been incredible to watch is how quickly Rome has picked up ASL, determined to speak to his little sister in her own language. They're inseparable, as if they've been siblings their whole lives.

I run a hand over my still-flat stomach. As much as I love their bond, I secretly hope my sister and Troy decide to have a baby so my little one has someone closer to her age.

And yes, *her*, because I'm fairly positive I'm going to have a girl. I may not have evidence to back up my claim since it'll be weeks before I get that ultrasound, but call it mother's intuition.

What surprised me was Patton's genuine excitement about the possibility. In fact, he'd grinned as we lay tangled in my sheets this morning and I mentioned it, as if he was already preparing to be wrapped around her pinky finger.

I'd been nestled against him, my bare back to his chest, as we both tried to catch our breaths. He'd tucked a sweaty strand of hair behind my ear before kissing the shell of it, sending a fresh wave of goosebumps tingling down my arms.

"You take my breath away, Little Borealis."

"Careful there, Mr. Pierce," I'd teased, brushing my lips against the back of his hand. *"Keep saying things like that when I'm a sweaty mess and I might never shower again."*

"And you think I'd object to that?"

I shook my head. *"You're crazy."*

"Always, when it comes to you."

I'd pressed my cheek against our intertwined fingers, feeling the metal from our matching bracelets against my skin. I still couldn't believe that after all these years, neither of us thought to take it off. I guess we both knew, regardless if we'd ever be in each other's lives again, our friendship wasn't something we ever wanted to forget.

My heart swelled at having him back in my life—a man I'd never stopped thinking about, never stopped loving, even when I'd only recently started admitting it to myself.

But admitting it to him was different.

We'd thrown those words around when we were young and thought love was the only ingredient to conquering everything. But now I know better.

While love was an essential ingredient we had plenty of, reliability and follow-through were the two others I wanted to see more of. Because when I finally told him I loved him this time around, I wanted to make sure I'd never have to compete with Hollywood for his attention.

"What do you think we should name her?" I asked, breaking the comfortable silence that had settled around us.

I could feel his smile against my neck. "Her, huh? You seem sure about that."

I turned in his arms, looking up at him. "You don't want a girl?"

"Baby, I will take whatever you give me." His hand lowered to my stomach. *"But if she's anything like you, then I hope she has your eyes and your stubborn streak."*

Pine For Me

"That's what you want our daughter to inherit from me? My stubbornness?"

"Yep. Otherwise, how else would I know the sheer joy of having two women in my life who always think they're right?"

I poked him in his stomach for his sarcasm, pretending to be annoyed before he swallowed my giggles with his kiss.

The sliding door whooshes open, bringing in the scent of grilled meat and pulling me out of the reverie. I hadn't realized I'd gotten lost in my thoughts while the kids dissolved into giggles, chasing Bob around the living room.

I turn to find my devastatingly handsome ex-husband filling up the doorway, holding a pair of tongs in his hand, his hair a little windswept and his eyes crinkling around the corners. His gaze sweeps from the kids and Bob, turning warm when it finds me.

I can't even help the chuckle that escapes my lips as my eyes scroll down his form, magazine-cover worthy, if magazines featured Hollywood heartthrobs in frilly aprons that barely touched their muscular thighs.

The plaid apron has "My Aunt is a Baddie" written in glittery cursive. Pearl's sheer pink fairy wings can be seen sprouting from his shoulders, while her sparkling plastic tiara sits atop his dark hair and one sparkling earring hangs off his left ear.

Honestly, this picture of Patton, domestic and so fucking adorable, on a magazine cover would send the world into a tizzy.

He looks absolutely ridiculous, and yet, I've never wanted him more. The way he patiently sat there while the kids poked and prodded him, getting him ready for our barbecue? God . . .

I know some of this is likely from the pregnancy hormones, but watching him get fake blush and eye shadow smeared on by my niece literally made me want to take him to my bedroom and ask him to knock me up again.

It isn't the first time the kids have hung out with Patton, having seen him practicing pitches with Troy at the old stadium nearby for Patton's upcoming film. And though they're still getting to know him, they definitely got comfortable with him today.

"How are those burgers coming along?" I ask, pursing my lips when I see the pretend stern look on his face.

He acts like he's exasperated wearing the costume, but he's not fooling anyone. I know he secretly loves that this gives him a chance to rebuild connections with a nephew whose life he missed out on, a nephew I kept him from getting to know, if I'm being honest. And Pearl, who has become family through Troy.

It's a guilt I don't know if I'll ever forgive myself for, but looking at him now, seeing the way the kids just accept him as their own, I wonder if he's already claiming the space his absence left behind.

He straightens his skewed tiara, walking inside and putting the tongs down on the counter. "They've got a few minutes to go." He gently wiggles the serrated knife from my hand, placing it on the cutting board before cradling my face. "How about I get you some sparkling water and you go put your legs up on the couch? I can take over here. Once the burgers are done, we'll head out to the yard."

"There's macaroni baking in the oven, too."

"I can get it out once it's done." He leans over to look inside the oven. "Jesus, sweetheart, you planning to feed an army?"

"I made extra to box up for a few of my friends at the shelter," I say, thinking about Hector and Abby.

Abby's been on my mind lately. And though I still don't know why she's here or what she's looking for, she's getting more comfortable being around me, different from the fidgety, almost-silent woman I first met. Part of me thinks I could even broach the subject . . . offer to help her find whatever it is she's looking for without her clamming up on me.

I reach for the knife. "Patton, you don't need to do everything. I can slice a few vegetables. I'm pregnant, not an invalid."

"I never said you're an invalid. But I'd hate for this sexy apron-tiara-wings combo to not reach its maximum potential. Let me show you how good I look cutting vegetables."

I tilt my head, giving him a be-for-real look.

Patton pinches my chin, tilting my head up to brush his lips over mine. "Please? Let me feed and water you."

My chest squeezes as memories of him saying that same silly line to me so many times dances in my vision. And just like that, between his gentle caress and those ridiculous fairy wings, I cave faster than a five-minute Target run that ends with three cartfuls of throw pillows I didn't need.

Ugh, the man makes it so hard to negotiate. Or think straight.

"Ew! Aunt Nisha?!" Rome cries, flinging himself onto the couch with his hands plastered over his eyes like he has sand in them. "You and Uncle Patton kissing is making my eyes burn."

Pearl immediately copies him, launching herself next to him. She has no idea why she's doing it, but if her brother is being dramatic, then she's going all in.

I take in the one-earringed fairy-man still cradling my face, the two melodramatic kids in my living room, and the horse-like dog with Darth Vader's head sticking out of one end of his mouth and wonder where it all went wrong. How did I end up with this off-brand cast of The Muppets movie directed by Tim Burton?

And yet, I wouldn't have it any other way.

"Fine!" I say, throwing up my arms. "But only because you

look cute, and apparently, I have a weakness for men with wings."

Patton kisses my forehead. "That's my girl."

I settle onto the couch between the two drama queens, who are still covering their eyes like they're shielding themselves from a gruesome scene in a horror movie.

"You two are ridiculous," I say, tickling both their sides and making them wiggle until they're squealing. When they catch their breaths, I look over at Rome, signing as I speak. "That reminds me . . . I made you both something."

"What is it?" Pearl signs, her red hair now a complete mess. *"Is it another friendship bracelet?"*

"No." I shake my head, recalling how the three of us strung friendship bracelets together the last time they were here. I sign the rest to both Rome and Pearl, my hands moving to form each word. *"It's in the bottom drawer of my dresser. Want to go hunt for it? You'll know which one is yours."*

"Yes!" Rome calls out, already heading to my room with an excited Pearl in tow.

Bob gets up from his spot near the window to follow the kids, coming back when he's halfway there to pick up the dildo he forgot. It continues to say, *"I'm your father,"* all the way to my room.

I sigh, leaning my head back on the couch, watching Patton move around in the kitchen, his fairy wings getting in the way of practically everything. When he catches me watching him, he shakes his shoulders and waggles his brows at me like he's Tinkerbell's weird and inappropriate cousin.

I burst out laughing, feeling my chest flood with a warmth I don't think I've ever felt before, not even for him. It's like someone snuck a space heater inside my ribs. I thought I'd felt it all before when it came to this man, but this . . . this feels different. It's not a new feeling per se, but one that feels like it's been dialed up to the max setting.

Rome's voice fills the room as both he and Pearl come running back, having found their gifts. "You knitted all the planets in the solar system on this scarf!"

"Not just that," I say and sign. Both kids are admiring their new scarves with so much love, you'd think I'd gifted them their own ponies. "The planets should all be proportionally correct. I did my research, little man."

Rome flings his arms around my neck. "Thank you, *masi*."

I lift a brow. "Wow, you finally call me masi when your mom's not around to hear you, huh?"

Masi, the word for aunt in Hindi and many Indian dialects, in fact, is something my sister has been trying to get him to call me. But the little booger refuses to do it, until now, apparently.

Rome shrugs before we both look at Pearl.

"You like your scarf, Pearl-girl?" I ask, using the nickname I've given her.

She nods, signing. *"It has fairies with wings and dresses in all the colors! I can't wait to wear it to school!"*

Bob's sharp bark has us jumping out of an embrace. He's sniffing the corner of my front door with so much interest, I'm worried he's going to get lightheaded.

There's a knock on my door, and I start to get off the couch, announcing, "I'll get it."

"Absolutely not," Patton calls from the kitchen, already moving to my door. "You stay put. I've got it."

I roll my eyes at him, feigning exasperation, just as he swings the door open, revealing my dad and Emanuel on the other side.

Wearing one of his many Hawaiian shirts, Dad's holding a covered cake dish in one hand and a paper bag in the other. His giant of a boyfriend holds Sapphire's mesh carrier in his hands. Not exaggerating, that carrier probably costs more than some high-end Chanel bags. Sapphire's disapproving white-furred face can be seen looking out from the mesh window, her eyes darting from the fairy-man to Bob. I don't have to be an animal mind reader to know she's wondering how the high-society likes of her got stuck coming to this circus.

"Patton, darling!" Dad exclaims, walking inside without needing a formal invite. He sets the cake dish and paper bag on the table in my foyer before pulling Patton into a huge hug. "Look at you. Still devastatingly handsome as ever, even in . . ." He steps back, taking in Patton's ensemble. "Well, this is certainly a new look for you. You're giving haute couture meets forest woodland creature. Honestly, I love it. I may even have to commission a painting."

Patton rubs the back of his neck sheepishly, the tops of his cheeks a little red. "I've had to do a lot of costume changes in my line of work, but I can't say I've ever worn something quite this . . . sparkly. Your grandkids are very persuasive, Suraj."

"I'd say that was less persuasion and more welcoming you back into the family."

Emanuel places Sapphire's carrier on the ground, and she immediately launches into her signature snarl at Bob. Patton's droopy-eyed dog just stares at her for a moment like he couldn't be bothered before trotting back to get his prized possession. He places the dildo in front of her crate like a peace offering, making her bark when Vader's mechanical voice streams through it.

"I'm your father."

Dad frowns down at the object near his precious dog-daughter like it's going to slither its way into her carrier and contaminate her royal bloodline before he's distracted by two pairs of little arms around his legs.

"Grandpa!" Rome says happily. "Are you here for our barbecue?"

Dad runs gentle hands over both Pearl and Rome's hair

before signing for Pearl's benefit. "Oh no, darlings. Emanuel and I are headed to the winery for a tasting of their reserved wines. We're just dropping off my famous French toast bundt cake and *ladoos*."

"Ooh, I love your bundt cakes, Grandpa!" Rome's hands work as he speaks, peeking inside the paper bag. "But what are *ladoos*?"

"They're Indian sweets made with flour, ghee, and sugar. I used your grandma's recipe, which was passed down to her by her mother. These *ladoos* have walnuts and dried fruits as well, which are supposed to help during pregnancy and even postpartum." Dad bops Rome on the nose. "But don't worry, you can eat them even if you're not pregnant."

Rome's eyes light up. *"Can we have some now, Aunt Nisha?"*

"Before lunch?" I ask, making my way over to them.

"Please?" Rome and Pearl sign the same word like they're telepathically communicating.

I sigh. *"Fine, but only if you call me masi again."*

"Oh, fine," Rome grumbles, hands moving as he signs. *"Can we have a piece of cake and a ladoo before our burgers, masi?"*

I smile. *"Okay, but you can't tell your parents when they call and check in from Cabo."*

The kids squeal, rushing toward the kitchen with the cake dish and paper bag.

I wrap my arms around my father, breathing in his floral cologne, before placing a kiss on his cheek. At five-foot-four—three inches shorter than me and Sarina—he's not a tall man, but where he lacks height, he makes up for in personality.

"Thank you for the cake and *ladoos*, Dad. You really didn't have to do all that."

He flicks a hand at me, his bangles jingling. "Oh, you stop. In your condition, I want you to eat everything your heart desires." He pats my cheek before looking at Patton. "And how is my son-in-law treating you?"

Patton and I exchange an awkward glance. It's been ages since Dad's referred to him as his son-in-law—at least in Patton's vicinity—but something in his tone suggests it wasn't a slip of the tongue.

I narrow my eyes at Patton. "He's not letting me lift a finger, if that's what you're asking."

Dad squeezes Patton's bicep with mostly affection, and perhaps a little flirting—because, of course, he does. "That's exactly what I wanted to hear. I was just telling Emanuel how much I've missed our monthly calls."

My head snaps to Patton, who looks like he's been zapped by a live wire. "Pardon? Your *monthly calls*?"

"Oh, my." Dad places his fingers on his lips, feigning innocence. "Did I accidentally say that out loud?"

"Dad—"

"Now, before you get that look on your face, darling," Dad cuts me off. "You should know that divorce or no divorce, I have loved this boy like he was my own since you were sixteen, watching *Family Guy* reruns on our couch. Just because you two couldn't figure out your crap, didn't mean I was ready to lose a son."

Vulnerability and gratefulness shines in Patton's eyes.

"You had people, Nisha," Dad continues. "You had me, your sister, and Piper. Yes, you went through something extremely traumatic, but so did this man. And he repented every single day for the hurt he caused you. But what sort of father would I be if I left him with no one to talk to during the worst time of his life?"

Patton runs a hand down his face, taking in a shaky breath. I know him well enough to know he's holding back tears.

Jaw tightening, he nods at my dad with so much affection in his eyes, it squeezes my lungs. "Thank you, Suraj. I"—

he clears his throat—"I wouldn't be standing here without you."

My eyes widen. "What does that even mean? That you wouldn't be standing here without him?"

Patton squeezes his eyes shut, taking a moment to ground himself. "I went through some dark times, Neesh. Times when I needed someone who knew me—*actually* knew me and wanted nothing from me. Your dad was . . ." He pauses, his throat bobbing. "He was always a phone call away. And when I told him how much I still wanted you back, he told me how you'd be at that tournament in L.A. He's also the one who gave me your new phone number."

My mouth drops open as I look at my dad, who simply shrugs.

"Oh, I know you're my daughter, but stop with your theatrics, darling. I kept my mouth shut for six years when it came to your whereabouts, aside from generally letting him know you were doing okay. But the man would not shut up about you. And you were no better . . . what with your online stalking and watching each of his movies dozens of times. I decided that enough was enough. I had to do something! So, I may have casually suggested that he show up at that tournament to win you back. But, of course, my daughters are nothing if not stubborn mules. The poor guy had to pitch an entire movie idea and move in across the street from you just to get your attention."

"Oh. My. God," I say slowly, placing my hand over my forehead, wondering if I'm coming down with a fever. "I was wondering how you got my number and texted me with the 'Hey' all those weeks ago."

Patton squints at me accusingly. "Which you never responded to, by the way."

I point a finger at my dad. "You scheming, underhanded—"

Completely ignoring my meltdown, Dad turns to my ex-husband. "Yes, well . . . Patton, I think you can take it from here, can't you, son? My work is done, and I do believe that wine is calling my name."

"Dad!" I call at his retreating back, half-shocked, half-amused. "Are you serious right now? You're going to drop a bombshell like that and just . . . leave?"

"Sweetheart, let this go." Dad flicks his wrist again. "Focus on your present and future. The past has weighed you down long enough, don't you think?"

My shoulders slump as the truth in his words land like gentle slaps. For a moment, I'm frozen and then, all at once, a stream of tears rolls down my cheeks like a damn waterfall. *Stupid pregnancy hormones!*

But it's not just the hormones; it's the realization that Dad spoke to Patton regularly. Comforted him, cared for him when my ex needed someone. And he did so while respecting my boundaries and wishes but understanding my heart.

Dad rarely meddled over the years, though he did call me a stubborn mule on more than one occasion. So as much as I want to be angry about his hand in this, I can't be. Because my dad—someone both my sister and I have always agreed is the greatest father in the universe—has wanted nothing but the best for us.

So yes, he schemed a little. But I'll forgive him for it.

Dad gathers me into a hug. "Oh, sweetie, I'm so sorry. I didn't mean to make you cry."

I sniffle into his collar. "No, I'm not upset."

"Are you sure? Because you seem perfectly intent on ruining my four-hundred-dollar handwoven shirt with your snot."

I snort-laugh. "You have a hundred of the same ones in your closet."

"And now, it seems, I'll have one less."

I squeeze him tighter. "I love you, Daddy. Thank you for . . . for being you."

He kisses my temple. "I love you, too, daughter. Now, go dry those tears and see if you can sneak off to get some vitamin D with your handsome Hollywood hunk here."

I groan, knowing he doesn't mean vitamin D from the sun.

twenty-six
nisha

Never Again, Baby

Whoosh, whoosh, whoosh, whoosh.

Patton's fingers tighten around mine as the sounds of her fast-paced heartbeats resound against the static, filling the silence inside the private ultrasound room.

The black-and-white image on the screen is almost indecipherable, but there's no doubt about it—our baby is in there. A baby girl, if my intuition is correct.

It's not typical to get an ultrasound at less than seven weeks, but with my history of fertility problems and miscarriages, my doctor wanted me to get a transvaginal ultrasound to ensure things were progressing as expected.

"Well, congratulations, Mom and Dad, everything looks perfect," Dr. Gilbert says, adjusting the wand slightly to get a better view. "The embryo is measuring at about seven weeks, with a strong heartbeat. I'd say you both could start cautiously celebrating."

I let out a breath, feeling a weight come off my shoulders. After my last miscarriage, I'd given up my dreams of becoming a mother, just like I'd given up knitting tiny baby booties and sweaters. I never imagined I'd be lying on another ultrasound table, listening to the beating of another heart, confirming life growing inside me. But hearing Dr. Gilbert's words floods me with so much relief, it's almost disorienting.

For years, I've lived with the belief that pregnancy wasn't in the cards for me, and I'd trained myself to stop wishing for something I couldn't have, content to just be a good aunt to my nephew, instead.

But now, hearing that strong heartbeat and knowing she's really in there, I'm remembering all over again how desperately I wanted this.

But celebrating and making big announcements? I'm not nearly ready enough for that. I'll celebrate my heart out once this baby is actually in my arms, when this constant fear has finally transformed into the joy I'm too afraid to feel right now.

Patton brings our joined hands to his lips, brushing a kiss over my knuckles. His eyes stay fixed on the grainy image. We've been in this exact spot twice before, but this time feels fundamentally different. He's completely present and invested, like nothing matters beyond this room.

The last time we were here, his phone vibrated nonstop in his pocket. And though he didn't answer it, I remember his attention being split with each vibration, putting a damper on the moment.

Today, it hasn't buzzed once.

In fact, I've noticed he puts it on some sort of hibernation mode whenever we're spending time together, as if he's creating a protected bubble just for us.

I remember writing those words on a list years ago—that I wished I meant more to him than any phone call, that he'd be present instead of just physically there. I hadn't intended for him to find that list, and not only did he find it, but he took my words to heart and is showing me with every action how committed he is to me and our baby.

"We're doing this, Little Borealis," Patton whispers against the back of my hand, his eyes slightly glassy. "We're really doing this."

"I think so." I swallow the fear creeping into my words. "I hope so."

Because I don't know if I can handle another loss...

"I'll give you two some privacy," Dr. Gilbert says, setting the wand aside and dimming the lights. "I know it's a lot to process. Given your history, I can understand the trepidation as well, but I want to reassure you that things seem to be looking good. The less you stress, the better it'll be for both you and the baby."

I nod. "Thank you."

"There are wipes on the counter right there for cleaning up." She tips her chin toward a box of wipes. "Take your time. Just press the call button when you're ready, and I'll come back with your photos."

She's just about to exit when Patton stops her.

"Dr. Gilbert, just another question. Nisha and I are headed to Cabo in two weeks for her sister's wedding. Are there any precautions we need to take?"

Dr. Gilbert glances over at me with a smile. "Congratulations to your sister on her wedding."

"Thank you," I say. "I'm looking forward to it."

"I bet. And you'll be nine weeks along by that time, so travel is fine as long as you're feeling well. Just remember to be careful with sun exposure, don't overexert yourself or lift anything heavy, and just listen to your body."

"I will."

"How has your morning sickness been? Still pretty rough?"

My thoughts go to this morning and the two times last night. I'd spent the night at Patton's, and each time, he'd followed me into the bathroom, holding my hair back as I heaved into the toilet. Then, he'd wait until I drank some water before wrapping a protective arm around me until I fell asleep.

"It's been challenging," I answer, my hand squeezing Patton's. "But manageable."

Dr. Gilbert nods knowingly. "The nausea should wane in the next few weeks. In the meantime, eat small but frequent meals and stay hydrated."

"I will," I assure her with a smile, but I can't help the prick of fear inside my gut. My hand travels down to my stomach instinctively, protective but trembling.

What if something goes wrong?
What if I lose this baby, too?
What if I get sick and need medical attention?

My spiraling thoughts must be evident on my face because as soon as Dr. Gilbert leaves and the door clicks shut, I feel the warmth of Patton's hands framing my face.

"Hey." His eyes search mine. "I can practically see those wheels turning. What's going on in that head of yours?"

I guess there's something to be said for someone knowing you as long as Patton and I have known each other, because he can read me like a book.

I try to force a smile, but it wobbles. "I'm scared. What if something happens while we're in Cabo? What if I—"

"Neesh." Patton's voice cuts through before I can ramble, firm yet gentle. "Look at me, baby. You're going to be fine. I've hired a private nurse who'll be on call while we're there. And if anything at all feels off, we'll be on the first flight back home. I promise."

I nod, letting the certainty in his words anchor me.

This isn't going to be like last time. None of it is going to be like last time.

I'll have my husband there, and one day soon, I'll have my baby, too.

Patton's thumb skims the top of my cheek, a glint of

something mischievous in his eyes. "Now, did you hear what the doctor said about not overexerting yourself?"

"As if you'd even let me."

A sly smile quirks up his lips as his hand travels down, skimming the side of my breast. His thumb grazes my nipple through the thin material before sliding lower, his fingers disappearing beneath the hem of my hospital gown, finding my bare center.

"Guess that means I'll be doing all the work."

"Patton—"

"Shh." His lips brush mine as his fingers circle my clit. "Let me help you relax, baby. You don't have to do anything but lay back for me."

My eyes bounce between his, hesitation and desire at war inside me.

This is completely reckless and utterly inappropriate. We might be in a private room and told to push the call button when we're ready, but if someone walked in here right now . . .

"Patton, the door isn't even locked," I whisper, feeling my body revving up despite my protest.

"Then you'll just have to be quiet for me."

Putting a halt to my train of thought, his tongue sweeps against the seam of my lips, parting them. And when it collides with my tongue, I moan into his mouth.

His fingers continue their ministrations, dipping down to find the wetness at my entrance. "That's it, baby. Now, spread your legs wider."

I do as he says, lacing my fingers through his hair, feeling his mouth ravish mine. My core tightens, begging to be filled as my desire coils tighter.

God, what are we doing?

Yet, I don't want him to stop.

Patton dips the tip of one finger into my entrance, and with just that slight pressure, I go from simmering to high heat. It's been like this ever since I got pregnant, my hormones rampant and my body ready to ignite with the slightest touch.

I bow against the ultrasound table, trembling and hungry for more. "Oh, God. Patton . . ."

Patton makes a satisfied growl deep in his chest, telling me how much he loves when I gasp out his name. His large hand cups my entire pussy, covering it with his palm like he's rewarding me.

"God, this pussy is so soft," he murmurs against my throat. "So wet and ready for me."

His fingers roll slow, torturous circles over me like we're not on a time limit, like there isn't a doctor outside, probably wondering when we'll push the call button for her.

Finally, a finger slips inside, gliding in deep and slick. It's slightly wetter than usual, a subtle reminder of the ultrasound gel I never wiped off. A gasp escapes my lips as my walls clench around him, and I lose myself to the moment and his adept touch.

Gone is the worry about anyone outside; gone are the fears about the present or the future. Because right now, all I want is for him to make me forget my own name.

I swivel my hips, urging his finger in and out.

"More," I beg. "I need more, Patton."

He takes my nipple in his mouth, sucking it through the gown's fabric, and I groan. God, he's always been so good at giving my body the kind of attention it needs. He gently bites and tugs, and my hips grind against his hand.

He licks and flicks my nipple, now visible through the wet fabric, making me arch again when he blows on it, making it feel cold against my skin. "Want me to add another finger?"

"Yes. Maybe add two more."

He laughs, kissing my collarbone. "Always so greedy for me."

Pulling out the finger inside me, he pushes back in with one more, testing and teasing as I writhe against him.

"What do you think?" he asks, rocking his fingers in and out of me. "Can you really take another?"

I can barely think, my chest rising and falling, feeling like I'm about to explode. "If I can take your cock, I can take three of your fingers. Hell, just put me out of my misery and give me your dick."

He chuckles, his shoulders shaking under my palms as he adds another digit. "I'm not getting inside you, baby; I just want you to get off. I'll fuck you as many times as you want once we get home."

Brushing kisses over my neck and jaw, he finger-fucks me while my eyelids flutter closed. My head tips back and my mouth falls open as the first flickers of euphoria crest inside me, rippling from my core like a broken dam. Every nerve ending sharpens as the need to culminate this delicious burn of pleasure takes over all my senses.

His bergamot and minty scent mixed with the scent of my own arousal, the sounds of our heavy breathing—Patton as turned-on as I am, even though I'm the one getting all the pleasure—along with the slick sounds of him pumping in and out, has me so revved-up, I'm sweating.

A part of me wants to prolong the moment, to edge myself from coming, even though we've been here way longer than any "private moment" should be. But I know I won't be able to, not with his fingers thrusting inside me like it was what they were made to do. And then, I know I'm doomed in the best way when he curls them.

The tips of his fingers stroke my front walls, and I slam the back of my hand over my mouth to hold back my cry. I'm whimpering, shuddering, crumbling into pieces.

"That's it, baby," Patton coos. "Give me what I want."

My hands fist his shirt as I pull his mouth to mine. My

toes curl and my thighs tremble as my pussy contracts around his fingers. I rock my hips up as Patton continues to pump his fingers inside me until, just like that, I come undone.

Hovering over me, his mouth against mine, he swallows my scream as every muscle in my body constricts and loosens. I'm practically drowning in a flood of heat. My heart thumps against my chest, but what brings me even more satisfaction is feeling his heart beating just as hard against mine.

"Fuck, I love making you come," Patton rasps, his fingers still working the last sparks of my orgasm until I'm completely spent.

Our kiss lingers, becoming sensual and tender, until I can finally take a satiated breath. "Good, because I never want you to stop."

"Never again, baby. I want to own every single one of your orgasms."

My eyes are half-hooded as I feel him gently remove his fingers from inside me before reaching over to get the wipes. Rounding the table, he lifts the hem of my paper gown and glides the warm wipe down my seam. My cheeks flame, knowing I've likely made a mess on the paper sheet covering the table I'm lying on.

But I don't interrupt him, nor do I ask to take on the task myself. I know the type of lover he is, the kind who worships my body *after* lovemaking just as much as he does during it. While I'm usually the type to spring out of bed the minute my body recharges, Patton loves to hold me hostage, coaxing me to cuddle a little longer.

Once we're all cleaned up, I slip back into my clothes, tossing the hospital gown into a bin. I press the call button, then catch my reflection on a glass armoire and frantically start patting my hair down, praying it doesn't scream "just got finger-fucked by my ex-husband in an exam room".

The door opens and the doctor walks in, her eyes flicking

between me and Patton. His hands are in his pockets, hip leaning against the table, looking completely unmussed, like he's just posing for a photoshoot.

Dr. Gilbert smirks. "I'm glad to hear that you took my advice to celebrate seriously." She hands over the printouts of the sonogram. "Congratulations again."

It's when she leaves that her words, "I'm glad to hear," register, making my face flame with mortification.

twenty-seven
nisha

We're A Forever Kind of Thing

"Is my hair frizzed out? Can you tell I'm sweating?" Sarina fans herself with her hand, her enormous engagement ring glinting. "God, it's hot. I should have expected that for a beach wedding, but this *lehenga* is making it worse."

Outside the entrance to the beach, where guests are gathered—where her groom stands awaiting his bride at the beautiful make-shift altar in front of the ocean—my twin swishes said *lehenga*, her Indian bridal skirt, from side to side, seemingly trying to get air underneath it. Unlike her first wedding, where her ex-husband demanded she wear a white dress at the church where his mother insisted they marry, Sarina is wearing a soft pink two-piece ensemble with a flowy chiffon skirt, a bejeweled strapless top, and a sheer red veil, passed down from our mother's wedding. Like a true Indian bride, she looks radiant and colorful from head to toe.

"You look breathtaking, and no, I can't tell you're sweating." I squeeze my twin's hands, smiling at the intricate henna flowers adorned on her palms. My eyes glisten just from looking at her.

"I don't think I've seen a more beautiful bride in my life,"

Piper says, taking a quick selfie of the three of us with her phone. "You look like a princess, babe."

"You really do, love," Dad says, taking out a floral-print handkerchief from his pocket and dabbing his eyes. "I am so happy your mother and I had such gorgeous genes to pass on to our daughters."

At that, we all laugh, and my tears stay at bay. Of course, our dad would manage to be emotional and vain at the same time. He's always known how to make us laugh, even when we were at the edge of tears, but he's never been good at holding back his own.

Dad is wearing a pink and red, traditional *sherwani* ensemble, his long embroidered silk coat the same colors as Sarina's *lehenga*. He looks more dapper and handsome than I've ever seen him.

When he sniffles, wiping the corner of his eye, Emanuel pulls him into a hug, rubbing his back gently. And just like that, my eyes prick again.

Perhaps it's all the emotions in the air, or my wild hormones. Or perhaps it's because I barely got any sleep last night, even with Patton's comforting arms surrounding me all night. I just wanted this day to be perfect for my perfect sister, and my nerves just wouldn't let me settle.

The more I tried to sleep, the more my mind raced with stray thoughts, like which room I was going to choose to make into the nursery. Would the baby have a room in both our homes or would we move in with each other?

We hadn't talked about moving in together. And when that thought surfaced, so did that familiar fear—were we moving too fast? Were we repeating past mistakes? Did Patton even want to live with me again?

We had a good rhythm right now. Though the baby was a surprise, I didn't want to make hasty relationship decisions based on the pregnancy. But if I was pressed for the truth, the idea of living with him again didn't seem all that scary, either.

My racing thoughts weren't helped by the packed schedule, and though my body needed the rest, I knew my brain would take a break only when it wanted to.

We hit the ground running since we got to Cabo yesterday. Troy booked out the entire resort for the next few days to keep the paparazzi at bay, not just for him and his Blazers ex-teammates, but for Dev and Patton, too. He also beefed up the security with all the A-listers and celebrities in attendance, not wanting any interruptions from the media.

Between yesterday's rehearsal, the meet-and-greet, the *mehendi* party—where all the women got henna painted on our palms—the cocktail hour, and dinner, I don't think any of us had a moment to breathe.

Well, Sarina and Troy definitely didn't.

I, on the other hand, was whisked away for "down time" every chance my ex-husband found me on my feet for more than fifteen minutes.

Whether it was keeping me hydrated with pineapple margarita mocktails, rubbing my feet during the cocktail hour while telling me about the Mexican Revolution, or bringing me fruit and crackers when I couldn't keep anything else down, the man hovered over me like a mother hen.

And though I feigned annoyance, I found myself looking for him anytime he was missing from my side.

My sister pulls both me and Piper in for a hug. "I love you both so much. You're not just my best friends and sisters, you're part of my entire world. It spins because you're in it."

And there go my tears.

"God, you lunatic. Why do you have to make us cry right now?" Piper sniffles, pressing a kiss to my sister's temple. "You're going to ruin our makeup!"

I squeeze Sarina's shoulders. "I don't know what I'd do without you. I was blessed to have been born with my best friend, my other half in so many ways. And to see you get married today to the man of your dreams, a man who has brought you and Rome so much happiness and love, after everything you've been through? There's no other joy like it."

"I love you, Neesh," she says again, a tear threatening to escape. "I can't wait to see you here, in a spot very much like this again one day, waiting to walk up that aisle to reunite with the man of your dreams."

I lift a brow, not missing the sparkle in her eyes with the word "reunite," but before I can say anything, Dad cuts in.

"Oh, she will. I have no doubt about that. With the way that gorgeous Hollywood hunk looks at her, I have a feeling we'll be planning another wedding very soon. And honey, I am so ready for another excuse to wear my good jewelry." Dad waggles his fingers, each adorned with rubies and diamonds, just to make his point.

Piper giggles. "I just want it to be known that I predicted this last year after you and Troy got engaged. After we all saw through Patton's scheme to film his next movie in San Jose, only a few miles from your house and our salon. I predicted that we'd be attending two weddings for the Arora sisters."

I roll my eyes, but there's no denying the smile that's crept up my face, making me feel warm and tingly inside.

While I don't want to dampen their hopes of attending another huge wedding—especially since I have no inclination toward something as fancy—the idea of marrying Patton again . . .

God, it would be like getting back a piece of my heart that I thought was gone forever. And just seeing how different we are now, I know it wouldn't be like the first time. We're older, wiser, and definitely more careful with each other's hearts . . .

So marrying him again, though I'm terrified to dream it

too early, would be like returning home after a very long and arduous journey.

"And I know you don't want to jinx anything, but I can't hold myself back any more." Sarina places her hand on her lips before touching my stomach. "I can't wait to meet my niece or nephew one day soon. But you've got time, little bean. Come out when you're ready and healthy."

"We're ready, Mom!" Rome's voice has us all turning to look toward him and Pearl, walking in with one of the coordinators. Pearl is wearing a soft pink dress, while Rome looks handsome in his dark suit and pink tie.

Sarina leans down to give them hugs, signing and speaking. "You both look so cute. Are you ready to get on with this wedding? Remember, you'll both go out first. Aunt Nisha and Aunt Piper will be right behind you."

Right on cue, the music starts, and Sarina's wedding coordinator comes inside to tell us it's time and that Troy is waiting at the altar.

Dad tucks Sarina's hand inside his elbow. "Ready for me to walk you down the aisle, darling?"

Sarina smiles, eyes shimmering. "I'm so ready, Daddy."

I blink away my tears as Piper and I follow Pearl and Rome out to the beach. I worked too hard on getting my winged liner just right to mess it up this early in the day. The kids wave at the guests, big smiles spread across their faces, before they wave at Troy.

Holding our bouquets of red roses and pink peonies, which match Sarina's outfit, Piper and I step out carefully onto the red carpet that's been rolled over the sand.

The late afternoon sun casts a golden light over everything, making the ocean sparkle behind the altar, and I can see Troy in his embroidered gold *sherwani* with pink accents, beaming as he watches Pearl and Rome make their way toward him.

Dev meets Piper at the end of the aisle, placing a kiss on

her lips before murmuring something in her ear that makes her blush almost as bright as the bouquet she's holding. She elbows him in the side before threading her arm through his.

My gaze locks with Patton next.

With his hands tucked inside the pockets of his dark suit pants, his hair slightly gelled, and his stubble a perfect shadow on his sharp jaw, my ex-husband looks every bit the movie star he is. But it's the way he's looking at me that makes my knees wobble. His dark eyes rake down my body, taking in the gold saree with pink flowers wrapped around me before they settle on my face, looking at me like I'm the only person on this entire beach.

Originally, Troy had decided against having groomsmen at all. With as many close friends from both his playing days and the Seven Schlongs, he said it was impossible for him to choose. Dean had been the most devastated by this decision, saying he'd been dreaming about standing next to his "best friend and idol". Apparently, he'd gotten "special underwear" for the occasion.

But Troy and Patton have gotten close over the past few months, so when Sarina decided it would be nice to have Patton and Dev escort her two bridesmaids, I'm almost positive Dean shed actual tears.

Patton steps forward, his trademark grin in place, but there's something softer in his expression. I'd say it's new, but I can't be sure anymore. Maybe he's always had that same tenderness in his eyes when it comes to me. Maybe it's I who's taken this long to acknowledge it.

Instead of offering me his arm when he reaches me, he pulls me in, one hand settling on my waist, while the other curves around my neck.

I should remind him we're in public, or that people are recording us, but before I can say anything, his mouth captures mine in a firm, unyielding kiss. It's claiming and possessive. And though it's over in seconds, it steals my breath, along with any coherent thought.

When he pulls back, his thumb brushes over my jawline, and he murmurs low enough so only I can hear. "We're a forever kind of thing, baby."

With my heart still beating out of rhythm, Patton pulls my hand to the crook of his elbow, and we fall into step beside each other. But I barely remember how I got to the other end of the aisle.

We hadn't talked about making things public, but I guess kissing me in front of everyone settles that question. And while I'm not worried about pictures being posted, given all the vendors signed NDAs and close family and friends were requested not to share pictures publicly, there's something both thrilling and terrifying about not hiding anymore.

Thrilling, because it seems like he's making a statement. Terrifying, because once this goes public, the media will have a field day—speculating, dissecting, and keeping everyone guessing as to if we'll actually work out this time.

But we'll worry about that when the time comes.

Once I kiss Troy's cheek, Patton and I take our places opposite each other, next to Dev and Piper, respectively. The soft ocean breeze lifts my dark shoulder-length hair as I sweep my gaze around the beach, looking at everyone who came here to celebrate this momentous occasion.

Troy's parents are in the front row, with Pearl and Rome sitting on each side of them. Each of the Schlongs, aside from the three standing at the altar, are sitting next to their Clam Jam wives. Rani and Kavi wave and blow a kiss my and Piper's way, and I do the same in return. Dean, being Dean, also blows an exaggerated kiss my way using both hands, complete with a wink and a hand gesture, telling me to call him.

Mala elbows his side, giggling, because only Dean's wife can put up with his idiocy. But that's a testament to how secure she is in their relationship. She knows Dean is absolutely feral for her, regardless of the show he puts on to get laughs.

I shake my head, but as soon as my eyes find Patton across from me, I bite my lip to hold back my laugh. He's gone rigid, jaw locked and eyes aiming missiles at Dean. I swear, if it wasn't for the respect he has for Troy and Sarina, my ex-husband would have committed murder by now.

Thankfully, his homicidal thoughts are interrupted when Sarina's favorite Hindi song, "Jashn-E-Bahaaraa" by A.R. Rahman, starts and everyone in the audience turns to watch Sarina appear at the end of the aisle with my dad. The sensual blend of the sitar and flute immediately sets the mood, and I swear goosebumps rise along my arms when I look at my beautiful sister.

Soft gasps erupt, along with sniffles, but all I hear is the way Troy takes in a shuddering breath. His eyes are glassy with unshed tears, and his love for my sister is written as clear as the skies above when he takes her in.

"Fuck." He swallows, visibly holding himself together. "She looks like an angel."

Sarina kisses our dad on the cheek before he hands her over to Troy, giving Troy a hug. Holding Sarina's hand above her head, Troy spins my sister around so her *lehenga* flares, making the guests holler and clap, before he pulls her to him, planting a kiss on her forehead.

He looks completely mesmerized by her, and the look on his face, completely love-struck and in awe, sends me back to the moment Patton saw me on our wedding day.

Where Troy is visibly holding back tears, I'd wiped my ex-husband's tears with the pads of my thumbs, breaking protocol and kissing him before we were supposed to.

Because love was never our problem . . .

Life was.

And perhaps our youth, too.

Feeling his gaze on me, my eyes drag over to Patton. And it's as if he can read my thoughts because the look on his face suggests he was there with me in that moment, reminiscing about that day, wishing everything had turned out differently.

There's pain there, but there's something else, too. Something that looks a lot like hope and faith. Something I've only recently started feeling after years of being comfortable in my hopelessness.

It's as if he's telling me to hang on, to have faith that this time will work out differently. That this time we won't let life get in the way. That we'll fight this time—for us and our upcoming little bundle. Because this time we're ready and exactly where we need to be.

And for the first time in years, I start to believe him.

Sarina passes me her bouquet with a smile that lights up her entire face, and I tell her I love her once more.

She turns to Troy, hands entwined with his. "So . . . we're doing this."

"That was never a question in my mind. I was going to get you to this altar even if I had to carry you over my shoulder, crying and screaming."

"Caveman."

"I prefer husband."

"I prefer that, too," she says, eyes sparkling.

"Good, because I'm going to ask that you scream that for me tonight when I'm buried—"

"Troy!" she gasps, making Piper and me giggle, and Troy's fellow cavemen groomsmen give him fist bumps like they're his frat brothers.

The officiant, an Indian priest who has clearly heard the

exchange, clears his throat, giving Troy a stern look. "Shall we proceed before you over-share any more with all the guests?"

I purse my lips, holding back my laugh as Sarina flushes brighter than her dress. Patton coughs into his fist, and Dev's shoulders shake, not able to hold back his chuckle.

Troy straightens up. "Sorry, yes. Ready when you are."

twenty-eight
patton

Are You Waiting For A Meteor Shower!?

It's not an Indian wedding if there's no dancing.

And by that, I don't *just* mean hitting the dance floor custom-built for a former MLB player and his new wife's wedding on a private beach in Cabo with tiki torches and a fully stocked open bar, because there's plenty of that. I mean, full-blown choreographed routines done by the groom and his best friends and the bride and her best friends.

That's right. I'm happy to say that tonight, I checked that off my bucket list as well.

I wouldn't say dancing comes naturally to me, but given my time in Hollywood and having made more than a few films where I had to dance, I thought I knew my way around a stage.

Fuck, was I wrong.

Turns out the form of dance the choreographer taught us, *bhangra*, isn't just jumping around with our arms up. It tests your core strength and makes your legs feel like jelly.

But seeing the look on everyone's face, especially the only woman I've had my eyes on all night, made a week of learning the damn dance worth it.

Unlike our high-energy dance, which Dean insisted we

fuel with shots of what tasted like gasoline, the girls' routine was a lot more graceful. Sarina never said it outright, but I could tell she purposely chose the softer movements with Nisha in mind, making sure her sister never felt left out and could participate without any stress.

And now, I watch my ex-wife from the bar where my friends are congregated, drinks in hand. The tattooed sleeve, that mid-thigh gold dress hugging every curve, and that ebony hair waving softly in the wind all makes her impossible to miss, and impossible to wonder what she's wearing underneath.

She's still on the dance floor, swaying to a Bollywood song spun by the DJ. He's no ordinary DJ, either. Troy flew in the world-famous Logan Miller, better known as DJ Access. The guy sells out arenas, so I can only imagine what it took to book him for this wedding.

My eyes stay glued to my breathtaking wife, who's laughing at something Piper has said. Yeah, I know. But it's just a matter of time till that "ex" portion of her title is dropped, so it makes sense I refer to her as my wife, at least in my head.

"You okay there, big guy?" Dean asks Hudson, who's quietly sipping his drink, eyes locked on his wife on the dance floor. "Are your old joints hurting after all that *bhangra*? Want me to flag down a server with some Icy Hot? I think I saw an extra walker somewhere, too. It had a pretty cool cup holder, so I thought of you."

Hudson takes a slow sip of his drink, eyes never straying from his wife. "Bold words coming from the guy who walked over to my room earlier to ask me to unscrew his wife's Stanley travel mug."

"That was a one-time thing! I told you my hands were slippery; I'd just used them to lube myself."

Hudson doesn't even flinch, just shakes his head because no reaction is the best reaction when it comes to Dean.

Chuckling and knowing he'll never get a rise out of Hudson, Dean swings an arm around Troy. "Man, I can't believe you're married. Fucking *married*! I'm so happy for you, bro. And that ceremony was beautiful. Seriously, this was the best day of my life."

"The best day of your life was *today*?" Dev asks, eyebrow raised. "At *Troy's* wedding? Not your own?"

Dean rears back like he's dealing with lunatics. "Of course, the happiest day of my life was my own wedding day; I married a goddess. But, fuck man, you can't just have one happiest day, you know? It would be like saying only one of you is my best friend, which would be completely ridiculous."

Hudson lifts his glass. "I'm sure Mala will be thrilled sharing the top spot with Troy's wedding."

Dean shrugs. "There are many things on my happiest day list, bro. Like the day I was born, though it was short-lived once I realized I had to share it with this asshole here." He jerks a thumb at Garrett, who flips him off. "Along with the birth of each of my kids—also on the happiest day list. And, of course, that one day when I orgasmed for almost an hour straight."

"Jesus Christ." Darian pinches the bridge of his nose. "Why can't we go one day without a reminder of your dick, Dean?"

"Because, little brother, my dick deserves to be remembered, memorialized even . . . unlike yours."

Troy grimaces. "I assume you ended up inside a hospital."

Dean grins. "Nah. I ended up *inside* my wife."

I drain the last of my bourbon, setting my glass on the bar. "And this is why you weren't allowed to give a speech."

"Bro, you're all just jealous because you can't say the same."

"Nor do we want to," Garrett says. "Anyway, back to Troy.

Congratulations, man! You married the woman of your dreams."

Troy shakes his head. "Kind of surreal, but fuck, I feel like the happiest bastard alive."

We all raise our glasses, and Troy grins, finding his new bride on the dance floor, dancing with her hands in the air.

They'd sent the kids back to the hotel with Troy's parents so the newlyweds could party as long as they wanted. Though with the way Troy has been eye-fucking his wife—similar to the way I've been staring at mine—I have a feeling he's planning to call it a night soon.

As if Sarina can feel his pull, she turns, beaming at him. Then, her eyes find mine. She glances around, noticing Nisha wrapped in a conversation with Bella and Mala, before tugging on Piper's hand and striding over.

As soon as the two women reach us, they're pulled in for long kisses by their husbands that have me averting my gaze back to the dance floor in search of Nisha. Damn, I wish they'd brought her along, too.

"Patton, have a minute?" Sarina asks, nodding toward a quiet area past the bar. Piper is standing right next to her with a contrite expression.

I look between the women I spent a portion of my teen years with, my gut telling me I have an inkling as to what this conversation might be about. We've talked over the past couple of months, but we've avoided talking about the elephant-sized crater our friendship became after Nisha and I split.

Both girls give knowing looks to their husbands before we walk to find a quieter spot. For a few moments, only the ocean waves fill the silence between us, but I can feel the weight of seven years hanging in the air.

Sarina stares down at her henna-painted hands. "I don't even know where to start..."

"You don't have to," I say, giving her an out. "We're all good now. We were never not good. And ever since I moved to San Jose, we've spoken, haven't we?"

"That's exactly it," Piper says quickly. "We were never not good, which means we could have kept in touch all those years. Fuck, you even tried to." She swallows, and I can see the emotion in her eyes. "But we cut you out."

Sarina's voice shakes like she's barely holding it together. "After seeing how broken Nisha was when she came to live with Dad, I thought the only way to support her was to choose a side. And I chose hers. I thought I was doing the right thing, but I realize now how much that must have hurt you."

"I understand," I say.

And I do, I really do. But, fuck, there were days I wished they'd have answered their phones or even their emails. Days I needed my friends. Days that were darker than nights.

Aside from Hollywood's superficial relationships, I didn't really have anyone else. My foster parents had their hands full with other kids, and I didn't want to burden them any more than necessary.

Joe and Molly had always been good to me and had encouraged me to pursue my passion for theater from a young age. And while they were the closest thing to what I'd call family, we didn't talk often. I visited them a couple of years ago when I had to film in Boston, but my career often meant years between real visits. And since they were also always busy raising a new generation of kids, they understood.

Thank God for my father-in-law, though. Because, without him, I probably would have drowned in bottles of whiskey and lost sight of everything, especially my plans to win Nisha back.

My eyes drift back to the dance floor where Suraj is doing

what looks like a version of the Macarena with Emanuel, and I can't help but smile.

Sarina's hand touches my arm. "I went through my divorce soon after you guys, and I guess I was jaded, too. It's not an excuse, though; I still should have kept up with you. You were important to me, too, Patton."

I place my hand over hers. "That asshole never deserved you. I'm glad you gave Troy a chance. He's one of the good ones."

"You are, too. You've always been one of the good ones." Her voice cracks, and fuck, the last thing I want is to make the bride cry on her wedding day. "We should have realized everything you were grieving as well: the miscarriages, the end of your marriage, losing all of us. But instead of being there for you, we abandoned you—"

"Hey," I talk past the knot in my throat. "She needed you more. After what she went through . . . " My jaw hardens, the familiar prick finding the corners of my eyes. "She needed you more."

Piper steps closer, gripping my bicep. "We just want to say we're sorry, Patton. You deserved better from your friends."

I pull them into a hug without any hesitation, like we used to when we were kids. When everything was simpler. "There's nothing to forgive. You're my family, always have been."

At that, Piper sobs against my shoulder. "Fuck, now you're making me ugly cry the same way Dean did when Troy didn't choose him as a groomsman."

We separate on a chuckle as Sarina wipes a tear from her cheek. "I'm so happy you and my sister are working things out again."

I look toward the dance floor where "I Gotta Feeling" by Black Eyed Peas pounds through the speakers. In the distance, Nisha's still swaying to the beat, and fuck, I want to be close to her.

"Thanks for tipping me off when the house in front of hers went on the market."

Sarina winks. "I couldn't see you both being separated any longer. Plus, her 'Crying in My Car' playlist was really getting out of hand."

I blink. "Crying in my what?"

"Nevermind. The point is, you two belong together."

"I've always been crazy about her."

Piper smiles. "You still love her."

There's no question about it. "I never stopped loving her, if I'm being honest."

"Does that mean you'll be walking down the aisle again?"

"Fuck yeah," I say without missing a beat. "I'd marry her tonight if she'd have me."

Both women squeal, bouncing on their toes.

"Have you told her?" Sarina asks.

I scoff. "That I want to marry her tonight? Um, no. She'd think it was wedding fever talking and all her stupid doubts would creep back in."

"Fair point." Piper laughs. "But have you told her that you love her?"

"Not in those exact words . . ."

Piper throws up her hands. "What, are you waiting for a meteor shower!? A solar eclipse?"

"Life's too short, Patton," Sarina says, squeezing my arm again. "You've already lost so much time; don't waste any more looking for the perfect moment."

They're right. What the hell am I waiting for?

~

My hand trails down her arm, fingertips tracing the tattooed designs there, as my mouth finds the shell of her ear, feeling her shudder in awareness. She knows there's only one person who would dare to touch her like this. "Have I told you how beautiful you look tonight?"

Her hips sway, pressing against my growing need. "Not in this hour."

I pull back her shoulder-length hair, brushing the curve of her neck with my lips, and feel goosebumps rise over her soft skin.

The ocean breeze mingles with the perfume of flowers decorating the dance floor and the faint smoke from the tiki torches drifts through the air. But I can't smell anything but pomegranates, sweet and enticing.

"Then let me remind you. You are the most devastatingly gorgeous woman, and the only one who owns me completely." My arm curves around her, my palm covering her belly protectively. "I love you, Little Borealis. I've *always only ever* loved you."

A soft gasp falls from her lips as Nisha spins in my arms. Her hands glide up to cup my jaw as her eyes bounce between mine like she's wondering if she heard me correctly.

I'm aware of the eyes on us and the soft squeals leaving her friends' lips, but none of it matters at this moment. For all intents and purposes, no one else is even here. We're all alone under the dark painted sky, so much like that night we climbed a hill in Boston to chase the rare flickers of the Aurora Borealis. That was the night I knew no one could ever own my heart the way she does.

"You love me?" Her sweet breath skims my lips.

"I never stopped, and I never will. I love you more than life itself, baby. Living without you was sheer torture, and it's a hell I won't survive again."

Her eyes pool, her chin trembling as she nods.

"I don't ever want to be without you, Nisha. Not years, not months, not even a moment. I'll choose you over everything else, myself included."

She shakes her head. "I don't want you to. I want you to have your career, your ambitions. I just wanted to see some . . . balance."

"And have you?"

She nods, holding my gaze silently for a moment. Her fingers trail through my hair as she rises on her toes, bringing our lips closer. "I love you so much, Patton Pierce. I've never known a moment where my heart didn't beat just for you."

Fuck, I want to sob, to drown in her arms. But instead I capture her lips with mine, pouring all the words inside my chest through a kiss. It's desperate and consuming, the kind that tastes like years of missed "I love yous" and vows I want to relive again.

Her fingers twist through my hair, pulling me closer, like she's trying to rid herself of the same ache I feel pulsing through my body.

But she never will.

Because this is a forever kind of ache, and we're a forever kind of thing.

I swear I've never tasted anything sweeter, felt anything deeper, held anyone tighter. This isn't just a kiss. This is a promise—a plea, and a prayer embedded in our souls—not just written on some meaningless papers. And I know, without a shadow of a doubt, I'll spend the rest of my life making sure she never forgets how wholly she owns me.

She tugs on my bottom lip, and I know she feels the groan rumble inside my chest. Pulling our mouths apart, her swollen lips form the words I've been waiting to hear all day. "Take me to bed, Hollywood."

twenty-nine
patton

Suck On It Like It's A French
Toast Popsicle

Her dress is hiked all the way up her thighs, her legs parted and straddling my lap. The scent of her arousal sweetens the air between us as my tongue snakes into her mouth, making her hum in agreement. I swear I live for her hums of pleasure, the sounds that say what entire sentences can't.

Having said our goodbyes to the newlyweds and our friends as fast as possible, we rushed back to our hotel suite in record time.

Her lips were on me the second we got inside. And before long, my girl was taking charge, pushing me onto the sofa before climbing into my lap, ravenous for my touch.

I cup the back of her neck, driving my fingers into her hair as my other hand skims her side. I brush the soft skin of her thighs, pushing the hem of her dress up further, my lips continuing to devour hers.

My hand rounds the globe of her ass, and it's then that I notice it . . .

She's not wearing panties.

I take a shaky breath and drop my gaze to where her bare

pussy glistens between us. My nostrils flare. "Tell me you were wearing panties during the reception."

She twirls a strand of her hair, blinking up at me with feigned innocence. "This pregnancy has made me so forgetful . . ."

"Nisha."

She giggles, brushing her lips along my jaw as her fingers thread through my hair. "Calm down, Mr. Jealous-and-Possessive. I slid them off when we got inside."

My fingers clasp her chin, pulling her mouth back to mine. "That's fucking more like it." My other hand trails down, fingers teasing her slit and making her whimper. "This pussy stays hidden from everyone but me. Got that?"

"We're going to have a baby, you big Neanderthal. Pretty sure there will be others looking at my vagina."

"Fine, but it doesn't mean I have to like it. And I'm coming to every appointment. Gotta keep my eye on anyone who gets too *handsy*."

Nisha rolls her eyes exasperatedly, but there's a smile on her lips when they find mine again. And then, in an instant, all the teasing flies out the window, leaving nothing but heat and desire behind.

My hands roam the curves I've memorized as her fingers dig into my shoulders, and our bodies writhe together in a rhythm all our own.

Her hands skim up my chest and, without unlocking our lips, she pushes off my suit jacket, throwing it behind her, before tearing at my shirt like someone possessed. Once it's unbuttoned and lying in the same heap, she drags her lips down my neck, peppering in tiny moans as she kisses and licks my skin.

Her hips roll over my bulge as her mouth skirts down to my pecs, her thumb teasing one nipple as the tip of her tongue plays with the other. She lets out a soft laugh when my hands tighten on her thighs and my abs contract, knowing exactly how she's affecting me.

"You like that?"

My jaw tightens as I struggle to keep my body in check, praying to God I don't come with just her hands and lips on me. "You know I do."

She scoots off my lap, getting on her knees in front of me, and I immediately start to protest. She's fucking carrying my child, the last thing I want is for her to be on her knees for me. My heart clenches at the sight of her—so breathtaking and so completely mine. Every flutter of her lashes, every curved smile, every fucking heartbeat feels like it belongs to me, and I ache to show her how much I'm hers in return. Fuck, I'll happily spend the rest of my life on my knees, worshipping at her altar, because she deserves nothing less.

But before I can say anything, her index finger presses over my lips, telling me she still wants to be in charge. Pushing my legs apart, she starts to unbuckle my belt, and before my brain engages again, she has my pants and boxer briefs pulled off.

My cock shows no sign of shame, lying thick and hard over my abs, twitching when she licks her lips.

"I need your hands on me, baby," I croak.

She doesn't waste another second, scooting in close and grabbing my shaft with both hands. The warmth of her small palms around my velvet skin has my balls pulling in tight.

"Fuck," I grit out, my head tilting back against the top of the sofa. It'd been years since I'd been inside a woman before I got back with Nisha, and it's been years since someone has touched me like this.

Bringing it to her lips, she darts her tongue out, dragging it over my tip to taste the pearls of pre-cum there, making my abs contract.

"Mmm." *There's that hum again.* "You taste good."

"Yeah? You want more?"

Her eyes stay locked on mine with every movement, and fuck if it isn't the hottest sight I've seen. And now that I have her here, her arms resting on my lap and her head hovering over my raging hard-on, all I want to do is mess up that cherry lipstick so it's smeared all over her lips and my cock.

"I want everything you can give me."

A haze drifts over my sight, mind, and senses as my heart rate ticks up. "Good. Because that's exactly what I plan to do. Now, spit on it."

Her eyes flare at the command, but a sexy smile draws up her lips. Dipping her head, she does just that, spitting on the tip and watching as it pools at her fingers. Her lashes flutter before her eyes draw back up to my face, awaiting more instructions.

"Suck on it like it's a French toast popsicle."

She giggles, but like the good fucking girl she is, she stuffs me into her mouth, sucking in as much of me as she can take.

I draw in a breath, feeling her tongue rolling over my length. Her cheeks hollow out, and she makes a sound so guttural, my hand reaches out to fist her hair. It feels so fucking good, I'll be shocked if I can last even two minutes.

She continues to bob over me, making slurping noises like I'm the best thing she's ever tasted while her hand drifts down to play with my balls. And when she takes me all the way to the back of her throat, practically gagging, I know I won't be able to make this last unless I pull out of her. But, fuck, a part of me considers not doing so with the way she's stroking and sucking me.

Sitting forward, I pull on her hair until her pouty mouth comes off me and her questioning eyes meet mine. Jesus, fuck, her swollen and ravished lips, with that lipstick smeared around her pretty mouth, are a vision I'll never forget.

My voice sounds raw and husky even to my own ears. "I need to be inside you, baby."

"But—"

"I will gladly have you suck my cock any day of the fucking week, but today, I need to finish inside you."

Her eyes are half-lidded when she nods.

I carry her bridal style to the bed and lay her down. I take in the soft curves of her hips, the wetness that coats her inner thighs, and the swollen pussy just waiting for me to fill it.

Her hips haven't filled out yet, as I suspect they will, the same way her stomach will swell in the coming weeks, making her look even more beautiful than she does right now. Which honestly feels like an impossibility.

Her finger crooks, beckoning me forward. "You planning to do anything more than stare at me all night?"

"I'm memorizing the way you look before I ravish you in all the ways running through my head."

"Might want to hurry up then, Hollywood, or I'm going to have to finish this all on my own."

I gently pull her down the mattress so her ass is on the edge. Getting down on my knees the way I wanted to earlier, I nudge her legs apart. "Sweetheart, the only thing you'll be doing is begging me not to stop."

Dragging the tips of two of my fingers through her slit, I circle her entrance before I lay my tongue over her clit, rolling it until she's restless and whimpering. I suck her hard bud into my mouth as I glide my fingers inside her, loving the way her pussy molds to them.

Nisha tips her head back, her fingers tugging at the strands of my hair. "Oh, God, Patton. That feels so good. Your mouth . . . oh, my God."

I pump my fingers in and out before I draw them forward, brushing down the front of her walls just the way she likes. She writhes and mumbles, placing her feet on my shoulders as I bite and suck her folds into my mouth before I tease her clit with my teeth.

Pine For Me

My cock begs to join the fun, so with my fingers buried inside her and my mouth still feasting on her, I give him a few tugs, not satiating his need but keeping him entertained.

Nisha moans as her hands find her tits. She pinches her nipples as she arches her back, chasing more of my mouth and touch.

I lave her needy heat, lapping at her juices while siphoning out soft cries with each drive of my fingers.

It's right when her walls give a quick flutter and I know she's close that I drag my fingers out of her, sucking them clean so as to not waste a drop of her juices. I climb onto the bed, chuckling when she whines.

She's not a fan of me edging her, but she knows there's a silent promise there to make it good for her when it happens.

I hover over her on a forearm, rubbing her slit before rolling my fingers at her opening. "You doing okay?"

She nods with an exhale. "Yes."

"You'll tell me if anything doesn't feel good?"

"Yes, I promise."

My eyes skim her features, lingering on the way her mouth falls open when I dip my fingers inside her once more. She is exquisite and has only gotten more beautiful over time.

"Good. Then open up wide for me, baby. I need to fuck you."

With her legs spread wide, Nisha takes me in, her slick heat clenching around my cock as I push in deeper until I'm buried to the hilt. The sound of her pleasure rips a groan out of me. And when my eyes find hers and our hard breaths mingle, the mood shifts between us.

Gone is the playfulness from a few moments ago, replaced by the declarations we made today, the vows we made seven years ago, and the promises our bodies are making now.

My thumb sweeps back a strand of hair clinging to her forehead, and I drive in slow and deep, savoring the way her body yields to me. I dip my nose to her hairline, trying to fill my lungs with her scent as I breathe her in.

"Show me how much you love me, Patton."

As if her whispered words strike a match inside me, I thrust deeper, but keep my pace unhurried, drawing out her pleasure without overwhelming her. She's carrying my child, so I move with intention, grinding into her just right, making sure every roll of my hip is deliberate without being painful. And though I know she loves a little pain with her pleasure, we both agreed there will be time for that after the baby is here, safe and sound with us.

My teeth graze her jaw before my mouth trails over her shoulder, leaving love bites in its wake. With every thrust into her and every blemish I leave over her skin, I plan to make her feel me inside her all the way to next week.

My hand clamps the back of her thigh, lifting and anchoring her as I drive inside. The slight change in position makes her gasp, and my control dangles by a thread.

I glide through her only to draw back and drive forward with precision and a goal in mind—to nudge that spot deep inside her that always has her shattering around me so beautifully.

Her eyes glisten as her hands come up to cradle my face. It feels like she's holding a lot more than me physically. Like she's holding my heart and soul, my entire damn existence in her cupped hands.

"Nisha . . ." My voice sounds raspy even to my own ears. "Fuck, baby. I love you so much. I'll never stop. Not in this life and not in the next."

"I know," she whispers, her nails gently dragging down my back, sparking heat inside me even as she squeezes her lids shut. A single tear slips free before she peppers kisses along my collarbone. "I know you won't . . . just like I could never stop loving you."

I find her lips again, our kiss pulling us into a binding spell, making me moan into her mouth. My hand trails down to her belly reverently, protectively, as I grind deep inside her, brushing that spot that has her entire body contracting.

Her fingernails bite my flesh as her hips come up to meet mine. Her voice shakes as she throws her head back, revealing the length of her neck. "I'm going to come, Patton."

I chase my own orgasm as I roll my hips, each thrust inside her making my vision blur. "Come for me, baby."

Two seconds later, she's screaming my name, her body clenching as her walls flutter around me, pulling me in deeper and milking me for everything I've got.

I hold her flush against me, burying myself in her like I'm trying to brand her. And then my entire body is tensing, a spark igniting at the bottom of my spine and zipping through me like lightning.

In what feels like a succession of explosions, I shatter inside her, spilling into the woman who owns every molecule in my body.

I fall onto the mattress, pulling her with me in a tangle of arms and legs, holding her until our breaths even out. Minutes go by as we stare at each other, her fingernails gently tracing paths down my back while my fingers glide down the inked lines of her tattoos. Neither of us says a word until my eyes find something I hadn't noticed before—two pairs of angel wings hidden between the stars and flowers.

My hand halts. *How did I miss this?*

"I got them soon after each one . . ." she whispers, reading my thoughts.

Each miscarriage, she means.

I clench my jaw, nodding. *I should have been there.*

Her fingers run through my scruff and, as if sensing my turmoil, she murmurs, "You're here now. That's all that matters."

I brush my lips along the inside of her wrist. "I'll be here. Always."

We continue the gentle caresses, lost in our own thoughts as we gaze at each other, until her soft voice breaks the silence. "Can I ask you a question?"

"Anything."

She rubs her lips together, hesitant. "Were there others?"

I open my mouth to answer, but she waves me off. "You know what? You don't have to tell me. You'd have been well within your rights to have been with others. I mean, I've seen pictures . . . and all sorts of women. But it's honestly none of my business."

I chuckle. "The first year after you changed your number and told me not to reach out, right after we finalized the divorce, yeah . . . there were a few. They were women I thought I could lose myself in, but no one I ever remotely wanted to be serious with. No one was you. No one even compared. So I just . . . stopped altogether."

Her brows knit. "What do you mean, 'stopped altogether'?"

"I haven't been with anyone in five years."

She blinks before slowly rising, like sitting upright will help her understand this conversation in a way lying down could never. "*Five years?* You were, what, celibate for five years before me?"

I shrug, looking up at her from my spot on the pillow. "Yes."

"But what about those photos I saw? All those women who looked cozy with you at the premieres and galas?"

I smile. "Geez, you were obsessed with me, weren't you? And here I thought you'd forgotten all about me."

"Patton."

"They were nothing. Just dates my publicist encouraged me to take to stir up buzz."

"So . . . in the past five years, you haven't even *kissed* someone?"

"Aside from when I kissed you after the taekwondo tournament last year? Nope."

"But . . . but what if I never came around? What if things didn't work out between us, despite your plan?"

"Then I would have waited. I don't know how long—two years, ten years, my whole life? It doesn't matter because I didn't want a replacement, Little Borealis; I wanted *you*."

Her lips part, and for a moment, she just stares at me, like she's caught between disbelief and reverence. "But that's . . . crazy, Patton."

"Yeah, maybe. But so is love."

She's quiet for another long moment before she clears her throat. "I've been wondering . . . about the nursery."

"Yeah?"

"Where should we have it?" She licks her lips. "What I mean is, do you think we should have one at my place and one at yours, or . . . ?"

I suppress my smile, knowing my girl well enough to know she wants me to fill in the third option because she's too proud to do it herself. "Or we could *just* have it at your place."

Her shoulders slump, and she gives me a resigned nod. "Right. Because you might move back to L.A. again."

My brows furrow. "Baby, do you know why I flew to L.A. last week?"

"I figured it was something to do with work."

I take her hand, brushing my lips across her knuckles. "I went there to sign some paperwork. I put my L.A. condo on the market."

"You . . . what?"

"I told you I was all-in. And considering the fact that I'll be putting my San Jose home on the market, too, I might be homeless soon."

Her fingers find her lips as she stares down at me in shock. "Patton, is this your very roundabout way of asking me if you can move in with me?"

I grin. "Baby, I'm selling two properties, not exactly being subtle here."

She blinks rapidly. "You're really doing this? You're choosing us over everything else?"

"You're not a choice or an option for me, Neesh. You're a necessity."

She swallows, eyes brimming with unshed tears as she lets my words sink in. When she looks back at me, a teasing smile plays on her face. "What if . . . what if I'd moved on with someone else?"

My jaw tightens, the thought of someone else touching her making me see red.

I pull her back down to the mattress, rolling us so she's pinned under me. "Then I would have made his life very, very uncomfortable until he decided you weren't worth the trouble."

She giggles, thinking I'm joking.

I'm not.

thirty
nisha

Not A Dessert

I brush the tiny bits of hair from John's shoulders, unbutton his cape, and turn his chair so the big mirror is behind him. Handing him a small handheld mirror, I smile at how handsome he looks. "There. Tell me what you think. How does the length look in the back?"

He turns his head from side to side. "It looks good, Ms. Nisha. Thank you."

"Just Nisha," I remind him, taking the mirror back. "I'll see you in a few weeks. Don't forget to add your name to the calendar, okay?"

"Will do. Merry Christmas again." He waves before heading out, tossing another in Hector and Abby's direction.

"Merry Christmas," I call after him before getting my broom and sweeping the area around the salon chair.

The shelter has been buzzing over the past month. The holiday season always brings in a surge of more people needing a hot meal and blankets, children's choir groups spreading cheer, and more volunteers bustling through with Santa hats. Instead of the usual sting of disinfectant, the sweet scent of cinnamon rolls and coffee lingers in the air.

When I finish sweeping, I make my way over to the

loveseat crammed in my closet-sized salon. Hector and Abby are right where they always are when I work here, yarn on their laps and hands focused on their needles. They'd rather sit with me than be out in the dining area mingling with others, and I don't mind that one bit.

They've been getting closer lately. Hector told me Abby's even been teaching him to knit. I doubt he cares about purl stitches, but the man would learn anything she was interested in if it meant spending time with her. Apparently, she even let him hold her hand on their walk in the park recently. For Abby, that's not just progress, that's basically her baring her soul. And yet, the way she still keeps her eyes down, sleeves tugged all the way to her palm, I know her walls aren't all the way down, at least not yet.

Hector rises to his feet, waving at the seat he just vacated. "Ms. Arora, please sit. You've been on your feet for hours."

Settling in beside Abby, I don't argue because he's right. It's been a nonstop morning. "Hector, you've got to stop calling me Ms. Arora."

He flashes me the same sheepish grin that says he has no intention of changing a thing before heading to take a seat on my salon chair until the next customer comes in.

Abby shifts beside me, rummaging in her worn cloth bag before taking out something wrapped in green tissue paper. She hands it to me with a small smile. "I . . . I hope you like it."

My chest squeezes. "You got me something? Abby, that's . . . that's so kind of you."

"It's nothing fancy. Just something for"—she nods to my now obvious baby bump—"the little one."

I swallow thickly, gently unfolding the paper, and a breath catches in my chest.

Nestled inside is a tiny knitted jumpsuit in every shade of pink with intricate stitches and neat handiwork. My fingers brush over the oversized buttons along the front and back for easy diaper changes.

My eyes water, and I quickly dab the tear threatening to escape at the corner of my eye. "You made this? Abby, this is . . . beautiful." I turn to her, brows furrowed. "But I only just told you about the ultrasound a couple of weeks ago. How could you have made this so quickly?"

She gives me a hesitant smile. "You'd mentioned you thought it was a girl well before the ultrasound." She shrugs. "I trusted your intuition and started making this weeks ago."

Placing the jumper on my lap, I wrap my arms around her, feeling her stiffen for a moment before she yields to my embrace. "Thank you. This is the most thoughtful gift I've ever received."

She pats my back, letting me hug her. "I'm glad you like it."

I wipe my cheek and marvel at the little outfit in my hands.

I'm almost twenty-two weeks along. *Twenty-two*. And though I can still hardly believe our little bean is now the size of a sweet potato, I can finally feel her moving inside me. They started off as tiny flutters but have recently turned into little kicks that Patton swears are directed at him because they always commence whenever he's around. It's as if she can't wait to leap into his arms.

Life has shifted so quickly over the past couple of months, I can hardly keep up. Patton and Bob moved into my house soon after we got back from Cabo, and I can honestly say it has never been as warm or chaotic.

Just this week alone, I've found my underwear and camisole hidden under Bob's bed. Besides the barely-functional dildo and my old bra, our four-legged klepto is basically operating a drool-soaked lingerie store in our house. I'm not going to lie, it's a little unnerving that both Beaver and Bob have shoplifting tendencies.

Oh, and my previously straightened throw pillows? Those are a thing of the past, since Bob has made it his life's mission to dig under them like he's hunting for gold.

I've also learned a few more things about my ex-husband during this time. Like that he has very strong opinions about whether the baby needs blackout curtains or sheer ones in her room, or whether I should be "allowed" to take showers unattended.

So, aside from assembling cribs and researching the safest rocking chairs on the planet—all while finishing additional scenes for his film, officially named *The Winning Pitch*—Patton has basically transformed into a very attractive helicopter husband. He's made it impossible for me to do almost anything alone, insisting that someone be around me twenty-four/seven. It's equal parts ridiculous and annoying, but also kind of sweet, and I have to remind myself that this is exactly what I asked for, what I wanted all those years ago.

And this time, he's here for all of it. He's here for me.

As soon as he moved in, Patton's team descended on my house like a team of covert operatives, wiring it with a state-of-the-art security system that probably outshines the Pentagon's. They claimed it was "non-negotiable," given who Patton is and how even more important our privacy is now.

I grumbled about the intrusion at first, but I've come to understand its importance. We live in a gated community and stay low-key, but given how crazy fans can be, it's never a bad idea to be extra careful. Let's face it, some of them make Bob's underwear obsession seem normal.

But despite all the hovering and treating me like I'm made out of glass, I have to admit this chaotic little life we're building might be the perfect one for me. I'm completely gone for the man who assembled our baby's crib at two in the morning, argues about curtains, and protects me like he's my personal bodyguard. We're also having a baby together. So, if I'm not the luckiest woman alive, I don't know who is.

I'm folding the baby's first outfit back inside the tissue paper when I realize Hector has left the room, leaving me and Abby alone. Taking the opportunity to ask her what's been weighing on my mind for some time, I turn to look at the woman whose hands are once again busy with her needles.

"Hey, Abby?" I clear my throat. "I was wondering if you ever found the thing you were looking for? You know, the reason you said you moved here?"

She sets down her needles, her tired green eyes examining her hands. For a moment I don't think she'll answer, but then, like she has a few times before, she surprises me.

"Yes and no." She takes in a soft breath. "There's this restaurant downtown. I found what I was looking for there, but I couldn't find the courage to go in and ask for it."

My brows knit. "What you're looking for is inside a restaurant?"

She nods. "It was, yes."

I study her face, trying to read between the lines.

"Is it like . . . a dish or dessert or something?"

She shakes her head. "No. Not a dessert. Forgiveness."

I moan, my eyes rolling to the back of my head, feeling myself sink deeper into the sofa. "Oh, God. That feels so good."

"That's it, baby. Relax for me," Patton murmurs, his voice low and approving. His thumb presses into the exact place I need him.

The arch of my foot, that is.

I crack one eye open, smiling when I see the smug look on his face as he massages my swollen feet like he's a trained masseuse. He might as well be because the man's hands are currently performing magic.

"You know, if you keep this up, we might just make baby number two before this one's even out."

He smirks. "Can I have that in writing?"

I giggle, tilting the magazine in my lap and showing him the photographs of us there. "Speaking of writing . . . Did you know that we're apparently having triplets?"

Before Patton can examine it, Bob saunters over to see what I'm pointing at. He places his large head on my swollen belly, effectively covering the magazine photos, and stares at me with those droopy eyes I've come to love so much.

It's his way of asking for pets. That, or he somehow senses when I'm even slightly worked up.

I scratch his long ear. "I'm fine, buddy. Just annoyed that, with all their fancy cameras, the paparazzi always manage to make me look like a troll."

Bob heaves a dramatic sigh, and I can practically hear him say, "*I hear you, sister. They never get my good side, either*". Then, as if he's been reminded of his great misfortunes, he trudges back toward his dog bed with his head lowered to find one of his many treasures.

Earlier this month, Patton helped me get the house Christmas-ready. After so many years of not having a real tree, we picked one out and decorated it while one of Patton's films, *The Claus and Effect*, played in the background. It's the one where he played a marriage counselor helping Santa and Mrs. Claus through their tumultuous relationship. We laughed, nibbled on peppermint bark, and sipped cider.

It took us twice as long as it should have to get the tree up, given we took frequent breaks to give each other orgasms, but we got the job done. Not to mention, we even had help from Bob. Thanks to his generosity, three of my bras are artfully draped over our classy Douglas fir.

That definitely made for an interesting conversation with my family when we hosted Christmas Eve dinner at our house a few days ago.

"Sweetheart, I'm glad to see you've 'chilled out' a bit, like you kids like to say," Dad had remarked, giving our tree a once-over like a high school mean girl. *"You know, limited checklists, less organizing, fewer over-fluffed pillows . . . all progress."* His eyes slid to the bras dangling off the branches and then to Bob, snoring near the fireplace. *"But letting the dog turn Christmas into a lingerie yard sale might be taking things too far, don't you think?"*

I'd pursed my lips because what Dad didn't know was, just that morning, we'd caught Bob marking one of the lower branches with a well-aimed tinkle. Let's just say once we cut the branch off and cleaned up the floor, I had to light some additional cinnamon-scented candles just to make the house smell extra festive before everyone arrived.

Patton leans over to glance at the glossy photo spread of us from Cabo with a headline that reads, *Hollywood's Heartthrob Jumps Headfirst into Fatherhood with Estranged Ex.*

Despite all the security, the pictures are from our afternoon walk on the beach in Cabo. I wasn't even showing back then, but sure enough, there's a red arrow directed at my then-flat belly.

The caption reads: *Insiders speculate that the couple is expecting not just one, but three babies! Could this be a ploy for ex-wife Nisha Arora to claw her way back into the glamorous life of the multi-millionaire, multi-award-winning actor? Sources say she's been in dire financial distress, having seen her come out of a homeless shelter.*

I snort. "Oh, please. First of all, that wasn't a baby bump, that was the burrito I inhaled for lunch. The only real food I was able to keep down all weekend, mind you. Second, 'dire financial distress'?! I love how, apparently, I'm gunning for your bank account. Joke's on them because I'm only in this for the orgasms and foot massages."

Totally not the whole truth, but I can't deny that the pregnancy hormones have made me insatiable. I literally want the man twenty-four/seven.

Anyway, unlike my sister, who hates everything to do with being in the spotlight, preferring to stay as far away from the media as possible, I've never been too bothered. Even when Patton and I were married, I'd wave at the hidden camera poking out from a bush or smile at the flashing lights when we stepped out for dinner.

It was part of being with someone as high-profile as Patton. It still is.

Do I enjoy being watched or having dumb articles written about me? No, but I also don't stress about it, and I definitely don't let it get to me.

For all intents and purposes, they're just doing their job. Sure, they're spreading rumors, but in the end, that's exactly what they are: rumors. As long as the close small circle I trust knows the real me, I don't give two shits what anyone else thinks.

"Just orgasms and foot massages, huh?" Patton tickles the bottom of my foot, making me squeal. "And here I thought you were with me for my Adonis looks and irresistible personality."

"Please. Your personality is seventy percent ego and thirty percent historical trivia."

He clutches his chest like I've physically wounded him. "You're telling me you didn't find it fascinating that men with mustaches in the Victorian era used special cups so their mustaches stayed dry? Or that Americans called hamburgers 'liberty steaks' during World War II because hamburgers sounded too German?"

"Yes. *Riveting*. Truly, you're the master of pillow talk."

He tickles me again. "And seventy? Babe, my ego should get at least ninety-percent. It's my best asset!"

"Dear God, what if our child inherits your humility? Or your obsession for random facts."

Still chuckling, he pulls me closer so my back is to his chest. Placing a kiss on my temple, his hand finds my belly. It's something I find him doing often, even waking up with his hand at my belly protectively. "I hope she inherits everything else from you, because then she'll be perfect, just like her mom."

I look up at him. "I'm going to need you to kiss me now."

I feel the movement inside my stomach as soon as his lips drop against mine, like she knows her dad's hand is right there for her to touch.

Both our gazes drop to where his hand rests, and Patton starts to rub his thumb on the spot where he feels her.

"She's saying hello," I whisper.

"Hey, Starlight."

I smile, feeling a rush of warmth flood my chest. "Starlight? You haven't called her that before."

"Not out loud. I guess I wanted to test it out. I call you Little Borealis so . . . Starlight feels like her."

I press my hand over his. "It does. It's a perfect nickname." I run the tip of my nose over his scruff. "Now, about that kiss."

His eyes darken as they meet mine, his fingers finding their way to my hair, and I melt into him. The gentle twist of his fingers inside my hair sends currents down my spine as his mouth claims mine, sure and insistent. I tilt my head, letting him deepen the kiss, hungry for more of his taste, the delicious scrape of his scruff against my skin, and the way his heartbeats quicken underneath my palm.

When he groans, I swear the sound travels straight

through me, settling deep inside my chest where it mingles with all the love I have for this man.

We're both breathless when our lips part, our foreheads resting against each other as our breaths collide. I can't help the soft laugh that bubbles out of me. "How do you make every kiss feel like that?"

"Like what?"

I shake my head, searching for the right words. "Like I've just run every red light and somehow made it out alive."

He chuckles. "I guess you can add that to my repertoire of all the reasons you're with me."

"You mean right next to the orgasms and foot rubs?"

"Precisely." He looks into my eyes for a long moment, his thumb tracing my jaw. "I love you."

I place my hand right above his heart, feeling its steady and solid rhythm beneath my palm. *Here with me.* "We're a forever kind of thing."

A hint of surprise flits across his features, noting I said the words he's been whispering for weeks, before they soften and his lips find mine again. "That we are, Little Borealis."

thirty-one
nisha

You Might Have
Competition

"Hey, assholes? The lights are about to dim so, look over here, will you?" Dean yells, holding his phone camera high for a selfie so it can catch the entire row of us. "Now, everyone say, 'Troy's nipples are the sweetest'!"

Troy groans, dropping his head into his hands, making a few of us giggle.

"What is wrong with you?" Mala hisses through her laughter, smacking Dean's thigh.

"Oh, come on," Dean fires back. "Don't act like anyone here hasn't thought about his nips."

"Can't say that I have," Hudson drawls from a few seats over, sitting hand-in-hand with Kavi.

"Oh, that's right. I forgot you're loyal to Patton's nips." Dean looks at Mala, grinning. "Not sure if I ever told you, Sprinkles, but our geriatric friend here has 'Team Patton' tattooed on his ass cheek."

Hudson doesn't miss a beat. "Right alongside your mom's name."

Kavi shakes her head, pressing her fingers to her lips to cover her laughter while the group erupts.

"Watch it, asshole," Garrett says, pointing at Hudson. "She's my mom, too."

Dean flexes into his phone's camera. "But she loves me more since I inherited all the good genes."

"Weird, because I inherited all the brain cells," Garrett deadpans.

"You mean the three you have?"

Piper snorts next to Dev, looking over at Darian, who's snuggled under a blanket with Rani. "Dar, I don't envy you growing up with these two as older brothers."

Darian takes a long breath as if searching for inner peace. "I'm still in therapy because of it."

We all chuckle when Patton speaks. "Dean, are you going to take this picture or what? The movie's about to start."

"Only if we all say the magic words."

Groans ripple through the group as I settle further into Patton's side with my legs up on the electric footrest. One of my hands rests over my thirty-week pregnant belly while the other entwines with his. Over the past few weeks, my belly has gone from cute little cantaloupe to full-blown watermelon-sized.

My feet look like swollen sausages, I pee like a leaky faucet, and I've developed a distaste for foods I used to enjoy, like Pad Thai, anything with garlic, and—wait for it—pineapples.

Freaking *pineapples*!

And while that shouldn't be a big deal in the grand scheme of things, do you know what it's like to suddenly hate the star ingredient of your favorite drink? Obviously, I'm not drinking anything alcoholic right now, but I'm not going to lie, I'm a little worried pineapple margaritas are permanently off the menu for me.

At least the morning sickness took a hike. And thank God I haven't developed an aversion to French toast. More often than not, Patton makes it for me every morning, but on the weekends, he'll swing by my favorite restaurant to pick up their almond-coconut French toast with apple and berry compote.

I look up at my gorgeous, talented, and infuriatingly perfect ex-husband, mesmerized by the way his eyes glimmer in the soft golden light from the sconces. He's . . . beautiful. Not just in the obvious way, the way that makes strangers throw themselves at him like he's handing out free food samples at Costco. I mean the beauty they can't see, the beauty only I get to witness: his heart, his warmth, his soul.

Even after months together, I still have to pinch myself to make sure it's real and that he's here.

I reluctantly disconnect my gaze from ogling his jaw and that scruff I felt in between my thighs mere hours ago, to glance at our friends seated next to us.

Garrett and Bella sit next to Dean and Mala, while Darian sits with Rani on Garrett's other side. Next to them, Hudson remains as stoic as ever, except when his gaze falls on Kavi, softening the same way Patton's does whenever he looks at me.

Troy is brushing a kiss along Sarina's knuckles while she just stares at him like he hung the moon, and Piper is whispering something in Dev's ear that makes his nostrils flare. At first I think he's angry, but on closer inspection, I'm pretty sure that's not anger on his face. It's . . . lust. *Ew*! If they try anything under that blanket before the lights dim, I'm going to file an official complaint with management here.

At first, Patton had planned to hold this private screening of his upcoming film, *The Winning Pitch*, at the baseball stadium where Troy helped him learn to pitch and where several of the game scenes were shot. But with the February breeze dropping temperatures so low—though the bright sun would make you think it's summer—it didn't make sense to ask everyone to be uncomfortable for two hours. So, he moved it here, to a private theater he rented out, complete with blankets and unlimited snacks and drinks from the concession stand.

"Magic words, people." Dean waves his phone in the air like he's at a concert. "Come on, don't be dickholes."

More groans, audible curses, and an inappropriate hand gesture later, and everyone smiles like they're being held at gunpoint.

The lights dim, sparing us from Dean's attempts for "one more shot" because apparently, he didn't hear Dev and Hudson say, "Troy's nipples are the sweetest".

Jesus Christ. If I wasn't almost eight months pregnant, I would have roundhouse kicked the annoyingness right out of him. Except, I also know what a formidable friend, father, and husband he is. How much life he brings into a room, even at his own expense through self-deprecation. He's also played a huge role in making Patton feel part of the crew, despite only joining a few months ago. And for that, I'll always spare him bodily harm, albeit begrudgingly.

But I won't deny I get a sick sense of satisfaction from making him wither under my glares and side eyes.

What? I'm allowed hobbies other than just knitting.

A hush blankets over us as the theater screen brightens, and we all face forward as the opening credits start. My hand moves over my belly when our little starlight seems to jump at the sound of the loud musical score playing in the background.

Patton glances down, pulling me closer to him and whispering in my ear, "What's wrong? Are you in pain?"

I shake my head. "I think the music woke her up."

He starts to move. "Fuck. Let me tell them to turn it down."

"No." I grab his forearm before he can get up. "It's okay. She'll settle down."

His brows bend. "Are you sure?"

Tilting my head so it's lying on his shoulder, I place a kiss on his jaw. "Yeah, baby. I'm sure."

His eyes find mine, an intensity as warm as the sun shining through them, before his lips meet mine.

"Hey lovebirds?" Dean whisper-hisses, leaning around the group, breaking our trance. "Who's playing me in this movie?"

Patton schools the smile only I know is there. "You'll see his name in the end credits. But he's aptly labeled 'overenthusiastic spectator number three'."

Dean's jaw falls. "Number *three*? That's bullshit! I'm Troy's biggest fucking fan. I literally have his used underwear framed on my altar!"

Bella almost chokes on her popcorn as Garrett pats her back while Troy bolts upright, hollering to anyone who will hear him, "Nope, nope! Security! Anyone? Someone, please escort this lunatic out."

Sarina shushes Troy, pulling him back down to her side while the rest of us shake with laughter. The rest of us, except for Mala, who is covering her face with her hands, shaking her head. God bless the woman.

Hudson mutters without glancing away from the screen. "It would have been more fitting for you to be number two."

"Oh, hardy-har-har," Dean mocks, rolling his eyes. "Look at the old geezer pulling out jokes from elementary school. When was that for you again? 1922?"

The opening credits fade, and the group falls silent as Patton comes on the screen. He looks larger than life, standing on the pitcher's mound in a crisp Boston Breakers uniform. The stadium lights beam across the screen, catching the sweat rolling down his temple as he kisses a photograph in his hands before placing it in his pocket—a ritual Troy was known to do of kissing his daughter's picture. In his last World Series game, however, that picture included two more people he loved: my sister and nephew.

My heart swells, practically demanding to be let out. My God, the man looks unfairly good out there, like he was born to play this role. The crowd roars as the Brooklyn Bats' slugger steps up to the plate. It doesn't take a genius to see the rivalry between the two teams through the screen.

The camera cuts to Patton, his jaw locked and eyes sharp, as he winds up for a curveball that Troy taught him. Even knowing how this scene ends—with the legendary pitcher sustaining a potentially career-ending injury—my stomach still rolls.

Beside me, the real Patton pulls me closer, placing a kiss on my temple.

For the next few minutes, the group is quiet and immersed in the movie, but I can't help admiring the man next to me. The man who was once my teenage best friend with huge dreams of Broadway lights and silver screens. The man who achieved all those dreams, and now lives with me in a modest home, far from the glitz and glamour of Hollywood.

He has more money than he'd be able to spend in several lifetimes, yet not once in the time I've known him has he ever been hungry for it, preferring to drive his truck most days, wearing the watch his foster parents gave him for his high school graduation instead of the countless Rolexes actors of his caliber flaunt on their wrist.

That's not to say he doesn't enjoy the occasional splurge, but money was never his goal. His drive was always for the craft itself, to become the best at it. So much so that, once upon a time, he lost me to it.

But now, finally, I think we can all coexist the way I always imagined.

And then *she* appears, the actress playing Sarina and Patton's counterpart in the movie.

"Oh, my gosh. She's so pretty," the real Sarina says beside me, dipping a french fry into mustard before bringing it to her mouth. "I loved her in *Bridgerton*, but she's even prettier here."

She being Simone Ashley.

All long legs and beautiful curls, she struts to the baseball field with a little boy who's supposed to be Rome, and banters with my husband with all the haughtiness of British royalty. The chemistry between them is so palpable that, for a decently long moment, I forget that I'm watching a film.

"Damn, Nisha," Dean whisper-yells from the end. "I think you might have competition."

"Not even close," Patton clips beside me, brushing his hand over mine, but I'm already too far inside my head.

Heat burns the tips of my ears and a haze of green clouds my vision as I shift in my seat, pulling away from Patton. Is it completely irrational that I feel a burning need to jump into that screen and gouge out the eyes of the woman daring to touch my husband? Yes. But try telling that to the pregnancy-hormone-fueled territorial beast that's taken over my brain.

And yes, I know I said husband. For all intents and purposes, she doesn't need to know he's my ex. All she needs to know is that he's *mine*.

Logically, I know it's part of his job and that natural chemistry sells romance flicks. But it's the hypotheticals that have me in a chokehold.

What if they aren't faking it? What if he finds her prettier, easier to be with, or worse, less of a hormonal mess than me? I mean, I literally bawled when I saw Vajayjay, Beaver, and Snatch yesterday, snuggled up with each other in their cat bed at the salon. If that doesn't scream mental patient, I don't know what does.

But before I have more time to spiral, Patton rises to his feet, tugging me up with him.

"Wh–where are we going?" I whisper.

But he doesn't answer, speaking to no one in particular as

he starts to make his way down the aisle with me in tow. "Excuse us. We'll be right back."

"But there's still an hour left," I protest, following after him.

A minute later, I'm being ushered into another theater. This one is silent, empty, and pitch-dark.

"Patton—" I start, half-question, half-demand, when he turns me around so I face the wall.

Without preamble, he threads our fingers together, places both my hands above my head, and tugs on my hip so my ass meets his groin. A second later, the heat of his body closes in around my back, enveloping me, pinning me against the wall without any force.

His breath ghosts over the shell of my ear, low and panty-melting. "Do you need reassurance of who I belong to, beautiful?"

My pulse skitters, my breathing unsteady. I try to look over my shoulder to catch his eyes, but the theater is too dark. "What are you doing? Someone could come in here."

He may have booked the entire theater, but there are still ushers and staff around. All it would take is for one overachieving teenager to open the door and, bam, we'd be headlining tabloids for weeks.

Patton presses closer, dragging his tongue in a wicked line along my neck. "Then let's give them something to see."

And just like that, all thoughts of Simone Ashley go flying through the nearest exit.

My nerve endings come alive, my nipples pucker, and molten heat pools low in my belly, seeping into my panties. The depravity and risk of it all courses through my veins like jet fuel.

"Oh, God," I whisper shakily, any further protests scattering when I feel the ridge of his cock nuzzle in between my ass cheeks.

Sinking to his haunches, Patton wastes no time dragging my panties down in one urgent motion, before rising again like a large cat reclaiming its prey. He hikes up my cream-colored, thigh-length sweater-dress to expose my ass before sliding his fingers through my folds. His groan is low and guttural.

His other hand grabs a fistful of my hair before he yanks my head back just enough for his lips to graze my ear. "All that fear and worry, yet your pussy is dripping for me. Now widen your legs. I need to remind this pussy to never doubt her worth."

Oh, God. This man's filthy mouth.

A strangled sound leaves me when he slips two fingers inside, meeting no resistance, as if my body was waiting for him to fill me all this time. My eyes droop and my knees wobble as I try to stay upright against the wall, but he's right there behind me, holding me up with his hard body pressed against mine.

"Patton," I gasp, even as my body contradicts my protest, my hips jerking against his hand, needy and desperate. "We can't—"

"We can," he growls, his voice vibrating against my skin. "And we will. I'm just getting started, beautiful."

And before I can even begin to form any more thoughts, his fingers are thrusting inside me, wreaking havoc in my core, my chest, and all my senses. His other hand comes around me to circle my clit while his mouth continues to suck and bite my neck.

The man knows my body like no one ever has, anticipating my needs before even I can, giving me way more than he's ever asked for in return.

My hands tighten into fists against the wall as my body undulates over his fingers. Patton brushes that sweet spot deep inside me with focus and precision, like making me unravel isn't just a desire, it's his calling.

A few more perfect strokes and I'm shaking around him, because of course I am. The man is a god amongst men, capable of making my body do his bidding with nothing more than his touch.

I'm just catching my breath when I hear the unmistakable sound of his zipper dropping before the head of his cock nudges against my entrance.

His hand comes around, splaying over my belly. "Bend over for me, beautiful. I don't want your stomach hitting the wall while I fuck you."

I do as he says, but have to widen my legs even more to give him access. I nearly sob with relief when he plunges inside me in one long stroke, filling and stretching me to mold around him. Then, grabbing my chin with the same hand that was inside me, he presses his fingers between my lips.

"Suck. Taste how much your pussy loves me."

I do as he says, moaning around his fingers and licking up my juices as our bodies collide, making the most obscene sounds in the empty theater.

Every snap of his hips ricochets through me, getting me impossibly wetter and flooding me with illicit heat. My legs shake as my walls contract as a hum of electricity builds around us, ready to strike.

His grip in my hair is unrelenting, every stroke inside me both claiming and possessive, but also careful and aware. Like he's purposely holding himself back from going as hard and fast as we both want because I'm carrying our most prized possession.

"Say it, baby," he pants in my ear, his breaths as ragged as mine as he pulls his fingers out of my mouth. "Whose pussy does this cock belong to?"

"M-mine," I stutter, my eyes rolling back from the pleasure sparking inside me from the tips of my toes to the roots of my hair where his fingers are still tangled.

"That's right, sweetheart. And who do I belong to?"

"Me."

"Just like you belong to me."

I nod, swallowing the groan that would echo down the hall for anyone to hear. "I know."

"You think any other woman could make me this hard? Could any other woman turn me fucking celibate for years?"

The heat inside my chest intensifies, threatening to leak out as warm tears. I swallow, even as I struggle to breathe. God, I love this man with every fiber of my existence. I think I have since the moment I laid eyes on him, since the moment he called me Little Borealis.

"My cock has only ever wanted you," he continues, rocking into me with that perfect balance of strong and gentle. "It will only ever want you for as long as I live. Tell me you understand that, baby?"

A lone tear rolls down the bridge of my nose. "I do."

"Good."

"Patton?"

"Yes, baby?"

"I love you."

I feel him smile against my neck as I shatter once more around his hard length. "I know."

I can't think, can't form words beyond ragged gasps as pleasure courses through my body, igniting a wildfire that spreads from my core to every inch of my skin. It's a blaze so intense and deep, no ocean would be able to quench it.

And whether it's my throaty moan or my complete surrender to him, my orgasm triggers his. He jerks inside me, his hips pistoning erratically until he's caught in the throes of his own release, until his body goes rigid behind me and his guttural roar echoes off the dark theater walls.

His chest heaves, and his heartbeats knock against my back as if trying to fuse with mine. Except they don't need to try... our heartbeats feel one and the same.

Before I can collapse, Patton wraps an arm around me, holding me tight. His lips brush my ear, making me shudder. "Worth the risk."

Five minutes later, we've managed to get our clothes back on and in order. I've patted my hair down as best as I can in the dark, hoping I haven't smudged my eyeliner.

Clutching my hand, Patton opens the door to exit the theater when we both come to an abrupt stop. Standing in front of us is our entire group of friends, looking at us with a range of expressions. Garrett's jaw is on the floor, Kavi's fingers cover her mouth in shock, and Dean mutters, "Called it".

No one speaks for a moment, and then Piper shakes her head, lips pursed to hide her grin. "You guys missed the best part of the movie. Hope it was worth it."

Heat rises to my cheeks, but Patton smirks, waggling his brows. "You mean the climax? Nah, we got to that on our own."

Sarina makes a strangled noise, shaking her head as she walks away. "Thanks for that. I'm going to go bleach my brain now."

thirty-two
nisha

The Bone-deep Ache of
Acceptance

"Beaver, buddy, we've talked about this. You can't go around stealing from our clients." I wince at the glittering Cartier watch lying at my feet. "This is how Netflix documentaries start. You're going to get us into serious legal trouble."

Beaver's sharp blue eyes narrow on me for a beat, his hairless white tail thwacking the air like a whip in challenge, like he knows I'm not happy with his "gift". Before I can bend down to pick up the watch, he springs forward to snatch it back and bolts across the room. By the time I've straightened—because when you're as pregnant as I am, it takes a while to "unbend"—he's already perched on his cat tree with the watch dangling from his mouth, staring at me like a hairless, lifeless, motionless wax statue.

I sigh, waddling over to him. Yes, waddling, because that's my mode of transport now. At thirty-nine weeks, I'm officially a beach ball with legs. And a pair of enormous boobs that Patton definitely enjoys more than I do. I've had to size up my uniform of black leggings and tunic, but at this point, the fabric is so stretched out, I mostly resemble a balloon animal on the verge of popping.

Okay, so the balloon example isn't my finest because . . . well, balloons. *Cue a full-body shudder.*

I haven't shaved my legs or seen my toes in weeks. Well, unless you count yesterday, when Patton painted them.

I smile at the memory of him hunched over with the focus of a neurosurgeon performing his very first surgery. I'd insisted I could do it myself, but he'd simply smirked like I'd lost my damn mind, brought my feet to his lap, and brushed each of my nails with my signature black polish. And the sweetest part? He even blew on them afterward like the world's sexiest nail tech.

Thinking of him reminds me he's in San Francisco, meeting with producers about a foster system documentary he's passionate about. With how far along I am, he said he didn't want to chance not being here if I needed something, so he insisted the producers fly here, instead of making him travel to L.A.

He's decided to scale back in general with work, making only one major film a year, and focus on our new family, using any extra time he has left for matters close to his heart, like the foster system. When I asked him if that's really what he wanted to do, his response was, *"I've already done everything I ever dreamed of, except this—building a family with you. This was always the real dream, baby."*

And honestly, the balance works well. He still gets to do what he loves, and I get more of him being around.

Hands on my hips, I give my mischievous cat a stern look. "Beaver, I'm not kidding. I'm not doing one of those 'meet the inmate' interviews from behind bars. Now, give it back."

It takes some minor wrestling, along with him trying to make another run for it, before I finally manage to scoop him against my belly and gently tug the watch out of his mouth. He exits my suite, meowing sadly and giving me the kind of wounded look Shakespeare wrote about.

Great. I know I'll be paying for this with extra cuddles and treats for the next week.

"What did he steal this time?" Sarina's voice carries from down the hall, her footsteps approaching. She must have heard me talking to my pickpocket cat.

"Oh, only a watch that costs more than my car."

I rub the side of my belly, feeling a tightness there. Last week I experienced what are known as Braxton Hicks contractions, or "practice contractions". For a while, I thought I was going into labor, but after I drank something and walked around, they eased on their own.

This feeling, like my uterus is twisting, sort of feels the same, maybe slightly sharper, but I don't think it's anything to worry about. I brush my hand over my belly, taking in a long breath. I have another week left; I can't jump to the conclusion that I'm going into labor every time I feel a stitch.

Both Sarina and Piper appear at my door, taking in the scene of me holding the expensive timepiece while trying not to topple over.

"Jesus," Piper says, shaking her head before reaching for the watch. "I think that's the watch my last client was wearing. At this point, that cat of yours should have a criminal record and a dedicated parole officer."

Sarina winces. "How the hell did that menace take it off him?"

"God only knows," I say dryly, handing the watch to Piper. "I should have named him David Blaine or Houdini; his talents defy explanation."

The tightness in my belly catches me off-guard again. It's more insistent this time, and I inhale another sharp breath, fisting the back of the salon chair. *Okay, that felt a lot stronger than the Braxton Hicks from last week. Or maybe it's the same, and I'm not remembering correctly?*

"Neesh," Sarina gasps, placing a hand on my back. "Are you okay?"

"I'm fine," I say, waving her off. "Probably another Braxton Hicks. That, or all the stress from running this criminal feline empire."

"Maybe sit down," Piper says, eyeing my belly with concern. "You're close enough to the due date that it could be a real contraction."

"I doubt it," I argue. "The doctor said I wasn't dilated at all when Patton and I went for my checkup two days ago. It's my last day before maternity leave; I'll be out of here in a few hours, anyway."

"Still—"

But Piper is cut off when Joshua knocks on my door. "Hey, Nisha. Your next appointment is here. Want me to bring him back?"

"Yup, I'm all ready for him," I answer, getting the last of my tools arranged in size order.

Okay, so maybe I've also fluffed my throw pillows a few times over the past week and rearranged the magazines on the coffee table every time I've passed them. But at least I haven't cleaned every cupboard or rewashed baby clothes for the *third* time like I've wanted to.

Though, I did arrange them by color, size, and cuteness factor...

I can see the old obsessive, control-driven version of myself that I'd tamed over the past few months trying to poke her head through. And I'm proud to say, aside from letting her slip in here and there, akin to letting a little air out of an overinflated tire, I have kept her mostly at bay.

So what's the reason she's even trying to claw back in?

Because I'm terrified.

Terrified of giving birth, terrified of becoming a mother, and terrified that I'll screw it all up. Fear has always had a way of amplifying my normally manageable quirks into full-blown, color-coded and alphabetized antics. And right now, that fear of the unknown is as loud as a bullhorn inside a quiet church.

But I keep telling myself the same thing—once our little starlight is here, once we get to know each other and have a routine, those fears will subside. At least that's what I've been told through all the books and online forums I've read.

"Nisha?" The worry in Sarina's voice has me glancing over while Joshua goes to fetch my next client. "Want me to call Patton?"

"And tell him what? That I'm having cramps? If they turn into full contractions, which they likely won't, I'll call him. I'll be fine enough to get through one appointment, I promise."

My sister and best friend look at each other, wondering if they should argue, before they reluctantly leave my suite.

It'll be okay. These cramps are just a way of preparing my body for the real thing. I just need to breathe.

Except, ten minutes later, I'm standing behind Andy Honeyman, a thirty-something CEO with perfectly styled hair and an ego to match, who's been droning on about his start-up's latest funding round, when I feel my slacks dampen on the inside of my thigh.

I freeze mid-cut, my eyes going wide as I attempt to look down, seeing nothing past my big belly. That's when my stomach lurches again, and I grip Andy's chair to hold myself up. A sheen of perspiration starts to coat my neck and chest as I remind myself to breathe. Just breathe. But the warm sensation increases until my entire left leg feels wet.

My mind screams.

No. No, no, no! This wasn't supposed to happen today. She's full-term, yes, but I'm not mentally prepared to have her yet. Plus, Patton's not here. And I don't have my hospital bag.

But it's okay. Just breathe, Nisha. It's going to be okay. You just need to call Patton and let him know that he needs to meet you at the hospital.

Everything is going to be okay.

"—I mean, Andreessen Horowitz is calling us the next Tesla," Andy continues to babble, completely oblivious to the fact that I'm practically bowled over. "I told my assistant to book me a bigger jet. Can't have the CEO of a potentially multi-billion-dollar unicorn company flying economy."

I take a gulp of air. "Andy, I—uh . . . I think we'll have to reschedule."

Turning, Andy finally blinks, peering down at my drenched slacks, his face contorting with disgust. "Uh . . . is that *normal*?"

"That depends," I say through gritted teeth, stumbling to my door, "on if you consider going into labor *normal*."

"Oh, God." Andy jumps out of the chair. "Are you—are you having a baby? Like, *right now?*"

"Yes, I'd say the process has officially begun."

"Oh . . . it's just that I have this meeting I can't be late to, and—"

This piece of human shit.

"Yeah, I'm so sorry, Andy," I bite out. "Clearly, I should have checked your calendar before letting my water break."

I clutch the door handle for dear life as another wave of pain passes through me before finally flinging the door open. "Sarina! Piper!"

My sister and best friend appear almost instantly, taking in the scene—me still holding the door handle, doubled over, while Andy gapes like a fish out of water.

"Yup, her water just broke," Sarina informs anyone who might still be clueless, springing into action. Grabbing towels from a cabinet behind her, she points to our best friend. "Piper, you get the car, and I'll help her get in."

Pine For Me

I fumble for my phone in my pocket. "I need to call—" I pant, then groan in pain. "I need to call Patton."

"I'll call him from the car, Neesh," Piper says, running to her suite to grab her purse and keys. "Let's just get to the hospital."

Still, I press Patton's contact number, walking at a snail's pace toward the exit. It rings the standard four times before going to voicemail. *Dammit.*

"Patton," I say with as much calm as I can muster. "I'm . . . I'm on my way to the hospital. Our baby is coming."

Sarina places towels on the backseat of Piper's car, helping me inside as gently as possible before yanking the seat belt across my lap. She comes to the other side, sitting next to me. "Okay, Piper, hit the gas. We're ready to go." She squeezes my hand, a grin breaking over her face despite the chaos. "You're having this baby, sis! I'm going to be an aunty!"

"Me, too!" Piper squeals, gunning it like she's trying to qualify for Formula 1.

I sink into the backseat, my head against the headrest, groaning as I clutch Sarina's hand beside me. This isn't what I pictured for today, but I need to be thankful. Yes, Patton isn't here, but my two best friends are, and they jumped into action. I've made it this far without too many complications, and that's something to hold on to.

Now, if only my boyfriend, ex-husband, husband—whatever the hell he is—would just call me back!

A cry rips through my throat as another contraction makes me double over again.

"If I'm not mistaken, your last contraction was seven minutes ago." Piper glances at me through the rearview mirror. "Which means we're in the early-but-serious zone."

And yet, still no sign of my ex-husband.

Maybe it's the twin-telepathy she claims we have, but

Sarina seems to read my mind, dialing Patton's number and sighing when she gets his voicemail. "He's not picking up."

"Try texting him," Piper says, swerving onto the highway.

I do just that, typing out a similar message to the voicemail with shaking thumbs. But when my message just sits there on Delivered instead of Read, my ribs threaten to constrict everything they're caging—my lungs, my heart, my quickly diminishing calm.

He hasn't read it, nor has he heard the voicemail.

Maybe he's still in the middle of that meeting. Maybe he'll see it in the next minute or two. Oh, God, what if something is wrong? What if something happened to him?

No, no. We're not going down that road, Nisha. Nothing is wrong. He's alive and fine.

I mean, he won't be either of those things after he calls me and realizes how much of a panic he's put me in, but we'll deal with me murdering him later.

This isn't like last time.

He's been around, *present and doting*, these past nine months.

He's just . . . caught up. His phone is probably set to Do Not Disturb.

But it wouldn't be, would it? Not when he knows how crucial these last couple of weeks are, when any moment could be *the moment*.

Still, I press his contact name again, the tentacles of that old feeling wrapping around me like steel cables. Loneliness, fear, the desperate need to hear his voice and feel his arms.

And the bone-deep ache of acceptance when he never called.

He said he's changed; I've seen it. And I want to believe it. But as the minutes go by—twenty, thirty, forty-five—and multiple contractions tear through me while my phone remains silent, all I can think is, *Why am I never important enough?*

thirty-three
nisha

Come Through for Me

The private suite inside the Stanford Medical Center's VIP wing that Patton had arranged long ago feels more like a hotel room rather than a hospital, with its soft lighting, plush seating, and inviting decor. But neither the luxurious amenities nor the fully attentive medical staff can erase the smell of antiseptic or the dread growing inside my heart.

Two hours. It's been almost two hours and still no sign of Patton.

With my hand entwined with my sister's, I'm propped up on the bed, wearing one of those measly gowns that are more lace ties than fabric, with monitors strapped to my belly to track both mine and the baby's heartbeats.

And though the rhythm of her heart is comforting, knowing she's healthy, safe, and ready to come out, my fears overshadow the moment, repeating on a loop.

Why hasn't he answered my calls? What if something is wrong? What if he misses our baby's birth? How do I do this without him?

"How are we doing, Nisha?" Dr. Gilbert asks, checking the results from the fetal monitor. Thank God she was here when Sarina and Piper brought me in, instead of an on-call doctor I'm not familiar with.

"Oh, just peachy," I say sarcastically, clenching my teeth as another contraction twists my uterus like it's a fabric being wrung out.

This one seems to last longer, making me grip Sarina's hand so tight, I'm afraid I'll break bones. Piper comes to my other side, brushing a damp strand of my hair off my forehead.

I was prepared for the pain, and under no illusion this was going to be easy, but having these two women by my side as pillars of support has made me feel braver than I ever thought possible, especially since Patton isn't here. They've shown up for me time and time again, setting aside their own families and lives to hold my hand.

Which is a lot more than I can say for my ex-husband, the man who said he'd never let me face this alone. The man who promised this baby and I were his highest priority.

As soon as the contraction crests, I check my phone, praying that I'll see a missed call or text. But of course, there's neither.

It's then that I hear a change in the beeping from one of the monitors. It's jagged, slower than before. "Wh–what's happening? Why did the beeping slow down?"

Dr. Gilbert's brows furrow. "The baby's heart rate is dropping during your contractions and not recovering as fast as we'd expect."

"What does that mean?" Sarina asks on my behalf, seeing the way my face pales.

"Sometimes babies get stressed during labor. The lowered heart rate can be an indication of that, so we just need to keep an eye on it."

Stressed. My baby is stressed? Maybe from these contractions shredding me from the inside, but maybe because she's tethered to me, feeling the anxiety thrumming through my veins. While I'm here, eyes glued to monitors I don't understand, praying I don't lose another child, her father is in some conference room, laying out his dreams for the next project.

Acid churns in my gut as memories from all those years ago assault my brain. The bathroom floor. The blood-soaked sunflower pajamas. The idle phone clutched in my hand like a futile lifeline.

The endless and suffocating tears, like a dark, heavy, thunderous cloud that makes you believe all sunshine is lost. They're not the kind of tears that cleanse your heart, but the kind that annihilate your soul.

And then that raw, all-consuming numbness, as if all my emotions were dowsed with a general anesthetic, when the doctor confirmed what I already knew. That I'd indeed lost the baby.

Patton swore he'd never let me go through something like that alone again. That he'd be here every step of the way . . .

So where is he now?

"Neesh, I messaged Troy," Sarina says, the corners of her eyes creasing with worry. "He's trying to get hold of Patton's agent, hoping maybe he knows something."

"I'm going to try to call him, too," Piper states, already pulling out her phone.

I don't respond. Or maybe I do. Whatever leaves my lips is flat and toneless, a sound caught between resigned acceptance and a wail I don't have the strength for.

They exchange another look before Piper dials Patton's number, leaving him yet another voicemail with the same desperate message. "Patton, please call one of us back. Nisha needs you."

My heart plummets.

But I beg it not to shatter.

Sarina squeezes my hand. "He's going to be here, Neesh. I just know it."

Pine For Me

I stay silent, tears gathering behind my lids. I'm not going to argue with her, but every cell in my body wants to scream, *"You mean like the way he was here the last time?"*

"I called Dad, too. He's on his way," she continues, but her words barely register.

Another contraction slams into me, seizing my breath, my movements, and everything inside me as white-hot pain shoots through me. I grip the bed rails so hard, my knuckles turn white. Stars dance in my vision before my tears finally break free, streaking down my cheeks on a mission to set fire to my skin.

Piper's gentle fingers brush them away. "Breathe, Nisha. I know you're scared, but you're the strongest person I know. You're going to get through this."

A sob bubbles up my throat. "The only way I get through this is *with* my baby."

Because if that's not the case at the end of this . . . I won't recover this time.

Piper's eyes glisten. "You will, honey. I know you will."

But I can't answer. My fears are sitting on top of my chest like a boulder, pressing down until all I can manage is silence. Because even with my sister and best friend beside me, I feel that old suffocating loneliness creep in. The kind that can only be erased by one person.

It's always him who should have been here. And always him who's missing.

The baby's heart rate drops dangerously once more, and this time Dr. Gilbert moves with purpose, summoning my dedicated nurse.

"Let's change positions. Turn to your left side, Nisha; sometimes that can improve the baby's heart rate."

The nurse comes to my side, helping me roll before strapping an oxygen mask over my mouth. The movement sends a bolt of pain through my lower back, leaving me gasping and shaking. For a few moments, the change in position seems to help stabilize the baby's heart rate.

But then it dips even lower.

"What's happening?" My voice sounds hoarse to my own ears. "Please tell me she's going to be okay."

Dr. Gilbert gives me a look that has my spine straightening. "The baby's not responding, and her heart rate is at a sustained deceleration."

Not responding. Sustained deceleration.

Stressed.

With each inhale of oxygen, I send a prayer out to a woman I think about often. A woman I wish was here with me every day, but especially today.

Mom, if you're listening, please help her. We're almost at the finish line, and all I've done for the last nine months—no, practically the last decade—is dream about meeting her, about being the kind of mother you were to me. She's a part of you, so please, if you can do anything at all, please come through for me.

Because I can't . . . I simply won't be able to go through losing another baby again.

"What does 'sustained deceleration' mean, Doctor?" Piper asks impatiently. "What's the next step?"

Dr. Gilbert's calm exterior breaks for a moment, her mouth setting in a grave line as she sets her decisive gaze on me. "That means we need to prepare you for an emergency C-section."

The room spins, and my heart seems to cease beating momentarily. But I have no time to gather my thoughts or even let the panic set in. I have no time to look at my phone or wonder where Patton is anymore.

Because minutes later, I'm being wheeled into the operating room.

thirty-four
patton

Seven Schlongs Hen Party

TROY WINTERS

Has anyone heard from Patton today? Sarina's been blowing up my phone. He's not responding to any of his missed calls or messages, and Nisha is looking for him.

DEV MENON

Piper has been calling me, too.

DEAN MEYER

He's probably in the middle of filming a men's cologne commercial or some shit. The dude always smells so good.

HUDSON CASE

Not at all weird that you've sniffed him.

DEAN MEYER

Please, as if you haven't done it yourself. Everyone knows what a hard-on you have for him. Don't act like you wouldn't buy his post-workout sweat.

Swati M.H.

GARRETT MEYER

An article I read recently said Patton Pierce's used bathwater was in high demand. How much do you wanna bet that demand comes from one person in our group?

HUDSON CASE

Fuck off. I just admire the man's craft.

DEAN MEYER

Is that why you have his whiskey commercial bookmarked on your browser? The one where he's shirtless, wearing a cowboy hat, showing off his abs. Because of his CRAFT??

HUDSON CASE

I like that brand of whiskey!

GARRETT MEYER

I think you like that brand of shirtless.

DEV MENON

Hey idiots! No one's answered Troy's question. Nisha is in labor, and both our wives are looking for Patton.

GARRETT MEYER

Whoa! Nisha's in labor?

DEAN MEYER

Jesus, @Troy Winters, maybe lead with that next time.

DARIAN MEYER

Wow. Nisha's in labor and she can't reach Patton? Didn't he tell us about something similar? The reason she left him the first time?

Pine For Me

GARRETT MEYER

Shit. I forgot about that.

TROY WINTERS

Which is why Sarina is freaking out. This isn't just bad timing; it's literally the WORST timing. I called his agent, but he said they left the meeting this morning in separate cars.

DEV MENON

Wait, so he's not still in the meeting? Because that's where the ladies thought he was.

TROY WINTERS

No. Apparently, he left over two hours ago and was headed to the salon to surprise Nisha.

DEV MENON

Shit. This is even more ominous.

DARIAN MEYER

But if, God forbid, something terrible happened to him, it would be all over the news by now. The guy's a famous movie star.

DEAN MEYER

So either he's fine or choosing not to respond or was abducted by aliens.

GARRETT MEYER

Honestly, I hope for his sake he's been abducted by aliens. Because as much as we'll miss him, and Hudson will miss his "craft," the dude's not going to survive Nisha's wrath.

HUDSON CASE

Why did you type craft in quotations?

DEAN MEYER

Because we know you aren't watching his movies for the plot, old man. And for once, I understand you. I never watched Troy's games for his pitching.

TROY WINTERS

Please, no one ask what the hell he was watching instead.

DEV MENON

No one needs to. Pretty sure Dean has slow-motion footage of you stretching before games.

TROY WINTERS

Christ. I'm so glad I officially retired.

DEAN MEYER

@Patton Pierce? @Patton Pierce? Hello!? @Patton Pierce??

DEV MENON

What the hell are you doing, dumbass?

DEAN MEYER

What? I'm trying to tag him so he sees these messages.

HUDSON CASE

[GIF of Jeff Bridges from The Big Lebowski running his hand down his face]

TROY WINTERS

What do you think missed calls and direct messages do, Dean?

Pine For Me

GARRETT MEYER

> Bro, tagging him on a text thread isn't going to summon him. He's not fucking Beetlejuice.

DEAN MEYER

> That's true. Because saying Beetlejuice three times would mean he'd ACTUALLY show up.

DARIAN MEYER

> Just wait until Patton comes back and reads this thread.

DEAN MEYER

> Shit. How do I delete that previous message?? Patton, brother, homie . . . you know I'm just messing around. I say stupid shit all the time.

HUDSON CASE

> Finally, something we can all agree on.

TROY WINTERS

> Not sure you have to worry, Dean. If I know my sister-in-law, Patton might not live to see another day, even if he DOES come back. When we spoke earlier, Sarina said Nisha looked homicidal.

GARRETT MEYER

> I don't blame her. Shit, @Patton Pierce, get your ass to the hospital. I don't want to have to write your eulogy with "he had his whole life ahead of him".

HUDSON CASE

> I could call Patton's publicist. Or reach out to his personal trainer and his dog walker. Any of them might know.

Swati M.H.

DEV MENON

> You have his dog walker's number? And here I thought Dean was the lunatic.

DEAN MEYER

> Hey! At least I'm a CHARMING lunatic! Hudson's straight up stalking. He's not even as youthful as I am.

TROY WINTERS

> Call whoever, Hudson. We need to find out where he is. I'm heading to the hospital. Not much else we can do from here.

DEV MENON

> I'm headed there, too. See you in a bit.

GARRETT MEYER

> Keep us posted. And @Hudson Case? Maybe keep the dog walker thing to yourself? I wouldn't want Patton to find out.

DARIAN MEYER

> He's on the thread, dumbass.

GARRETT MEYER

> Oh, that's right. Well, @Patton Pierce, I hope you were sitting down while you read this.

thirty-five
patton

One of Pavlov's Test Subjects

The empty, backward-facing car seat in my rearview mirror catches my eye, making my lips curve up. I installed one in both mine and Nisha's cars just last week. And soon, it'll hold the most precious person in both our worlds. Just the thought of meeting our little starlight has me vibrating with anticipation.

Reaching over to the passenger seat of my truck, I grab the ball cap I always have there and tug it low over my head before slipping on my sunglasses.

My publicist wouldn't be thrilled knowing how often I've frequented this place over the past few months, but what he doesn't know won't kill him. And so far, I've managed to do it without getting photographed, which is a feat on its own.

Besides, I've become friends with the owners, Rachel and Rachael. The two women turned this hole-in-the-wall space into San Jose's *R&R's Waffle House*. To avoid confusion, Rachel goes by her full name, while Rachael goes by Rach. They're the ones who keep Nisha's favorite French toast waiting for me every weekend.

The ladies couldn't be kinder, bringing my order out to the curb when the restaurant is busy or tipping me off when it's quiet enough that I can sneak inside. On the early mornings that I know Nisha will sleep in—something she's been doing more of with all those middle-of-the-night bathroom visits that keep her awake—I'll even sit in a corner booth with a latte and a fresh donut that the ladies never charge me for, catching up on emails until Nisha's breakfast is ready.

What? Just because I have more money than I know what to do with, I shouldn't like free stuff? Anyway, I tip them triple the amount of my order every time, so I consider it even. Plus, since Nisha hasn't been drinking coffee throughout the pregnancy, I try not to drink it in front of her. So, this works out in both our favors.

I'm usually here earlier on Saturdays, but after my meeting with the producers this morning in San Francisco ended both positively and earlier than I expected, I figured I'd swing by to pick up brunch for Nisha instead. She should be at the salon by now, and I have no idea what she ate this morning since I left early.

Not before getting my fill of her, though. She'd stirred awake to wish me good luck on my pitch, and one thing had led to another, which led to me having my first breakfast between her legs. Fucking hell, I can't get enough of the woman. And the fact that she's swollen with my child only makes her more beautiful and me feeling more insatiable around her.

Having gotten the thumbs-up from the ladies, stating there's minimal foot traffic at this time since they're close to closing, I stride inside. My plan is to have a cup of coffee as I wait for Nisha's order.

The familiar and sweet scents of vanilla and cooked dough hit me as soon as I enter, and my mouth instantly waters. I'm like one of Pavlov's test subjects. Well, now I think I'll have to order one of their donuts, too, aside from just the coffee.

"Great to see you, Patton!" Rachel greets me from behind

the counter where she's wiping down the coffee machine with practiced ease. Her blonde and gray locks sit neatly on her shoulders. "Want your regular while you wait for Nisha's almond-coconut French toast?"

"Yup, and a glazed donut, too. Thanks, Rachel."

Her astute hazel gaze assesses me. "You're wearing a suit, and it's later than usual. Did you have a meeting?"

I smile, slipping my hands into my pockets. "Can't get anything past you, can I? I met with some producers about a passion project I'm pitching."

She polishes the steam wand with a white cloth. "Well? How did it go?"

"They seemed interested but said they'd discuss and get back to me."

"That sounds promising." She reaches for a steel container, filling it with milk and putting it under the steam wand before turning back to me. "And how's Nisha? She's what, thirty-eight, thirty-nine weeks now?"

"Hey, Patton!" Rach, the other owner and friend from the duo, emerges through the double-doors in the back, wearing an apron with their company logo. Her shoulder-length waves, a mix of chestnut, auburn, and gray, are secured in a clip at the back of her head. "Glad you were able to come by before we close. Well, actually, that's not true; we *technically* close in ten minutes, but both Rachel and I will be here for the next couple of hours, cleaning up and doing inventory and accounting."

"What she means is," Rachel says, pouring a shot of espresso into the cup she's making for me before lifting it toward me, "feel free to stick around. We won't be rushing you out."

"Thanks," I say, taking the cup from her. "And Nisha's good. Tired, but good. She's thirty-nine weeks. The home stretch."

Rach offers a wide smile. "That is so exciting! Now, not that I pay attention to tabloids or anything, but—"

Back at her position near the coffee machine, Rachel coughs discreetly, muttering what sounds like "bullshit," making me chuckle.

Rach lifts her chin, ignoring her friend. "As I was saying, I don't read gossip magazines, but I couldn't help but notice one when I was in the grocery line. You and Nisha were on the cover, and there were doulas and supposed doctors predicting you were having a boy based on the way she was carrying."

"What a load of crock!" Rachel rolls her eyes, dumping old espresso into a compost bin. "Those gossip rags have nothing better to talk about."

Holding my cup, I lean in over the counter conspiratorially. "Well, I'll tell you both, if you promise to keep it between us..."

Rach nods, making a gesture like she's zipping her lips. "We promise. You know you can trust us."

And I do trust them. These women have been nothing but friendly and dependable, keeping me under the radar from even their own families. It's a luxury fame rarely affords.

Rachel saunters to the counter. "We even made Abby swear not to tell anyone you came in here from time to time. She's the woman we hired a few weeks ago to help us over the weekends. We told her straight-up that she'd be out of a job if she blabbed."

I'm just about to tell them Nisha and I are having a girl when the double doors swing open and a woman steps out, balancing a plate on her hand.

"Um, Ms. Rachel? You said to bring out a glazed donut when they were ready?"

That voice. It's soft and hesitant, and...

Recognition scratches at the edges of my memories.

My eyes lock on her, though she hasn't lifted her gaze yet.

My breath stalls inside my lungs, and the cup threatens to crack in my hand.

"Ah, yes. Speak of the devil!" Rachel says brightly, oblivious to the way I've gone rigid. "Patton? Why don't you take a seat at your booth? Abby will bring over your donut."

And that's when she looks up—

Abigail Shaw.

Her eyes widen and her mouth falls open, revealing several missing teeth. Her feeble hands tremble so hard, the donut slides to the edge of the plate.

Rach rushes to Abigail's side, wrapping a hand around her wrist, making Abigail flinch. "Abby, what's going on? Are you okay?" She looks from Abby to me. "Do you . . . do you know each other?"

I blink, taking in the woman in front of me.

She's a shadow of her former self with hollowed cheeks, pale skin, and her frame lost beneath the restaurant's uniform that hangs off her like borrowed clothes. Her once thick mane is nothing but wisps clinging to her scalp. And yet, there's no mistaking those eyes.

They're muted now, dulled to the color of dry grass when they used to remind me of lush trees. The same eyes that sharpened on me as I asked if there was anything to eat when she came home an entire day after having locked me inside a one-room trailer. The same eyes that turned cold when I asked her about the sores on her arms. Or darted around the room, wild and paranoid, when her dealers broke into our trailer.

And the same eyes that glistened, resigned and grieving, at the sight of me sobbing, begging for the cops to let her go.

Those same eyes stare back at me now, wide with recognition.

"We used to," I say, squaring my shoulder and placing a mask over my face that would make me unrecognizable to myself. "Abby is my mother."

thirty-six
patton

Hope They Gave Her the Good Drugs

I don't hear the squeak of the vinyl as I slide into the booth, or the scrape of my cup against the wooden table. I don't hear Rachael and Rachel's shocked murmurs, wondering if they heard correctly. Nor do I hear the hesitant footsteps of the woman who birthed me, walking toward me after twenty-six years.

I don't hear any of that when all I can hear is the drum of my heart, the rush of blood inside my ears, and the catch in my throat with every ragged breath I take.

The delicious vanilla scent that surrounded me only moments ago feels suffocating, like it's too sweet for what's about to unfold.

"S–son."

My eyes snap to her, my hand fisting on my lap. Hot molten lava races through my veins. "You lost the right to call me that a long time ago, Abigail."

Seven years. She did seven years for possession and intent to distribute. It wasn't her first stint in jail, but it was her longest. And while she waited behind bars, having left her six-year-old son in the hands of the state, I waited for *her*.

Day in and day out, until I turned thirteen, when I knew

she was being released, I waited for her to come back and take me home, but she never did.

I remember waking up every day and checking the mail. Surely, she'd write if something had changed. Surely there was a reason she hadn't found me yet. She wouldn't have forgotten her one and only son.

But she had.

Because I didn't just wait at thirteen. I waited every year after that, on every birthday, every Christmas, and every first day of school, hoping that was the day she'd come back.

But by eighteen, I accepted she wasn't going to. I knew she'd been released from jail and had searched online obituaries to confirm she wasn't dead.

I could have looked for her, tried to find her myself, but I chose not to. Because that kid, who would scan crowds to find his mother's familiar green eyes and perk up whenever there was a knock on the door, had grown up. He'd accepted her decision, let go, and found peace.

Or that's what I thought until now.

Because right now, peace is the last thing I feel. Above that are feelings I haven't made use of in a long time, like anger, hurt, and betrayal. But more than anything is the reminder of how I was abandoned, not just when she was in jail, but when she wasn't.

"Patton—"

I lift a hand to silence her ragged whisper, even if it meets its mark inside my chest. "What are you doing in San Francisco, Abigail? How did you find me?"

She shuffles forward, plate still trembling in her hands. I can't tell if the shaky hands are just nerves or a permanent condition.

"I-I made my way to L.A. a couple of years ago, but I never found you. Then I heard you were going to be filming in San

Jose. I read about it when the shelter let me use their internet. So I took a chance and moved here."

The shelter. I look at her haggard visage, her gaunt and hollow face, and her lifeless eyes. Time and addiction have whittled her down to the bone.

I wish there was something, *anything*, that could help loosen the rock lodged inside my throat. I've often wondered about her over the years, and though my thoughts were usually bitter and unforgiving, I'd never wish to see her homeless, alone, or weak. Never.

I'm still processing her words and the fact that my mother is in front of me after all these years when she speaks again.

"A few months ago, I saw you walk into this restaurant. I thought I'd imagined it, but then I saw you here a time or two after that. So . . . I came here and begged them for a job, hoping I'd get a chance to talk to you."

"Why?" I ask, trying to keep my jaw hard. "What do you want from me? Oh, let me guess. You owe money to someone —your dealer, perhaps?—and you're here to ask for my help."

Her eyes turn glassy. "I've been clean for more than a decade, and completely sober for four."

I give her a condescending smile. "Wonderful. Do you want a standing ovation? A pat on the back, maybe? You know, the things you were never there to give me."

"I don't want your money or your help, Patton. That's not why I'm here."

"Then why *are* you here?"

She doesn't answer for a few long beats, her chin trembling as she tries to compose herself. She might think I'm being cold and dismissive—and maybe I am—but she doesn't know me well enough to know the wounds I've worked hard to mend. She has no idea how much internal strength and positivity I needed, day in and day out, without any biological family to speak of, to find myself. To *believe* in myself.

Pine For Me

Though I didn't do it alone, not after I met Nisha. She was there every step of the way . . . until she wasn't. But we've worked past that, and I'm never reopening those scars; not when we've finally moved forward.

Abigail nods at the seat across from me, sniffling. "Can I sit down?"

Before I can respond, Rach peeks around the corner. "We'll stay open for a while, so take as long as you both need."

I catch her wide brown eyes over Abigail's shoulder before she quickly busies herself, wiping down an already spotless counter. I don't doubt that the two women are listening to every word of this family drama unraveling in their restaurant, but I trust them enough to know it won't leave these walls.

Placing the plate on the table, Abigail uses the distraction to slide into the seat across from me, even though I never explicitly gave her permission.

My heart pounds like a stampede of wild horses inside my chest, my grip tightening around my cup as my gaze drifts over her.

For years I imagined what it would be like to see my mother again. At one point I even wrote down the questions I'd ask, aside from the obvious *"Why didn't you come back for me?"* But I can't seem to recall a single one right now.

She looks down at her hands on her lap. "I want your forgiveness, Patton. I'm not expecting your love—"

"Well, I'm glad we're on the same page, then, since I have none to give you."

Her sharp intake of breath is like a prick to my chest. I close my eyes, forcing myself to breathe. Maybe she deserves my words, maybe she doesn't. But despite everything, *this* is not who I am. I'm not this harsh or callous, this resentful or cutting.

I'll never defend her actions, but I also won't let them turn me into someone who clings to the past. Especially not when I've worked so hard to move forward.

Am I still hurt after all these years? Of course. But I've also learned that choices compound until one bad decision leads to another, and suddenly, you're so far down the rabbit hole, you can't find your way back to daylight.

I know because I've been in her shoes. Where her drug was meth, mine was ambition. I chased its high until it consumed me. Until I lost the one woman who saw me for who I was. To her, I wasn't the guy on dumb billboards or overrated red carpets, but the man she gave her heart to, the one who vowed to protect and honor her, but didn't.

The thought has me wishing I could turn back time, not just to swallow my harsh words to my mother, but to see the path I was on. The one that led to the dissolution of my marriage all those years ago. The one that led to Nisha and me being apart for so long.

"I didn't mean that," I say, my voice softer, my shoulders slowly releasing the tension gathered in them. "I . . . I don't know what you were going through at that time, but I also don't know how to sit here and pretend the last twenty-six years didn't happen."

She nods, a tear slipping down her cheek. "I know. I'm so, so sorry, Patton. I've made a lot of mistakes in my life, but the biggest was not being the kind of mother you deserved. I was really messed up at the time. It's not an excuse, but it's a regret I'll live with for the rest of my life."

She brushes her cheek with the back of her hand. "I'm not asking you to pretend. I know I can't undo the past or give you back your childhood . . . or all those moments I missed. But I am asking you to find it in your heart to forgive me." Her shoulders hunch. "And if you can't, I understand that, too. I probably deserve that."

My gaze catches Rachel's from behind the counter before

she pretends to remember something, scurrying off toward the double doors.

I look out the window next to the booth. "Why didn't you come back for me? After you got out of jail, I mean. I . . ." I trail off before clearing my throat, my voice softer. "I waited for you every day, Mom."

"Oh, Patton." My mother drops her face into her hands, her shoulders shaking with her quiet sobs. "You have no idea how long I've dreamed about hearing you call me that."

For a moment, I think about reaching across the table to grab her hand, but I'm not ready—honestly, I'm not sure I'll ever be. So instead, I tighten my jaw and look up at the ceiling, holding back my own tears.

Her sniffles subside before she lifts her face, red-rimmed eyes bouncing between mine. "I did come back for you."

My brows draw together. "What?"

"It was by pure chance that I found you, actually, since the state denied me your whereabouts, even after I petitioned. About three months later, I wandered into a county fair where kids from a local performance arts center were doing a play." A smile tugs on her lips. "I knew it was my boy the moment I saw you up there, playing the Scarecrow from *The Wizard of Oz*. You were so talented, even back then."

"Clearly not talented enough for you to want me back."

The words are out before I can stop them, bitterness crawling up my throat. I'd just told myself I was going to move past the resentment, yet here it is, rearing its ugly head again.

She flinches at my tone. "I *did* want you back. You were my son. You still are. I had every intention of approaching you and your foster family. But then I saw how happy you were . . . how your foster parents showered you with hugs and praise right after the show. They looked genuinely glad to be a part of your life. There were other kids there, too, high-fiving you for such a good performance. I'd never seen you so happy, so well taken care of . . . certainly never with me."

"Happy?" I ask incredulously. "The person who was supposed to love me unconditionally abandoned me—a thought I took to bed with me every night, thanks to you—and you thought I was *happy*?"

Yes, I was lucky to have been placed with kind and supportive foster families over the years, but they never replaced my mother. She'd made grave mistakes and terrible decisions with regards to my safety, but she was still the woman who'd sung me lullabies and hugged me the way only your own mother can.

"Aside from a criminal record, I had nothing, Patton. No job, no money, no place to sleep at night." Her voice catches as she tips her head back, placing the heels of her hands over her eyes. "You have no idea how much it broke me to walk away from you. But I did it because I thought it was the only way to give you a real chance."

"You had *strangers* raise me. Is that what you call giving me a real chance?"

Her watery gaze meets mine before she quickly averts it, biting her chapped lips. "Do you think you would have become the man you are today, the movie star, if you'd been raised in another trailer park? Those strangers gave you the schooling and safety I never could."

It was because of them that I met Nisha.

The thought tempers a bit of my incredulity and ire.

"When I tell you I had nothing, Patton, I'm not exaggerating. I couldn't have given you the life you deserved, but they could. They *did*." She waves a hand in my direction. "And look at you now; you're exactly as you should have turned out."

My stomach churns with mixed emotions as I lean back in the booth. A part of me understands what she means. I might even be able to empathize with her situation and her decision to some degree.

But forgiveness?

The other part of me knows I won't get there today.

I forget how much time passes after that, words spilling between us slowly, mixed with hesitation and moments of silence. My coffee turns cold, and the donut sits untouched between us, a sweet confectionary in the middle of a bitter reckoning.

She tells me about her time in prison and life afterward, hopping from one job to the next without a landing pad. She tells me that she kicked the addiction to hard drugs a decade ago, but alcohol was still a crutch until four years ago, when she decided to get sober and find me.

And as much as I want to ask why it took her so long to decide to find me, I bite back the words. Because the answer won't undo the damage, and it certainly won't bring back those lost years.

So I just nod and let her talk. There's something raw and earnest in her face when she speaks, like she's clutching her sobriety with both hands, proof that she's working harder than she ever has, proof that she deserves a second chance in both life and with me.

I get the sense that speaking about her past and being vulnerable doesn't come easy to her.

"What about now?" I ask. "You're working here at the waffle house. Why are you still living at the shelter?"

"I get more than just a bed at the shelter," she says quietly. "They have counseling, support groups, and meals." She smiles, playing with a strand of her hair. "They even have this sweet young lady who comes in to cut our hair on the weekends. Everyone at the shelter loves her."

"Wait a minute." My heart kicks my ribs like a soccer ball. "Are you at the shelter on the corner of Glen and Overton?"

"Yeah, the San Jose Safe Haven."

My pulse spikes, and for a moment, I'm completely speechless.

Holy shit, what are the chances? Of all the shelters in the city, and all the women my mother could have crossed paths with, she had to meet *my Nisha*.

My hand reaches for my phone inside my suit jacket and then my pant pockets, coming up empty. I honestly can't believe I'd forgotten about it all this time.

"How long have we been talking?" I ask, my voice sharper than I intend, a sense of foreboding churning inside my stomach.

Your girlfriend slash ex-wife slash the woman you want to spend the rest of your life with is about to have your baby any day now, dumbass! Why haven't you had your phone on you?

"About two hours."

Oh, God. I'm already sliding out of the booth. "I must have left my phone in my truck."

"Patton?" Abigail's soft voice barely registers over my racing thoughts. "What's wrong?"

"She's not just the girl who cuts your hair," I say, rushing toward the door. "She's my ex-wife, my girlfriend, the love of my fucking life . . . and she's having my daughter."

Outside, I yank open the door to my truck, spotting my phone right there in the cupholder. My stomach drops like a free-falling elevator when I see the numbers on the screen.

Thirty-one missed calls. Fifty-four text messages.

I remember checking my phone as soon as I got out of the meeting this morning, and aside from the usual "I love yous" exchanged with Nisha, there wasn't anything urgent. And then I had to go and leave the damn thing behind!

"Shit." My vision blurs as I scroll to the messages, all saying similar things, starting almost two hours ago.

Pine For Me

LITTLE BOREALIS

> Patton, where are you? I need you to get to the hospital now! The baby is coming.

LITTLE BOREALIS

> Patton, please pick up! No one can find you, and I'm really worried.

SARINA ARORA

> Patton, please call back. Nisha needs you. She's in labor.

PIPER MENON

> Dude! WHERE ARE YOU?? Once this baby is out, Nisha is going to spin-hook kick your face!

My throat tightens until every breath feels like it's being forced through a straw, and my world feels like it's shrinking to the point where I think I might faint.

Two hours.

Two hours of contractions, of pushing, and doing it all without me. My head swims.

How could I not have been there *again*?

I can only imagine what she must be thinking; how her past fears must all be rushing back, reminding her of all the times I wasn't there before. My chest burns with both shame and anger at myself.

For almost eight years, I made it a mission to cross off every wish she left me on that list. From the moment I moved in across the street from her, I wanted to ensure she knew she had all of me, and that there is nothing more important to me besides her. I've shown up, laughed until we cried, and made damn sure to be there every step of the way, no matter how big or small the moment.

And now I just threw her back into the same cyclone of fears I swore I'd end.

Fuck, fuck, fuck!

I hit her contact number, but it goes straight to voicemail. I'm not sure of the words that stumble through my lips, some rushed out garbage apology that I deserve getting punched in the face for.

Then I call Sarina, then Piper. When neither answer, I dial Troy before I can think better of it.

"Patton, what the fuck!" Troy answers on the second ring. "Where the fuck are you?"

"Are you at the hospital?" I snap.

Fuck, is the baby here? Has everyone gotten to the hospital before me? Did I miss the birth of my kid all because I left my fucking phone in the car?

"I'm on my way, asshole, but why the fuck aren't you there? Everyone's been looking for you."

I throw my ball cap to the ground. "Long story. I'm heading there now. Can you just tell me—" I take in a sharp inhale, scared to even ask. "Did she . . . did she already have the baby? Did I fucking miss my daughter's birth?"

"I don't know. Sarina said Nisha's contractions were getting worse half an hour ago, but I haven't heard from her since. But, Patton? You better hope they gave her the good drugs, because with this shit that you just pulled, she's going to murder you."

Yeah, and I deserve it.

As soon as I hang up, a pair of footsteps crunch behind me.

"Patton?" My mother's small voice is laced with worry. "Is everything okay? Can I help in any way?"

For a moment, I think of saying no, but to my utter surprise, the words that emerge from my lips are completely different. "Do you want to meet your granddaughter?"

My mother's face crumples, her trembling hands finding her mouth. "Yes, more than anything!"

"Then, let's go!"

With my mother in the passenger seat beside me, I put the truck into gear. I'm just about to gun it out of the parking lot when Rachel rushes over with a bag waving in the air above her.

She hands it through the open window, grinning from ear to ear. "So, you're having a girl!"

I give her a quick nod before peeling out of the lot, my tires spitting gravel, and my head spinning with the same prayer.

Please, please let me make it in time.

thirty-seven
patton

It Helps That You Look Sexy
In Scrubs

I'm not sure how many traffic laws I break. All I know is that my foot never left the accelerator for those fifteen minutes until I screeched to a halt at the hospital's emergency entrance.

Flashes go off as soon as I jump out, the sudden bursts of light blinding me. How the hell did the paparazzi find out I was going to be here? I shove past them, my hand protectively clasping my mother's elbow, urging her to keep her head down.

"Patton, we saw Nisha rush inside. Is she okay? Is it true she's in labor?"

"Who is the woman with you?"

"Smile for us, Patton! You must be so excited to become a dad!"

My breaths ricochet inside me as I rush through the hospital's automatic doors, my mother's hurried steps resounding behind me. I'm sure she's going to be all over the tabloids tomorrow because, if there's anything I've learned about the paparazzi, it's that they're better than intelligence agencies at digging up stories. It is what it is, though. They'll run with it for a week, then move on to something else.

Despite my annoyance with the photographers outside, I'm thankful the nurse at the front desk recognizes me immediately, waving us through in a rush without pressing us for paperwork.

My pulse pounds in my ears as I sprint behind her, every step feeling like I'm competing against time.

"She's being taken to the operating room for an emergency C-section," the nurse calls over her shoulder.

"What?" My feet nearly come to a jarring stop. "What do you—why? What happened?"

The questions tumble out of my mouth, every thought in my brain battling to be heard first. *An emergency C-section?! Did I hear her right?*

She gives me a look that's both panicky and sympathetic, pushing through a set of double-doors that swing with a soft whoosh. "Her contractions are causing the baby's heart rate to drop, and it's not recovering quickly between episodes. You can ask Dr. Gilbert more about it." She turns into a small prep room, plucking scrubs and shoe covers out of a shelf. "But right now, you need to get into these if you want to be in the OR with her."

I nod frantically, and within seconds, I'm shoving my arms into a sterile gown. My hands shake as I pull the surgical mask over my face.

The nurse gestures to a large waiting area nearby, looking at my mother. "Ma'am, you'll need to wait in there."

I squeeze my mother's frail shoulder. "I'll update you soon."

She wrings her hands, the motion betraying her anxiety, before giving me a tremulous smile. "Please tell Nisha I'm thinking about her. And that I can't wait to meet my granddaughter."

With a nod, I follow the nurse through another set of

double-doors, my stomach doing acrobatics fit for the Olympics.

And that's when I see the surgical team wheeling Nisha on a gurney, halfway down the hall.

"Nisha!" My voice echoes inside the corridor.

Her head angles toward me, and I take in her pale, sweat-dampened face, lined with pain and fear. Her eyes widen briefly at the sight of me, and I swear her entire body relaxes just a fraction. "You're . . . you're here."

"Yeah, baby, I'm here." I catch her free hand, interlacing our fingers like she's my lifeline.

I place a quick kiss on her knuckles, my apologetic eyes trying to convey all the words I need to say to her when we're not being rushed. Because "I'm sorry" doesn't even come close.

Against the frantic footsteps and murmured medical speak around us, Nisha gives me a faint, exhausted smile. "I'm glad."

I walk beside her gurney, every step a silent promise that whatever waits for us ahead, we'll face it together.

My lips find Nisha's forehead first before drifting down to our daughter's impossibly delicate temple. My chest warms with emotions so intense, it threatens to catch fire. They're a blend of overwhelming love, surging pride, and protective tenderness I never knew existed inside me.

"She's perfect," I murmur, the words barely audible.

I can't take my eyes off the beautiful miracle who's graced our lives, with her miniature features, her head of soft, dark hair, and rose-petal lips. I can't believe she's here.

After doing their initial assessments, the nurses gently wiped her clean and placed her on Nisha's bare chest for skin-to-skin contact. To our surprise, our baby instinctively found her way to her mother's breast, her tiny fist uncurling as she latched on with a determination that had both Nisha and me chuckling and glassy-eyed.

Nisha glides a gentle finger down the baby's back, infinite tenderness in her eyes. "What should we name this little starlight?"

We'd talked about her name here and there over the months, but had decided to put off the decision until we met her.

I brush a strand of damp hair from Nisha's face, in awe of her strength and her body. "What feels right to you?" You did all the hard work to bring this life into the world."

Nisha's expression is thoughtful despite her exhaustion. "I was thinking of Gia Estelle. Gia means heart in Hindi and God's gift in Italian, and Estelle means star."

"Gia Estelle," I repeat, testing out her name on my tongue. Something about it sounds exactly right, like she was always meant to be named that.

"Gia Estelle *Pierce*," Nisha says, leaning forward in a silent request for me to bring my lips to hers.

I don't hesitate, pressing my lips to hers before wrapping a hand around the nape of her neck and deepening the kiss. The moment is dense with all we've been through to get here, not just today but for years. However, it's relief, wonderment, and love—so much fucking love—that settles around us.

For a moment, with our lips exploring each other's, our hearts locked, and our baby in her arms, my entire world narrows until nothing else exists.

Then, a tiny coo breaks the silence, and we pull apart with a soft laugh. Fuck, my heart feels like it's going to explode.

"Looks like she doesn't want any competition," Nisha says, looking down at Gia, who has fallen asleep inside the crook of her tattooed arm, her lips wet and her expression serene.

"She knows who really matters."

Nisha threads her fingers with mine. "She's lucky to have you, and so am I. But she's going to need you to explain what happened today."

I run a hand through my hair. "I accidentally left my phone in my truck when I went to R&R's to get your favorite French toast. I thought I'd surprise you since my meeting ended early. But when I got there, my, uh"—I take a breath, still coming to terms with everything that's happened today—"my mom was there."

Nisha gasps, quickly glancing down at Gia to make sure she hasn't woken up. "What?"

"Yeah. Long story short, because I really don't want to take away from this moment, sweetheart, but apparently she's been looking for me for a few years. She started working for R&R because she saw me there a couple of times. And today, when I saw her . . ." I trail off, not able to put my whirlwind of emotions into words.

"It must have been so surreal for you," Nisha finishes for me. "After all these years, seeing her again. I can only imagine how overwhelming that must have been."

My brows draw together, my throat tightening in shame. "I . . . I lost track of time. We were catching up and . . . I just—"

"Patton, I get it." Her hand squeezes mine. "There's no way you could have predicted any of this. Not me going into labor a week early and certainly not your mom showing up out of nowhere."

I swallow, my eyes locking with hers. How is this woman so calm and understanding when all I feel is shame and guilt? "I'm so sorry, Nisha. I can't even—God, I can't believe I wasn't here *again* when you needed me. I promised you I'd never let you go through something like this alone again, and I failed. I fucking failed."

Pine For Me

"No." She shakes her head. "You didn't, Patton. Look around. You're here, you're with me and our daughter. Yes, it was close, but you made it. And that's what matters. And honestly? Even if you hadn't, we would have understood. It wouldn't have been intentional."

My brows furrow. "You're not mad?"

"It helps that you look sexy in scrubs, and I'm on drugs."

I smile, but even if she wants to let me off the hook, I'm pissed at myself. "Still, I can't forgive myself. I still haven't forgiven myself for all those years ago."

"You should, Patton. I have." She holds my gaze. "I won't deny that my fears reared their ugly heads today. Believe me, you would have gotten an earful if it was for any other reason. But this? Your mom catching you off-guard like that? I don't blame you. I'm just glad you made it."

"Me, too." I brush my lips against hers again before pulling back when I remember something. "You know her, by the way."

Nisha's head rears back. "What?"

"Her name is Abby. Abigail, actually. She goes to the shelter you volunteer at."

Nisha's mouth drops open, her eyes becoming saucers. "Are you—? Patton, she's—oh, my God! Abby's my friend! She's the one who knitted Gia's first outfit!"

My mouth opens and then closes, words escaping me. The fact that the universe conspired to have my mother and Nisha become friends under totally different circumstances feels impossible.

"To think," Nisha continues, her voice full of wonder, "she knitted it for her own granddaughter and had no idea!"

I run my free hand over my face, everything hitting me like a freight train. "She asked me to forgive her."

Nisha nods. "It all makes sense now. She'd mentioned you. Well, not you, specifically, but she said she moved here looking for something and mentioned wanting forgiveness. Holy crap, I'm just..." She shakes her head, seeming as dazed as me.

"Shocked? Stunned? Blown away?"

"All the above." Nisha laughs softly before studying my face intently. "And can you? Forgive her, I mean."

I take a long breath. "I don't know."

"I get it. A quarter century without your mom is a long time."

We both glance down at Gia, still sleeping in her mother's arms, as we take a moment to process everything that's just shifted in our world.

"She's in the waiting room," I say hesitantly. "I don't know what possessed me to bring her. You don't have to see her if you're not ready; you're probably exhausted—"

Nisha presses her finger over my lips, putting a halt to my rambling. "I already told you I'm friends with her. And now that I know she's Gia's grandmother?" She gives me that smile that always undoes me. "Bring her in with the rest of our family and friends. Actually, bring her in before everyone else, with my dad and Emanuel. I want the grandparents to have their own time with her, first."

My jaw tightens as I try to keep my emotions in check, my lips finding hers again. "Fuck, I love you, Little Borealis." I place a kiss on our daughter's head, relishing the sounds of her soft breathing. "You both are the best things that ever happened to me."

thirty-eight
nisha

The Clam Jam

NISHA ARORA

[image of baby with a knitted pink bow beanie and a scrunched-up face]

Welcome Gia Estelle Pierce to the chat. Our tiny bundle joined the world today, weighing a whopping seven lbs, eleven ounces.

BELLA MEYER

MY GOD! She is PERFECT, Nisha!

KAVI CASE

Ahh, we have been waiting for you to send pictures. Look at those cheeks and that adorable nose! She's gorgeous!

MALA MEYER

OMG, yes! I'm so jealous Sarina and Piper were able to hold her already. She is so beautiful, Momma! But then again, with your and Patton's genes, that was a given.

Swati M.H.

PIPER MENON

Not to rub it in, but I got two snuggles in, and I cried both times. And she spit up on her aunt Sarina, so clearly, she's already picked a favorite!

SARINA WINTERS

Lies. She just felt really comfortable with me.

RANI MEYER

Oh my goodness! Look at the tiny perfection! I love her name, by the way. Gia Estelle totally sounds like the name of a future CEO, or a mafia don. Either way, she's going to be running things.

MALA MEYER

Has the girl already perfected your death glare, Neesh? Look at her giving the camera all that sass!

PIPER MENON

Oh, she definitely has! She gave us all that 'I suggest you wash your hands before touching me or risk losing them' look today. Clearly inherited her mom's black-belt energy.

KAVI CASE

She's going to be breaking boards before she's even potty-trained.

NISHA ARORA

I wouldn't expect anything less.

BELLA MEYER

How are you feeling, Neesh? Heard you were taken in for an emergency C-section.

Pine For Me

NISHA ARORA

> Like I was opened up like a damn piñata and shook until all the contents came out. I'm going to stay here for a couple of extra days, but we're both good. Patton's currently sitting in the hospital chair, staring at Gia like she invented the sky.

SARINA WINTERS

> It's pretty adorable. Daddy Patton is a whole new era.

NISHA ARORA

> And she knocks out cold the second he holds her. Same as me. The man could put an entire room to sleep whispering facts about George Washington or the Battle of Waterloo.

MALA MEYER

> Are her eyes green, BTW??

RANI MEYER

> Holy crap, they are! Don't you and Patton have brown eyes? @Nisha Arora, do we need to book a paternity test and reveal it on the Maury show?

NISHA ARORA

> Relax. She's most definitely Patton's. The dramatic entrance alone screams she's a Pierce.

KAVI CASE

> Then where do the green eyes come from? And speaking of dramatic entrances, I heard Patton almost didn't make it to her birth.

Swati M.H.

MALA MEYER

Yeah. The guys were all talking about it this morning. What the hell was that about? Did he lose track of time fixing that gorgeous Hollywood hair?

NISHA ARORA

So, plot twist: Patton's long-lost mom sorta dropped in on his life hours before Gia's birth. He'd forgotten his phone in his truck and never saw all the missed calls. Yeah, 10/10 on timing.

RANI MEYER

WHAT?! Seriously?

NISHA ARORA

Couldn't make it up if I tried.

KAVI CASE

That's . . . wow. A surprise baby and a surprise mom on the same day. Patton's head must be spinning.

SARINA WINTERS

It's why she forgave him. Can you imagine if he said he was running late because he was stopping for snacks or something?

RANI MEYER

Nisha would have thrown him out the maternity ward window. [GIF of person being hurled out a window]

NISHA ARORA

I won't deny it. I was thinking about all the ways I'd end him until he showed up.

BELLA MEYER

And I assume his mom has green eyes?

Pine For Me

NISHA ARORA

Exactly the same shade as Gia's.

MALA MEYER

So, what's the deal now? Is his mom going to meet Gia? Is she sticking around this time?

PIPER MENON

Neesh, tell them the rest.

RANI MEYER

There's more??

NISHA ARORA

Remember how I do hair at the homeless shelter?

BELLA MEYER

Yeah. Which is so big-hearted of you, BTW. But also, not a surprise.

SARINA ARORA

Under my sister's tough exterior lies a big teddy bear.

NISHA ARORA

So, I became friends with this reserved woman there, named Abby. Gave her haircuts, knitted together, all that. I could tell she'd been through a lot in life and was looking for something. Well, surprise, surprise! Abby is Patton's mother.

RANI MEYER

SHUT UP!

MALA MEYER

No fucking way. That is too wild.

Swati M.H.

PIPER MENON

Doesn't it seem like something right out of a soap opera??

KAVI CASE

Literally one of those "my evil twin got plastic surgery to look like our dad and murdered our mom" moments.

RANI MEYER

So, you were your baby daddy's long-lost mom's friend before she found him again?

NISHA ARORA

I didn't know about it!

MALA MEYER

This is some crazy-ass shit.

BELLA MEYER

Wow, I have no idea what to say. How are you handling all this, Neesh? Has Abby met the baby yet?

NISHA ARORA

A part of me thinks I'm having a bad reaction to all the drugs. But honestly, I'm really happy for Patton. It'll take him time to digest this and forgive her, but he's a big believer in second chances.

SARINA WINTERS

Especially since he got one himself with you!

PIPER MENON

And you know he wouldn't have brought her to the hospital if he had no intention of forgiving her. The man's an Oscar-winning actor, but he isn't fooling anyone.

Pine For Me

NISHA ARORA

We had all the grandparents come and meet Gia just a few hours ago. Abby literally sobbed.

KAVI CASE

That is so sweet. But speaking of sobbing, when can we sob over our new baby niece in-person?

NISHA ARORA

Give me a couple of weeks to get this breastfeeding thing down and get the hang of things. I'd love to be able to wash my hair at some point, too. Then we'll have you all over.

MALA MEYER

Knowing you, you've already started a feeding and sleep chart.

NISHA ARORA

Color-coded, too, obviously.

PIPER MENON

You'd have laminated it if you weren't instructed by your doc to rest.

NISHA ARORA

Bold of you to assume I didn't bring my travel laminator in my hospital bag.

SARINA WINTERS

The scary part is, there's a 50/50 chance you actually DID bring one.

Swati M.H.

NISHA ARORA

There is nothing wrong with being prepared for any emergency. Alright, Gia's waking up again. Will send you details on get-together soon.

MALA MEYER

Sounds good. Dean's ready to bring the "special gifts" he ordered.

NISHA ARORA

Tell him that if this special gift makes noise, it's punishable by me making him hold Gia after a diaper blowout.

BELLA MEYER

Alright, we'll let you get back to baby snuggles. When you're ready, we'll bring food and our husbands.

PIPER MENON

And wine. Don't forget the wine.

MALA MEYER

And dessert!

KAVI CASE

Neesh, do you still hate pineapples? I could bring a pitcher of the pineapple margarita mocktails you loved in Mexico.

NISHA ARORA

Ugh, TBD. My tastebuds are all over the place. If I can't have pineapples again, we might have to hold a memorial service for my margarita era. But bring the pitcher anyway. Let's test fate.

Pine For Me

KAVI CASE

You got it. Oh, and dibs on the first cuddle with baby Gia.

RANI MEYER

Don't even think about it. I've been preparing for this moment since Nisha told us she was pregnant.

MALA MEYER

Yeah, get in line @Kavi Case.

[GIF of women catfighting]

NISHA ARORA

Nice. I expect nothing less than a full-on death match in my living room.

thirty-nine
nisha

Pierce Party of Three

Two Weeks Later

My backyard looks like Martha Stewart threw up on it.

Okay, so perhaps that wasn't the imagery I was going for.

What I mean is, it looks like the pages of a home and garden magazine came to life. There are twinkling string lights swaying under the pergola in the soft May breeze, flowers in large mismatched vases lined down the farmhouse table, and fluffy pink blankets artfully draped on Adirondack chairs like we're hosting a catalog shoot and not a baby meet-and-greet.

Oh, and throw pillows. Lots and lots of outdoor throw pillows. Would it even be a party at my house without them?

Though, I can't take much credit for the party or decor since Patton hired professional decorators and caterers for this event. And while I'd like to apologize for not putting a whole lot of effort in, I'm cutting myself some slack.

Ever since we brought our little girl home, both Patton and I have gotten roughly two-point-five hours of total sleep. I'm exaggerating, of course, but also, not really. It's as if Gia thinks she's living in another time zone. Or maybe she's already living her best sorority girl life, sleeping most of the day and partying through the night.

So yes, when Patton called in professionals, I didn't argue. Between cluster feeding, diaper blowouts, and baby spit up, I've barely had enough brain cells left to dress myself, let alone host people.

Thankfully, the temperature has warmed up, so while there's more pollen and insects in the air, the sun feels amazing after almost a week of rain, though rain in the Bay Area is always a welcomed event.

My eyes travel to Bob sitting beside Rome and Pearl, playing an intense game of Jenga on one of the tables. Ariana, Dev and Piper's almost two-year-old, is giving Bob a health exam using her toy stethoscope to check his ear for a heartbeat. Dev stands nearby, watching her. The man might be a no-nonsense billionaire whose negotiating skills in the boardroom rival that of a Supreme Court litigator, but you wouldn't know it based on the tender way he looks at his daughter. I can't blame him, either. The kid is so ridiculously cute, I'm ready to permanently change my doctor and find an appointment with her.

I smile at how patiently Bob lies there, but his eyes say what his lips can't: *I'll be giving her a one-star rating for her bedside manner after enduring this torture.* Though the real miracle has been that he hasn't seen one of his mortal enemies —a butterfly. I know the second that happens, he's going to want to beg to go back into the house with his tail tucked under him, the big baby.

These days, instead of the dreaded dildo or one of my underthings, Bob's been carrying around one of Gia's used onesies. One is currently lying under his chin like he's guarding a dragon's egg.

What can I say, our dog has always hoarded personal items as a show of his acceptance and affection. And he has loads of that affection for his little sister, sniffing and snuggling her every chance he gets. Not a single moment goes by where he isn't watching her like she's a government asset under his protection. And while it's strange in that slightly stalker way that he parades around her onesie, I'd rather it be that than my thong while we have company.

Speaking of thongs, all mine are nicely tucked away in the bottom drawer of my dresser, to be used one day in the future when my body no longer feels like it's being held together by stitches and prayers.

For now, I'm in my cotton, high-waisted era. The kind that comes in multipacks and could double as a sling or a parachute in case of an emergency. And honestly, given my boyfriend has never cared about what I wore under my clothes, so long as he could get to what he needed quickly, I have zero regrets about choosing comfort over butt strings.

And yes, to Patton's dismay, we now officially refer to each other as boyfriend and girlfriend. He would much rather we erase our past years of separation and go back to being husband and wife, but as I've told him before, one thing at a time.

The thought of not marrying him, when he officially asks me, hasn't even crossed my mind—there's no man I love more than him—but I'd at least want to look less like roadkill in the photos. *Not that it matters. The paparazzi will always do me dirty, no matter how hot I look that day.*

I look up, finding Patton's eyes on me. Gia, with a knitted pink bow half the size of her body that I made for her, is tucked safely in the crook of his elbow.

It's crazy how fast I melt when I see him like this with his broad shoulders relaxed, strong forearm and big hand holding her protectively, and that ever-present soft gaze, like he's still unsure if this is all real, taking us both in.

And she's no better. Just like she used to react to his voice and nearness when she was in my stomach, she coos and smiles whenever she's in her dad's arms. Like she knows she's in the safest place possible.

The sight of them literally makes my chest hurt, like my heart is trying to burst out of it.

Patton's gaze wanders down my face in that intense way of his. Nothing makes me as hot and bothered as when those eyes are on me. And from the slight smirk on his face, he knows it, too.

I give him that look—the one he knows means, *"don't you dare think those nefarious thoughts right now; we have a party to host!"*

I'm just about to voice the same thing when the back door to the yard opens and the Meyer brothers stream in with their wives, with Kavi and Hudson close behind them.

Sarina, Troy, Piper, and Dev, who arrived earlier, drift over as the newcomers join our circle.

While the guys mingle, Rani and Kavi reach for me, pulling me into a hug before Mala and Bella follow suit, all of them complimenting the loose pink dress I chose to match Gia's.

The ladies then gather around Patton, voices dropping to reverent whispers as they admire our baby.

"Oh, my God, you guys," Rani says, beaming. "She is so freaking cute! I see a lot of you in her, Patton."

I groan audibly, pretending to be annoyed, but honestly, I'm happy she looks so much like her dad.

"Just wait til she wakes up hungry," Patton says. "That tiny-baby rage is one hundred percent her mom's."

"Hey!" I elbow his side, making everyone laugh.

"Alright, hand her over, Pierce," Dean says, shouldering past the ladies to come stand in front of us. "This is a meet-and-greet for Gia, and you've literally hogged her the entire time."

Patton raises a brow. "You've been here all of three minutes."

"Exactly! That's three minutes my goddaughter could have been imprinting on her favorite uncle."

Troy snorts, halfway through his beer. "Technically, I'm the only one she will call uncle around here."

Dean waves him off. "Technicalities have no place when it comes to this group."

Probably the truest statement he's ever spoken, given how much we all act like siblings, except with our immediate partners, of course.

Dean makes grabby hands at Gia until Patton sighs and gently passes her over like she's made of glass.

Dean coos down at her, and I won't lie. While I've never been physically attracted to any man besides Patton, if Dean ever posed for a magazine holding a baby like that, every copy would be snatched off the shelves in seconds.

Objectively speaking, this backyard is overflowing with handsome men and their equally gorgeous wives. It's like being trapped in the most attractive group photo ever taken.

"Look at this tiny thing," Dean says, peering down at my baby. "She's probably already smarter than her uncle Garrett."

Garrett shrugs, pulling Bella against his side. "Considering she hasn't tried to high-five a spinning ceiling fan, she's got Uncle Dean beat, too."

Eyes closed, Hudson shakes his head like he's in physical pain. He plucks a glass of wine from a tray that a server has brought over. "That actually happened, didn't it?"

Kavi giggles next to him, taking a sip from her own wine.

Darian nods. "Just like the time he stepped on a wasp

barefoot . . . on purpose. When it comes to our brother, you can assume the most ridiculous stories are *actual* anecdotes."

Dean rolls his eyes, looking down at Gia. "Don't you dare listen to them, precious one. They're just jealous they're not risk-takers like your uncle Dean. They can't even try a new menu item without wondering if it'll give them indigestion."

Laughter ripples around us.

"Alright, Dean," Mala says, tapping her husband's shoulder. "You've had your time with her. It's my turn."

"But I just got her!" Dean says, turning his body away from her.

"Dean Meyer," I warn, "if you startle my baby awake with all your rushed movement, not only will you have a banshee to contend with, but I'll volunteer you as my sparring dummy for a week when I'm ready to get back to the *dojang*."

Dean grimaces, likely weighing out his chances of survival against one of my kicks, before reluctantly handing Gia over. "Fine, but just so you know, I'm taking her back as soon as you guys are done."

Mala ignores him, already melting as Gia curls into her. "Oh, my God. She smells so good."

"Like pomegranates," Patton declares before turning his warm gaze my way. "Just like her mom."

Dean drops onto an Adirondack chair with a dramatic sigh. "While the baby hogs are getting their fix, it's time I show you guys the gift Mala and I brought you guys."

"Don't pull me into this," Mala chides, gently handing Gia over to Bella. "I got them *normal* gifts."

Dean reaches for a bag next to him, sifting through the tissue paper to pull out three cream-colored onesies—a tiny one for Gia and oversized ones for me and Patton—that read "Pierce Party of Three".

"Oh, my gosh," Piper gasps, grabbing one of them. "That's *actually* really cute, Dean."

Patton smirks, looking directly at me. "One of us is not a Pierce yet."

"Just a matter of time though, right, brother?" Dean asks as if I'm not standing right here.

Patton's eyes stay on me. "Oh yeah. She doesn't really have a say in the matter."

I tilt my head. "Oh really?"

He leans down to press his lips to mine, making my heart skip a beat. "Really."

"Those are way better than the pajamas you made us all wear with Troy's face on the crotch," Dev says, breaking our spell.

Dean shakes his head. "You have no appreciation for the finer things in life, my friend. Those pajamas were epic."

"I'd like to make it clear that I didn't want my face on any of your dicks," Troy says.

"Damn, you should have said something before I got all my boxer-briefs with your face printed on them," Dean counters, making everyone cringe.

It's then that I notice both my sister and Piper reach for drinks from a server's tray. They give each other surprised looks before something like realization dawns over them.

"What's going on?" I ask, pointing a finger between my besties. "Why did you both pick up the mocktails when we all know no one could pay you to drink them?"

Sarina bites her bottom lip, flicking Troy a glance, to which he simply nods. She takes a breath, smiling. "I'm pregnant."

Piper gasps, a hand rising to cover her lips. "Me, too!"

Gasps and squeals ring out around us as we all start to gather Sarina and Piper in a hug before a voice resounds from near the side door.

"Did I just hear that my daughter is pregnant? And Piper as well?"

Pine For Me

My dad, wearing one of his usual Hawaiian shirts and a beige Panama hat, walks into the yard with his enormous boyfriend-slash-bodyguard in tow. Emanuel pushes their sassy Pomeranian's stroller ahead of him as if he's escorting royalty.

"Dad!" Sarina yells, launching herself into his arms while still clutching her mocktail.

He places a kiss on her forehead. "You know, I had a feeling when you came over last week . . . You were positively glowing."

Her brows furrow. "What do you mean? I just found out yesterday."

"Oh, please, darling. You should know by now that I was blessed with the highest paternal intuition." Dad opens his arm toward Piper, who falls into a hug right beside my sister. "And you, my honorary daughter, congratulations on another upcoming bundle. Lord knows you and that delicious husband of yours make gorgeous babies."

"Dad," I wince, walking over for my own hug. "What have we talked about with you checking out our husbands? You're lucky Emanuel isn't the jealous type."

Emanuel, the equivalent of a human teddy bear in a pink polo shirt, just shrugs. "Actually, we check them out together. We talk about how hot and muscular they are, and who we'd like to—"

"Yeah, nope," Sarina interrupts. "Don't need either of you expanding on that."

"Now, where is my newest granddaughter?" Dad claps his hands, his rings catching the sunlight as he heads toward the group of women holding Gia.

Despite all the commotion, the girl has slept through everything. But given it's been almost two hours since she ate, she'll be waking up soon, hankering for my boob.

New voices come through the side entrance, and we all look over to see Abby emerge, hands fidgeting in front of her.

Hector walks in behind her, wearing the sweater I knitted for him last year, beaming at me when our eyes meet.

Abby has come over to the house several times over the past two weeks to play with Gia, and each time I see both Patton and her make a little more headway into mending their relationship. And while I know Abby is ready to embrace her son, both physically and emotionally, he's still slightly guarded, more comfortable with side hugs than full embraces. But if I know Patton's immense heart and capability to forgive, he'll get there.

And given he just bought her a fully furnished apartment a block away from us, I'd say that forgiveness is well on its way.

The last time Abby visited us, she brought Hector along. And while their relationship is fairly new, it was adorable to see how happy they both looked together. Also adorable? The way Patton questioned him, more like a parent than her son, asking Hector what his intentions were with his mother.

I rush toward them both, pulling them into a hug. "I'm so happy you could be here." I look at Abby. "Want to head over to the group and get a snuggle in with your granddaughter? She's going to wake any minute now for her human milk machine."

Abby giggles softly, but before she can make her way over, Patton saunters to us, placing a hand on my lower back.

"Hey, Mom. Good to see you." He gives her a side hug before shaking Hector's hand.

"Thank you for having us," Abby says softly before handing him a gift bag. "I knitted her more clothes."

I can't help but embrace her again. "Thank you, Abby."

"Patton!"

We all turn toward the side door just as an older couple steps inside. There's a woman with gray curls and a portly man in a Boston Bolts hockey T-shirt who looks like he hasn't met a stranger in his life. The woman is practically bouncing with excitement, her arms outstretched in Patton's direction.

Bob, never one to let a potential security breach go unchecked, gives a warning bark before trotting over to do a full-body search. Sniffing the couple thoroughly, he seems to determine they're not carrying weapons, contraband, or treats before giving everyone an approving huff.

I immediately recognize them as Patton's foster parents, who I met first as a teenager, and then again at our wedding years ago. We've spoken on the phone here and there since, and more recently last week after Gia was born. I even had Abby attend that call, where tears gathered inside her eyes as she thanked them profusely for fostering Patton and helping him become the incredible man he is.

"Molly? Joe?" Patton's voice shakes slightly. "What are you—"

"Nisha sent us flight tickets to come see you," Molly says, her voice warm as she wraps Patton in a motherly hug. "We had to come see your little girl properly. Getting a glimpse of her through photos and videos just wasn't enough."

Patton glances at me over his shoulder, his eyes warm and grateful. While he and his foster parents may not see each other often, they hold a very special place in his heart, so I know how much it means to him that they're here.

"We brought gifts." Joe grins, giving Patton a back-slapping hug.

I'm just about to step forward to greet them as well when I see it.

Rising behind Joe like a ghoul from my nightmares is an enormous, helium-filled teddy bear bobbing in the breeze. Its shiny, vacant eyes catch the sun, and I swear—*swear!*—they gleam red for a second.

Okay, so perhaps it's not as large as I've described, and maybe it doesn't have dead eyes. But it's helium-filled.

And fucking scary.

The effect on me is immediate and catastrophic.

"No," I whisper, backing up so fast I nearly trip over Hudson's feet. "No, no, no."

"What's wrong with—" Joe starts, but I'm already in full panic mode, ducking behind Emanuel like I'm hiding from armed assailants.

Emanuel, bless his heart, has no idea what's going on but goes right into protective mode, positioning himself between me and the balloon like he's ready to take bullets for me.

"Should I tackle it?" he asks gravely.

"Yes!" I whisper-hiss. "Or burn it!"

"What's happening right now?" Hector asks, a tiny caprese hors d'oeuvre on a toothpick halfway to his mouth.

"I feel like I'm missing context," Hudson says, brows pinched and eyes taking in the spectacle before him.

"Nisha has a thing about balloons," Sarina explains, doing a shitty job of keeping the laugh out of her voice.

I peer around Emanuel's massive frame, watching my boyfriend move to retrieve the balloon from a very confused Joe.

"They're *unpredictable*!" I insist. "Float around all willy-nilly and hang out in dark hallways to catch you off guard in the middle of the night. They're freaking demons!"

By now my friends are openly laughing, Piper nearly snorting her mocktail.

Patton, my hero and savior, retrieves the string of Lucifer's floating plushy from Joe's hand with so much gusto, you'd think he was filming a stunt for an action movie. He starts to run it toward the side gate when the string slips from his fingers at the last second.

The balloon floats toward me in slow motion, menacing and mocking. Its eyes are locked on me, its frightening smile curving up to reveal blood-coated fangs.

Yes. I know this is all in my head!
And yet, I still scream.

My shriek rips from my lungs before I can stop it, startling Gia awake. She peers up at Dean holding her, and then lets out a wail that could shatter glass.

Dean's eyes widen. "Yeah, the banshee lungs are definitely from her mom's side."

epilogue

Nisha - Three Months Later

"Wait a sec," I say, glancing at our surroundings from inside Patton's car. "This is the same place you had me meet you a couple of years ago after the taekwondo tournament."

He smirks. "Stay put for a second. Let me come around and open the door for you."

I roll my eyes, knowing there's no point in arguing with him that I am, in fact, capable of opening the car door and getting out myself. His non-negotiable rule is, if we're in the same car together, he will always open my door to help me out and he will always carry the baby carrier.

Coming around the front of his 1956 Chevy Corvette, he pulls my door open, letting the warm August breeze travel over my skin. Yes, the man has other cars besides his truck—though that is still his favorite. And then there's the Land Rover he bought me as a "push gift". I told him all I wanted was sushi and a nap, but instead, I came home to a new car waiting in my driveway.

This Corvette, however, is only available to him when he visits L.A., which is what we're doing this weekend.

Patton had two talk shows to attend, both to talk about

The Winning Pitch and raise awareness for the foster programs here in L.A., so I decided to come along with him.

It's our first weekend away from Gia, and I won't lie, we've spent most of it missing her, FaceTiming my dad and Emanuel every chance we get in order to see her little face, hear her little coos, and watch her hands curl and uncurl. Every time she smiled at the camera, my heart skipped a beat and I wished I could snuggle her.

This afternoon, Abby and Hector were at Dad's house, too.

Since meeting them both at the hospital after Gia's birth, Dad and Emanuel have made it a point to befriend Abby and Hector, even going on hikes with them and inviting them over for lunch. The four of them have also kept in touch with Patton's foster parents, often video chatting with them, especially when Gia is around.

It's been incredible to see the six of them get closer, but honestly, it's not surprising, either. Sure, having a grandbaby to unite and dote over was the catalyst for their friendship, but I give a lot of the credit to my amazing dad, too. His heart is as immense and boundless as his personality.

With the sun low on the horizon, I let Patton pull me up, my chest colliding softly with his. The second the door shuts, he pins me against it, though I'm not exactly protesting. His gaze drops to my mouth before his fingers trace up my spine, bare under my backless sundress, sending waves of goosebumps skittering over my skin.

Goosebumps and butterflies.

My body has no shortage of them when it comes to this man.

His forehead meets mine as his hand cradles my face. "I figured we'd finish the date we were supposed to have that night before you rushed off like a scared kitten."

My head tilts up to meet his hungry eyes, reminiscent of

smoldering wood after a fire, and I take a greedy inhale of his masculine scent, that heady combination of bergamot and mint I love so much.

"I remember thinking nothing had changed. That you still belonged to the world."

"And now?"

Our gazes hold for a moment, charged with electric currents that feel otherworldly. Because how could two people have this kind of chemistry, this magnetic pull, on this earth?

"And now . . . you belong to me. To our baby girl."

His thumb drags over my bottom lip. "In my heart, in my soul, and in every fucking molecule that resides within me, I have always only ever belonged to you, Little Borealis. No one else."

My mouth finds his then, my hand curving around his neck to pull him closer. I suck his tongue into my mouth, swallowing the groan that rumbles from his chest, thundering through me. Heat barrels inside me, making my nipples pebble behind the fabric of my dress and my pulse rev, kicking my body into overdrive.

Our bodies press together, desperate and certain, as my hips fling forward, seeking the kind of friction and release only he can provide. I need more. So much more.

While he had to be careful about how rough he could be with me throughout the pregnancy and as I healed postpartum, we've now gotten back into the normal swing of things. Just last night, Patton tied my wrists to the bed in our hotel room while he fucked me so hard, I forgot my own name.

His hands curl over the backs of my thighs and suddenly, I'm airborne, pressed against him as he carries me to the hood of his car.

My chest heaves as my ass lands on the warm metal. My knees fall open, inviting him closer, as I brace my hands behind me to steady myself.

Patton moves forward, his dark gaze trailing down my body. "You have two options. My tongue or my dick. Which one is it going to be?"

A frustrated sound tumbles out of me, making him chuckle. "I can only choose one?"

"For now, baby."

"Ugh, fine," I say, reaching out for him until he's finally in my arms. I reach down to cup his erection, heavy and throbbing between my thighs. "I want this."

I fumble with the buckle of his belt before he takes over, rising only to unbuckle himself and lower his pants and boxer-briefs.

I watch his long length bob against his abs, his tip already glistening with pre-cum. My tongue darts out to lick my lips, and Patton's nostrils flare.

"Fuck. There is nothing sexier than seeing you salivate for my cock."

His fingers yank off my panties, and a needy whimper unfurls on my lips. "Patton, God, I want you so much."

And just as soon as those words leave my mouth, I'm being tugged down the hood of his car until he's situated between my folds. He guides his tip through my slickness, mixing our juices, before he inches himself inside.

"I love being inside you, filling you until you can barely breathe." His fingers trail down my stomach, his thumb rubbing circles over my clit. "I love the way your body always invites me in."

"Please," I say, panting. "I need you inside me right this second."

Patton grasps my hip, our matching bracelets glinting in the dimming light, before he pushes inside me with a rough groan. For a second, all my breath leaves my lungs before I feel him start to move.

My arms stay locked behind me, keeping me upright as he

fucks me hard and fast on the hood of his Corvette, thrusting so deep, my head rolls back. I mewl with each deliberate and punishing stroke, wondering if I'll ever catch my breath.

He releases one side of my hip before his hand curves around my neck, squeezing just the way I've always loved. "I love you."

I melt, closing my eyes before crossing my ankles behind him. "I know."

His hips thrust harder, and I get closer.

Closer to the infinite sky. Closer to our forever and ever. Closer to shattering only in the way this man can make me.

Patton's hand slides to the back of my neck, his hips continuing their assault against mine, before he melds our lips together. He kisses me as hard as he fucks me.

"We were written right under this sky, weren't we, Little Borealis?"

My body rocks and my hair sways behind me as I look up at the dusky sky, painted with hues of orange and pink. Distant stars sparkle through the haze like diamonds embedded on silk.

It's not the same as the night we watched the Aurora Borealis glittering like magical dust scattered across the heavens, but it's breathtaking all the same.

Because I'm with the boy I loved first.

And now the man I'll love last.

"Yes," I whisper, though I can't explain the pricks of tears at the corners of my eyes. Maybe it's because we've waded through so much to get here, or maybe it's because it still feels like a dream. Our lives, our baby, our love.

Patton's forehead presses against mine as he pummels me, the tip of his cock finding that place deep inside me. "We were always going to find our way back to each other."

"Like two halves of the same soul."

His jaw tightens, the blink of his eye telling me he's feeling the same emotion echo inside him, pure and unshakeable. *Ours.*

"I love you," I breathe, my fingers fisting the front of his shirt. "So fucking much."

His lips find mine as my orgasm crests and those same stars find the backs of my lids. "I know."

I moan, long and guttural, into his mouth as Patton finds his release inside me, both of us coming together like colliding ocean waves.

Our ragged breaths settle as our heart rates find normalcy. Patton peppers kisses over my jaw and neck before he finds my lips again.

"So," I say, a smile dancing on my lips. "Is this what you brought me here for? To defile the hood of your car?"

A snicker escapes him before he tugs my bottom lip between his teeth. "I told you I wanted to finish our date. The defiling was just a bonus."

I flick my nose against his. "I seem to recall that our last date here had Cheeky Mike's tacos and pineapple margaritas."

Thank all the gods I got my taste back for pineapples!

"Well, that's good, because this one does, too."

My heart fires off a strange beat. "What?"

He tips his chin down to our still-connected groins. "How about we get our clothes on and head to our spot? Actually, leave your panties off . . ." He adds quickly, "It'll make it easier for when I'm ready for dessert."

My cheeks heat. Yes, we just had wild sex on the hood of his car in the middle of nowhere. Yes, he's seen and felt me in ways I haven't let anyone else. And yet, he can still make me blush.

Five minutes later, Patton and I have crossed over that scary, rickety old bridge, and I'm too busy marveling at the glittering L.A. skyline against the darkening sky to notice what he's been leading me to. Until I do.

The same flannel blanket is laid out at the end of the cliff with almost the same rocks and large cooler flanking the sides, as if he recreated that night down to the last detail. Spread on the blanket are tortilla chips, bowls of salsa, and bags of tacos from my favorite food truck, all covered by an enormous glass dome so the wind won't steal our food. Also present are flameless tea lights, each one flickering like they're competing to outshine the other.

When did he...?

"Patton . . ." My smile tugs at the corners of my mouth even as my throat tightens.

I turn to my right, then my left to find him.

He was right here two seconds ago.

But then I feel him before I see him, his warm presence at my back. I turn around, gasping when my gaze dips.

There, in the middle of this cliff, illuminated only by the dusky sky, the city lights far below, and the flickering tea lights, is my ex-husband.

On one knee.

Presenting me with an open velvet box.

My breaths feel ineffective inside my lungs. My hand trembles as I brush my fingers over the back of his hand. "Patton . . . oh, my God."

His throat works before he speaks, his voice thick and rough.

"You're not just the mother of my child, baby; you're my best friend, my fucking heart and soul. You always have been. Losing you once nearly broke me, and I swear to God, I couldn't survive it again. I barely survived it the first time."

His voice shakes, his eyes shiny as they stay locked on mine. "I love you, Nisha, more than anything. Nothing comes before you, before our family. I am so damn grateful to be here, to be yours again, and to get a second chance at us. I vow to never ever fuck it up again."

A laugh bubbles out of me as I wipe a hot tear off my cheek.

Patton's lips tremble before he swallows hard and puts his other knee on the ground. "So here I am, Little Borealis, on my fucking knees for you, begging like the fool I am for you to give me another chance. To marry me again and make me the happiest man alive. Not because we have to, but because we get to."

Sobs wrack my body, and despite wanting to lunge at him, I sink to my knees in front of him. My fingers shake as they find his face, my thumb dragging away a tear that slips from the corner of his eye.

This beautiful, relentless man.

He fought for this . . . for us. He poured not just his time and effort, but his whole heart—along with a bit of scheming—into stitching us back together.

And he thinks he needs to beg me?

"In what universe, under which sky am I not yours, Patton?" I ask, sniffling.

He stares at me, shoulders loosening just enough for me to notice.

I shake my head. "Let me tell you, there isn't one. I'm yours. Heart, body, soul, and anything else that might exist. In every lifetime, in every universe, under every sky, I'm yours."

It's as if all the tension leaves his body. He takes a shaky breath, cupping the back of my neck to pull me closer until our foreheads connect.

"Fuck, baby. Your answer . . ." His throat works on another swallow. "It might have been better than the speech I worked my ass off to remember."

I can't help but laugh. I splay out my left hand, my eyes fully taking in the enormous, brilliant round diamond, haloed by smaller diamonds so it looks like a star.

My laugh is replaced by an intake of my breath. "Patton, that is . . . beautiful."

He slips the ring onto my finger before his brows pinch together. "What's wrong?"

I shake my head. "No, I absolutely love it. It's just that . . ." My eyes trace down his worried face. "I was thinking we could get matching wedding band tattoos this time."

Patton's smile is immediate, his thumb brushing over the edge of my jaw. "Then that's what we'll do. A ring, a tattoo, hell, I'll wear a neon sign for the rest of my life if it means telling the world I'm yours."

And that's when I finally launch myself at him, my arms circling his neck as I kiss him like if I don't, the earth may spin off its axis.

When we finally break apart, breathless and laughing through the tears, he nods at the blanket. "Come. Let me feed and water you."

bonus epilogue

The Schlongs Jam The Clams - One Year Later

HUDSON CASE

I know we barely use this chat with all of us, but this needed to be discussed:

[Link to Celebrity News Now article: Wedding Bells Ring Underneath the Northern Lights: Patton Pierce and Ex-Wife, Nisha Arora, Tie the Knot Once More!]

SARINA WINTERS

Wait, WHAT??

PIPER MENON

No way. This has to be clickbait. They aren't married yet.

DEV MENON

Celebrity News Now doesn't usually post without proof, though.

DEAN MEYER

Dude, look at this! I found one with pictures!

[Link to Celeb Gossip Glitz article: First Pictures of Patton Pierce's Norway Wedding]

KAVI CASE

Holy shit.

BELLA MEYER

Oh, wow. That's them.

DARIAN MEYER

It's a little blurry. Are you sure it's them?

SARINA WINTERS

Yes, it's fucking THEM! I could identify my twin from the International Space Station. And that's definitely our dad holding Gia in a tiny fur coat.

PIPER MENON

@Nisha Arora and @Patton Pierce, you guys better have an explanation for this. This is friendship betrayal on a criminal level.

RANI MEYER

And this explanation should be along the lines of "we were abducted by some aliens that came out of the Aurora Borealis and forced to perform nuptials at gunpoint".

DEAN MEYER

I suppose that's better than being forced to perform fellatio ON them.

PIPER MENON

Hmm. The jury might be out on that. Depends on the alien.

Pine For Me

DEV MENON

> <facepalm emoji> I forgot how unhinged this chat gets when both Dean and my wife are involved.

GARRETT MEYER

> Back to "The Pierces". I thought Norway was for their postponed babymoon?

MALA MEYER

> Same! When did this turn into an actual wedding?

DEAN MEYER

> And why weren't we invited?? I've been preparing a speech ever since they announced their engagement!

HUDSON CASE

> Do you actually think Nisha would have let you give a speech at her wedding?

DEAN MEYER

> Well, I deserved the respect of being rejected to my face!

SARINA WINTERS

> Now that I think about it, I did think it was odd when Dad called two days ago, saying Patton wanted to fly him, Emanuel, and Gia out on a private jet because they "missed the baby".

TROY WINTERS

> I can't believe Hollywood pulled off a secret wedding. I'm impressed.

PIPER MENON

> I'm not, and I'm pissed! Patton and Nisha, show yourselves, cowards!

PATTON PIERCE

Okay, before you guys collectively murder us, let me explain.

DEAN MEYER

Well, look who decided to finally grow some balls. I thought maybe they'd fallen off on one of the polar ice caps.

DARIAN MEYER

The polar ice caps aren't in Norway, dumbass.

DEAN MEYER

I'm sorry, baby bro, but ever heard of metaphors? I was making one about the frigid temperatures. You know, cold = balls falling off. Do you need a diagram?

HUDSON CASE

That's not a metaphor, you idiot. That's just you not knowing geography or anatomy.

DEV MENON

Can you morons shut up and let Patton explain?

PIPER MENON

This better be good, @Patton Pierce.

[GIF of woman crossing her arms over her chest]

PATTON PIERCE

Basically, I surprised Nisha with a wedding. She had no idea. I also knew we'd both want Gia there, so I asked Suraj to bring her out. That's it. That's the entire explanation.

Pine For Me

SARINA WINTERS

So my dad was in on this??

PATTON PIERCE

Not really. I think he had his suspicions when I asked him and Emanuel to bring suits, but he didn't ask me. But he did show up to the wedding wearing a ruby necklace he said was passed down to him by his Rajput ancestors, if that tells you anything . . .

SARINA WINTERS

I am messaging him on the side. I can't believe my dad knew and didn't tell me anything!

PATTON PIERCE

To be fair, I think he just suspected. Knowing him, he travels everywhere with his Rajput jewelry.

MALA MEYER

I'm genuinely impressed you surprised Nisha with a wedding.

DEAN MEYER

That's either the most romantic thing I've ever heard, or the dumbest, given what a control-freak your wife is. Probably both.

NISHA PIERCE

For the first time in both our lives, I think I agree with you, Dean. I was both swooning and slightly murderous when I realized what was happening.

PIPER MENON

Oh, look. Even your phone knows you're married now. It changed your name.

SARINA WINTERS

Nisha! Explain how you went along with this betrayal. NOW.

NISHA PIERCE

You knew we went to see the Northern Lights because they're such a part of Patton and my story. Well, one minute we're getting out of our car to see them and the next, there's an officiant standing there along with Dad, Emanuel, and Gia!

KAVI CASE

But in the picture, you're wearing a wedding dress! There was a place to change there?

NISHA PIERCE

Before we left our hotel, Patton had said he wanted to get "professional pictures" taken under the Aurora Borealis. I should have totally suspected when he had me wear a beautiful full-sleeved white gown, but I just never thought he'd do something like this!

GARRETT MEYER

Damn, Hollywood. That's some CIA-level covert planning!

SARINA WINTERS

I'm still mad at you, brother-in-law!

PIPER MENON

Same! I'm not sure I'll be over this any time soon.

Pine For Me

PATTON PIERCE

I accept that. But I was also thinking about the babies you both just had. I didn't want to inconvenience any of you by flying to such freezing temperatures. That's the reason I had Suraj fly Gia in just for that specific day, and we bundled her up just for the main event.

NISHA PIERCE

Which all went very quickly, BTW. Literally a half-hour with how cold it was. And, BTW, we're totally going to be throwing a proper reception as soon as we're back. With an open bar. We want all of you there.

DEAN MEYER

Open bar? Okay, I'm downgrading from pissed to mildly annoyed.

SARINA WINTERS

Alcohol won't cut it for me. I require groveling. Extensive groveling. I'm still processing that MY TWIN GOT MARRIED WITHOUT ME!

TROY WINTERS

I just watched a key fly off Sarina's phone from rage-typing.

NISHA PIERCE

I'm sorry, sis. I swear I didn't know, and I'm ready to grovel.

PATTON PIERCE

Same. What is it going to take to not be mad?

SARINA WINTERS

Full control of the reception. Guest list, theme, venue, everything.

NISHA PIERCE

Don't you think that's going a little, I don't know, overboard?

SARINA WINTERS

Was I your maid of honor at this wedding?

NISHA PIERCE

Well, no.

SARINA WINTERS

I rest my case.

NISHA PIERCE

Fair enough. Done.

SARINA WINTERS

I wasn't done. I also want the next baby's middle name to be Sarina.

NISHA PIERCE

We're not having another baby.

PATTON PIERCE

What if it's a boy?

SARINA WINTERS

Then he'll have some explaining to do when people ask him why his middle name is Sarina.

NISHA PIERCE

Again, we're not having another baby!

Pine For Me

PATTON PIERCE

We might have another baby <wink emoji>.

TROY WINTERS

Damn, Pierce is feeling bold today.

NISHA PIERCE

PATTON!

PATTON PIERCE

Just keeping our options open, baby. Plus, don't you want your sister to forgive you?

RANI MEYER

I think marriage made him fearless.

DEV MENON

Or stupid.

PIPER MENON

As for the demands, I'm pissed too. I should be getting something as well!

NISHA PIERCE

Sigh. What would you like?

PIPER MENON

I want to be Gia's godmother.

SARINA WINTERS

Absolutely not. I'm already her godmother.

PIPER MENON

Fine. I want to be the next baby's godmother.

NISHA PIERCE

Again . . . never mind.

DEAN MEYER

Since we're all making demands, I'd like Patton to ask Troy to give me his World Series jersey. The one he sweated in.

TROY WINTERS

Not gonna happen.

DEAN MEYER

Oh, come on! I'm sad that I wasn't invited to this polar vortex wedding. Nor was I asked to make the speech I worked so hard on. It's the least you can do.

HUDSON CASE

If Dean gets a jersey, then I want a personal screening of Patton's next film before it comes out.

DARIAN MEYER

This is getting ridiculous.

NISHA PIERCE

Look, we'll make it up to everyone at the reception. I promise.

PATTON PIERCE

Yes, we'll throw a party to remember. Just forgive us.

SARINA WINTERS

Fine. But only because I love you both, and I'm planning the most epic reception the world has ever seen.

RANI MEYER

I speak for the Clams when I say we're helping!

Pine For Me

SARINA WINTERS

Obviously!

NISHA PIERCE

Thank you guys. Love you all. We're going to get back to our honeymoon now.

PIPER MENON

You better call us as soon as you're back so we can schedule a ladies' night.

BELLA MEYER

Yeah, we want all the deets!

KAVI CASE

And better pictures. Not the blurry ones online.

NISHA PIERCE

Promise! But for now, here's one. We got them right after the wedding.

[Picture of Patton and Nisha's wedding band tattoos]

MALA MEYER

I love the matching stars around your fingers!

DEV MENON

Very on-brand for you two.

SARINA WINTERS

Oh, and @Patton Pierce? Welcome back to the family, officially. But if you try something sneaky like that again, I swear to God . . .

PATTON PIERCE

Got it. No more secret weddings. Scout's honor.

. . .

THE END!

But I want more!

1.) Read the rest of the HAIRCUTS AND HEARTTHROBS Series - If you haven't read the series, what are you waiting for??

2.) Read Darian, Garrett, Dean, and Hudson's stories: ELEMENTS OF RAPTURE Series!
Read ADRIFT—**Darian & Rani's** forbidden, single dad/nanny romance
Jump into ASCEND—**Garrett & Bella's** marriage of convenience, single mom romance
Don't miss ABLAZE—**Dean & Mala's** angsty brother's best friend, slowburn romance
Download ABYSS—**Hudson & Kavi's** enemies-to-lovers, best friend's dad, office romance

about the author

Swati M.H. writes stories full of humor, heart, and heartbreak that always end in an HEA. She lives in the Bay Area with her incredibly patient husband and two beautiful daughters. Her days start with caffeine and sometimes end with a glass (or three) of wine.

Swati loves staying in touch with her readers. Find her at www.swatimh.com or through Facebook and Instagram. Be sure to join her Sweeties reader group for daily fun.

acknowledgments

Honestly, I can't believe this was the last and final book in the Haircuts and Heartthrobs series. All I've done for the past couple of years is think about this cast of characters, so leaving them feels quite bittersweet. And now, having written each of their happily-ever-afters, I feel a little . . . untethered.

What will I do with all the time?!

Ha!

Write another book, of course!

I hope you enjoyed Patton and Nisha's story as much as I enjoyed writing it. So, before I thank anyone else, I'd like to thank you for taking the time and chance on reading my book. I appreciate you so much and I hope I was able to bring a smile (and a laugh or two) to your face.

Being a writer can be a lonely job, but I'm lucky to have found my tribe over the years. They make this journey incredibly fulfilling and a lot less lonely.

To my group of alpha and beta readers—Rachel Childers, Rachael Poxon, Michelle Mastandrea, Sarah Beth, Namita Sycz, Olivia Pace, and Daisy Salgado Pham—thank you for being so encouraging and supportive. I love bouncing ideas off you ladies and appreciate all your insight and suggestions.

Thank you to my lovely PA, Stephanie Rash, for always bringing joy and laughter to my life with hilarious messages, all while reminding me to get my shit together. You're not just a PA, you're a dear friend.

A big thank you to my editor, Silvia Curry and my cover designer Marisa-rose Black.

Thank you to my lovely and talented friend Rin Sher for being an alpha reader on this book and for putting up with my meltdowns when the characters refused to cooperate.

My friends Steffanie Blais, Emily Silver, and Stephanie Rose—thank you for the laughs, virtual pats on the back for writing even a hundred words some days, and all the love.

Kar, Suhani, and Sanika—you're my world. Thank you for being my constant cheerleaders and my rock-solid support system.

Made in the USA
Coppell, TX
27 January 2026

69217257R10233